TREES AND SHRUBS

Peter Hemsley began his career in Horticulture in private service and nursery work in Ripon, Yorkshire, and then as a student at Askham Bryan College, near York.

He gained further experience with Scarborough Corporation Parks Department before entering the Royal Botanic Garden, Edinburgh as a student. He successfully completed the course, gaining the Garden Diploma and the Royal Horticultural Society's National Diploma in Horticulture.

He was appointed to the post of Botanical Foreman in the garden at Edinburgh where he assisted the curator in designing the interior landscapes of the new plant houses. On completion of this project he was promoted to Education Officer and made responsible for the running of the horticultural course.

His keen interest in education led him back to Askham Bryan as a lecturer where he has spent the past ten years developing teaching in Amenity Horticulture and in his specialist subject of Arboriculture. During his spare time at the college he has gained the National Diploma in Arboriculture. He has also contributed a chapter on Garden Trees to Professor Alan Gemmell's *Practical Gardener's Encyclopedia*.

He is currently an examiner for the Royal Horticultural Society's National Diploma in Horticulture and The Royal Forestry Society's National Diploma in Arboriculture. Much of his spare time is spent visiting gardens and arboreta to observe and photograph specimen trees and shrubs to provide visual material for teaching purposes.

TEACH YOURSELF BOOKS

TREES AND SHRUBS

Peter Hemsley

Series Editor
Professor Alan Gemmell

Illustrations by
Oriol Bath

TEACH YOURSELF BOOKS
Hodder and Stoughton

First Impression 1980

Copyright © 1980
Peter Hemsley

All rights reserved. No part of this publication may be reproduced or transmitted in any form or by any means, electronic or mechanical, including photocopy, recording, or any information storage and retrieval system, without permission in writing from the publisher.

Published in the USA by David McKay & Co. Inc., 750 Third Avenue, New York, NY 10017, USA.

British Library C.I.P.

Hemsley, Peter
Trees and shrubs. – (Teach yourself books).
1. Trees 2. Shrubs
I. Title II. Series
635.9′77 SB435

ISBN 0–340–24788–6

Printed and bound in Great Britain for Hodder and Stoughton paperbacks, a division of Hodder and Stoughton Ltd, Mill Road, Dunton Green, Sevenoaks, Kent, (Editorial Office; 47 Bedford Square, London, WC1B 3DP) by Richard Clay (The Chaucer Press) Ltd, Bungay, Suffolk

Contents

Acknowledgements

I would like to record my sincere thanks to my wife Christine for her invaluable assistance in typing, proof reading and constant encouragement and to my daughter Julie for her uncomplaining tolerance.

Thanks are also due to all my tutors who have fostered my knowledge and passed on their enthusiasm for plants and gardens.

Introduction

The purpose of this book is to provide useful information for new gardeners and to increase the knowledge of gardening enthusiasts about the tremendous wealth of hardy trees and shrubs which are available to beautify the environs of our homes.

To summarise, I begin in Part One with a simple explanation of plant-naming, followed by a glimpse into plant structure and the elementary growth processes. This provides a basis for the practical aspects of raising new plants from seeds, cuttings or grafts. Then follows the important task of planting, from choosing and buying plants, site preparation and planting procedure, to the vital after-care. This leads naturally on to the maintenance of established trees and shrubs. The remainder of Part One considers pest and disease problems and concludes with a summary of the law relating to trees and shrubs.

Part Two of the book is devoted to the plants themselves, concentrating on their visual qualities, limitations and uses in the garden. For convenience these are arranged in appropriate groups beginning with the wealth of flowering trees and shrubs, arranged in the order of flowering. Next come the plants with distinctive or coloured foliage, followed by those with attractive bark, colourful fruits and distinctive shape. Conifers, with their special charm and elegance, are given a separate section. Then follow three utility groups devoted to climbing and wall-trained plants, hedge and screen plants, and ground-covering shrubs. Finally, there is a summary of problem sites with lists of suitable plants.

I hope that with this knowledge readers will become enthusiastic about this wonderful group of plants, and that their gardens will be improved by their efforts to put their learning into practice. Apart from getting involved in the practice of gardening, I also hope that readers will continue the process of education. They can do this by attending evening classes or by joining their national and local horticultural societies.

The most pleasurable way of learning is to visit other people's gardens. British gardeners are most fortunate in having the greatest heritage of gardens to be found anywhere in the world. There are superb national plant collections such as the Royal Botanic Gardens of Edinburgh and Kew, and famous gardens such as those of the Royal Horticultural Society at Wisley and the Northern Horticultural Society at Harlow Car, Harrogate. Many splendid gardens in the capable hands of the National Trust are also open to visitors. But gardens do not necessarily have to be large and famous to be attractive, and much can be learned from the many less well known gardens that are opened for charity under the National Gardens Scheme or the Scotland's Gardens Scheme. Details of openings are published annually in booklets that are available at most leading bookshops.

Finally, in introducing the book, I urge you to make time to enjoy your garden. There is nothing more refreshing to the spirit than admiring the beauties of nature, and there are no grander objects for our gardens than the trees and shrubs.

PART ONE

INTRODUCTION

1

Naming Trees and Shrubs

Learning plant names; common names and botanical names; the subdivisions of family, genus, species, variety and cultivar.

Learning the names of trees and shrubs is a challenge for both new and experienced gardeners. Initially the names may seem bewildering or confusing, especially when you read books or study catalogues which contain lists of unfamiliar-sounding names. Imagine your first encounter with the tongue-twisting *Metasequoia glytostroboides* or *x Cupressocyparis leylandii*! Such uncommon names may seem difficult to grasp at first, but in the same way that a teacher learns the names of new pupils, so the gardener quickly learns and remembers the names of new plants. This learning process is a continuing experience; rarely if ever will you meet the gardener who has complete knowledge of plant names.

The plant kingdom embraces a multitude of different subjects which have evolved over millions of years from single-celled structures into gigantic and complex multicellular vegetables. Since classical times learned men and botanists have laboured to classify plants into a systematic and sensible order; this is known as the science of Taxonomy. During the eighteenth century, Linnaeus, the Swedish naturalist, introduced the binomial system of naming plants, and from these beginnings there developed *The International Code of Botanical Nomenclature* and *The International Code of Nomenclature of Cultivated Plants*. The rules laid down in these codes determine how plants are named.

There are two quite different types of name that gardeners encounter – firstly the common name, and secondly the more correct, botanical name. Common names are usually local in origin: for example, *Sorbus aucuparia* is known as Rowan Tree, Ranty and Mountain Ash in different parts of Britain, but throughout the world it will be known as *Sorbus aucuparia*. Botanical names are usually derived from the classical languages of Latin, Greek or Arabic and it is for this reason that many sound unfamiliar to us.

The botanical name often informs us of the origin of the plant, *e.g. Acer japonicum*, the Maple from Japan. Sometimes it describes some feature of the plant, *e.g. Betula pendula*, the Birch with pendulous twigs, or *Jasminum nudiflorum*, the Jasmine that flowers before the leaves emerge. As you see by these few examples, the name reveals useful information about the plant, and consequently the learning of names can be made far more interesting by reference to a botanical dictionary which explains their meanings. (See Further Reading List.)

The family

Taxonomists have subdivided the plant kingdom into various groups, classes and orders. These are largely of academic interest, and it is only when the subdivision of the plant family is reached that the classification has a practical use. A family contains a group of related *genera* (plural for *genus*): for example, in the large *Erica* family (*Ericaceae*) we find about seventy genera including *Erica*, *Calluna*, *Pieris*, *Pernettya* and *Rhododendron*.

The genus

In books and catalogues all plants have at least two botanical names (binomial) – first the genus, and second the species. A genus is a group of species which have common structural characters; these characters are found in the reproductive parts of the plant, *e.g.* flowers, fruit and seed. Thus all species in the genus *Prunus*

(Cherry) have a basic flower structure that is common to all other species in the genus, although outwardly the plants appear to be very different; they range from deciduous trees like *Prunus avium* (Gean) which grow up to 20 m (65 ft), to the evergreen shrub *Prunus laurocerasus* (Cherry Laurel), which grows to 6 m (20 ft). You will notice that the generic name always begins with a capital letter. A simple analogy would be to regard the generic name as the surname of the plant.

The species

Species are a group of individuals which have the same constant and distinctive characters. Thus, when you look at a sea of Heather on the moors you are really looking at hundreds of individual plants of *Calluna vulgaris*. These are almost identical in terms of general growth characteristics, *e.g.* height, flower colour, time of flowering *etc.*, and seed from these plants would produce plants with virtually the same characteristics.

To return to our simple analogy, the species name can be regarded as the forename; thus, John Smith would be written as Smith (the genus) and John (the species). In plant-naming, however, the specific epithet always begins with a small letter, *e.g. Prunus avium*, and you will notice that the genus is always written first.

The variety

Species of some plants have evolved to suit specific geographical locations but are not sufficiently different to qualify for species status. These are referred to as varieties. For example, the type of Black Pine which grows in Austria is known as *Pinus nigra var. nigra*; that from Corsica as *Pinus nigra var. maritima*; and that from the Crimea as *Pinus nigra var. caramanica*.

The cultivar

A more important division of species to the gardener is the cultivar (meaning cultivated variety), and this name is enclosed in single quotes or prefixed by the abbreviation Cv. Cultivars are the choice selected forms of plants which may have arisen by hybridisation, *e.g. Rosa 'Max Graf'* (*R. rugosa crossed with R. wichuraiana*). Other cultivars arise as seedling variants. Many of the different types of Lawson's Cypress first occurred as seedlings and have since been propagated vegetatively (*i.e.* not from seed) and given cultivar names, *e.g. Chamaecyparis lawsoniana 'Ellwoodii'*. Cultivars also arise as 'sports', a term that refers to forms of mutation where a bud or shoot develops with abnormal characteristics. If these can be propagated vegetatively the offspring is given a cultivar name, *e.g. Chamaecyparis lawsoniana 'Ellwood's Gold'*, which is a sport from *C. l. 'Ellwoodii'*.

Learning plant names may at first seem tedious, but an eventual working knowledge of them will be a great asset to you, especially when you select and buy plants for your garden.

2

The Growth of Trees and Shrubs

The functions of roots, stems, leaves and flowers.

An understanding of the basic structure and the elementary growth processes of woody plants is a useful starting point for the successful cultivation of trees and shrubs. There are four basic parts to consider: roots, shoots or branches, leaves and the reproductive parts, *i.e.* flower, fruit and seed.

Roots

The roots perform two essential functions: firstly they anchor the plant, and secondly they absorb water and dissolved nutrients to sustain the plant. Most roots are found growing in the top 50 cm (20 in) of soil, which contains a greater abundance of oxygen, organic matter and nutrients, but trees have a few deeper-growing anchor roots. The extent of a root system varies according to the type and size of plant, but often they extend many metres from the base as they continue to radiate outwards in their search for water and nutrients. The diameter of a tree root system often exceeds the height of the tree.

A microscopic view of a root tip reveals the presence of many fine root hairs; these are the cells which are constantly absorbing water and dissolved nutrients. As the root elongates, old root hairs are worn away and new ones are continually produced just behind the root tip. Old woody roots merely serve to transport water and nutrients from the root hairs to aerial parts of the plant, but in trees, older roots close to the trunk also act as buttresses and give support against wind.

Stems

Roots are connected to the stem. In trees a stem develops into the main trunk, which in turn supports a framework of branches. The two main functions of stems are to conduct the sap, *i.e.* water and nutrients, to various plant tissues and to provide support and elevation for the canopy of leaves.

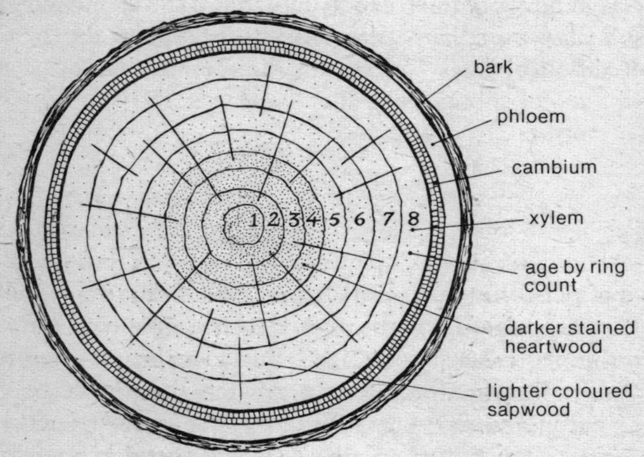

Figure 1 Cross section of a woody stem.

Fig. 1 shows the cross-section of a woody stem with its outer covering of bark, the papery, fibrous or corky material which protects the conducting tissues. A microscopic view reveals a tissue just beneath the bark called phloem; phloem is made up of elongated cells which facilitate the downward flow of sap. This serves to distribute the simple carbohydrates manufactured in the leaves to other parts of the plant. Moving inwards, we next discover a most important layer of cells, the cambium. These cells are continually dividing to produce new tissues, and in later chapters reference will be made to the importance of cambium in wound-healing. Cambium produces new phloem tissue to the outside, but its main product is new xylem tissue to the inside.

Xylem is the wood tissue, and its purpose is to provide strength and support for the stem. New xylem also conducts water and dissolved nutrients from the soil upwards to the leaves through its system of vessels and fibres. Each growing season a distinct new layer of xylem is added, and the stem increases in girth. In spring xylem vessels are usually larger than those produced in late summer and autumn; this differentiation produces the annual rings which can clearly be seen in the cross-section of a felled tree and which can be used to determine the age of a tree.

Leaves

Leaves are the productive parts of a plant, for it is here that the carbohydrates which provide energy and the basic chemicals needed for growth are manufactured. Leaves vary enormously in size and shape but their internal structures are similar (see Fig. 2). Beneath the epidermis (outer skin) lie rows of so-called palisade cells, which enclose an abundance of chloroplasts; these contain chlorophyll, the essential green pigment of plants. Lower layers of loosely arranged cells called mesophyll connect to openings in the leaf called stomata. It is through these openings that gases essential to various physiological processes move in and out of the leaf.

Most important of these processes is photosynthesis, also known as carbon assimilation. Photosynthesis is the manufacture of simple sugars (carbohydrates) within a leaf. The elements necessary for photosynthesis are water, carbon dioxide, energy from sunlight and the presence of chlorophyll; the end product is glucose, a simple sugar. Glucose is quickly converted into more complex carbohydrates through the action of enzymes and the presence of other chemical elements which have been absorbed by the roots. Oxygen released as a by-product is essential for the existence of both plant and animal life.

Manufactured carbohydrates within the cell solution are transported to wherever they are needed. Leaves are served by a network of veins which are made of various tissues, including phloem and xylem; these in turn connect to the phloem and xylem systems of branches, trunks and roots. Thus there exists a complex network of microscopic tubes extending from root hairs to the very top of a large tree.

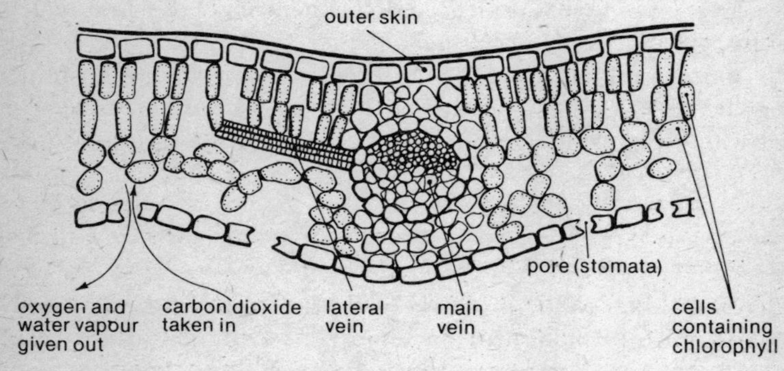

Figure 2 Cross section through a leaf.

Respiration is another essential physiological process in plants, that provides a continuous supply of energy for growth. Oxygen is the vital element for this. It is always found in abundance around the aerial parts of a plant, but occasionally there is an insufficient supply to roots and seeds beneath the soil.

Transpiration is the physiological process whereby water is lost from the leaves. Water movement through a plant is a physical action and whatever is not used in the plant passes out through the leaf stomata and into the atmosphere as water vapour. Living cells must be kept turgid if they are to function properly, and if a plant loses water too rapidly the cells will collapse. As most water is lost through stomata, the plant can regulate the rate of water loss by opening or closing these.

When the water supply to the roots is inadequate, *e.g.* in drought conditions, leaves begin to wilt and evergreen plants often react by premature leaf fall. This is the plants' safety mechanism to prevent complete desiccation and death, but both will inevitably occur if the water supply is not replenished within a short period. A similar reaction can occur when trees and shrubs are transplanted and the reduced or disturbed root system is unable to take up sufficient water for the plants' needs.

Flowers

Flowers are the sexual reproductive parts of trees and shrubs. These may be large and showy in insect-pollinated plants, *e.g.* *Rhododendron* and *Buddleia*, or relatively inconspicuous in wind-pollinated plants, *e.g.* *Pinus* and *Betula*. There are three types of flower: male flowers, which contain only pollen-bearing anthers; female flowers, which only contain ovules; and bi-sexual flowers, which contain both anthers and ovules. Flowers of many woody plants are of this latter type, and pollination (the transfer of pollen from anther to stigma) is therefore a simple process.

Some plants, such as Birch, Hazel, Oak and Beech, have separate male and female flowers on the same plant, and these are referred to as monoecious plants. Those which have male and female flowers on separate trees are called dioecious plants. This is an important point. The attractive berries of plants such as Holly and Skimmia are only borne on the females, but a few male plants are also needed to bring about successful fertilisation and seed production.

Seeds are dormant, embryonic plants which, given the right conditions, germinate into new plants and eventually grow into the complex organisms that we have briefly examined.

3

Propagation of Trees and Shrubs

Seed propagation – limitations of raising plants from seed; obtaining seed, collecting, cleaning and storing seed; dormancy in seeds; germination and after-care of germinated seedlings; vegetative propagation – time of taking cuttings; selection of material; preparation, treatment and insertion of cuttings; conditions for rooting; semi-ripe wood, hardwood and root cuttings; layering; grafting and budding.

Despite advances in horticultural technology many trees and shrubs remain difficult to propagate, and even professional nurserymen with sophisticated facilities and highly-skilled propagators find plenty of woody plants which challenge their ability. Fortunately, however, there are a great many plants which can be increased without much difficulty and without the need for elaborate facilities. Quite apart from the challenge to your own horticultural skill, there is tremendous pleasure and satisfaction in propagating your own plants.

Trees and shrubs can basically be propagated by seed, or vegatatively, by cuttings of roots or stems, layers and grafts. Choice of method depends mainly on the plant being propagated, the material available and the facilities at your disposal. Inevitably a few losses occur during the propagation process, so aim to produce a few extra plants to make up for these. Any surplus plants can always be exchanged with other gardeners or neighbours for different plants or stock material; this is an economic way of stocking your garden and an ideal introduction to new gardening friends.

Seed propagation

Limitations of raising plants from seed

The simplest technique of multiplying a stock of plants is by seed, but before choosing this method it should be realised that every seedling is a new individual bearing the combined characteristics of its parents. In addition, many characteristics of woody plants are not transmitted sexually, *i.e.* via the seed. As a result, seed from a selected parent plant will very often produce plants that have quite different characteristics. For example, aberrant forms of trees, *e.g.* erect-growing or weeping forms, will produce seedlings with a normal growth habit. Likewise, plants with abnormal leaf colouration will usually produce seedlings with normal green foliage, as in the case of seed from Golden Sycamore, which produces seedlings with the usual sombre green leaves. In nature, however, there are always exceptions – and some colour variants will produce coloured-leaf seedlings. For example, in a recent sowing seeds from Copper Beech yielded seventy per cent green seedlings and the remaining thirty per cent varied in intensity of leaf-colouration from diffuse green purple to very dark purple.

A large measure of seedling variation can therefore be expected when raising woody plants. But this need not be a disadvantage – a number of interesting new cultivars which have since been propagated vegetatively first arose as seedlings. As a general guide, aberrant forms, coloured-leaf forms, cultivars and hybrids will not breed true from seed; but true species will generally reproduce offspring with characteristics virtually identical to the parent plant.

Obtaining seeds

Success cannot be achieved without first having viable seed. This can be purchased from your garden sundriesman, but an enjoyable alternative is to browse through the catalogues of firms which offer seeds of trees and shrubs. Certain national and local horticultural societies also operate seed exchange schemes, which are an excellent way of obtaining some of the less common plants. For the enthusiast looking for rarities, there are occasions when shares may be purchased in plant-collecting expeditions; these are advertised from time to time in the horticultural press.

Collecting your own seed is a most satisfactory method, as this way you can see the qualities of the parent plant and also have complete control of the seed from harvest to sowing.

Collecting, cleaning and storing seeds

Seed-collecting is a skilful job. To begin with, seed has to be gathered at the right time of year, when the seed or fruit is mature. Seed maturity is often indicated by a change in colour of the seed coat. Such a change is familiar to anyone who has gathered 'conkers' from Horse Chestnuts; those that still have creamy-white patches are not quite fully mature. Immature seeds, if cut open, tend to be sappy or milky inside when compared with mature seeds, which are plump and firm.

Collecting goes on throughout the year but there is an intensive period in late summer and autumn when a great many seeds can be harvested. Plants which have dry fruits which burst open, like pods of *Cytisus* (Broom) or *Laburnum*, and capsules of *Rhododendron*, must be collected before the seeds are shed. Berries likewise must be gathered before hungry birds strip the plant bare; in cases of especially choice subjects, it is advisable to protect the ripening fruits by tying cotton or polythene bags over them. Before collecting seed in quantity, it is wise to cut open a few seeds with a sharp knife to ensure that they contain viable embryos and are not merely empty shells.

Some woody plants need several decades' growth before they bear seed, and many plants introduced from other countries will not produce seed in the English climate. Likewise, a good number of woody plants do not set seed each year like annual plants; this may sometimes be due to climatic effects, but it is now known that other physiological factors contribute to this phenomenon, known as cyclic bearing.

When collecting dry seeds, *e.g.* pods of legumes such as Broom and Bladder Senna, or ripened catkins of Birch and Alder, gather the seeds and place them into labelled paper envelopes. Larger seed structures such as cones of Pine, Spruce or Cedar can be placed into seed trays lined with newspaper. Collected seed needs time to dry before cleaning and will need a warm, dry atmosphere in which to do so. Certain cones will not open and release their seeds until they have had fairly high temperatures, *i.e.* 46° to 60°C (115° to 140°F) for a period of two or three days.

Cleaning is necessary to extract the seed and to separate the good seed from the chaff and other plant débris. Capsules and pods should be gently crushed; opened cones only need shaking. Extraneous matter is removed by sieving and by gently blowing the sieved material to disperse dust particles. Finally, the cleaned seed is packeted into clearly-labelled paper envelopes. If correctly stored, many seeds will remain viable for several years, and it is therefore useful to date each packet and note the origin of the seed for future reference. Packeted seeds should be stored in a cool, dry place where temperature fluctuations are minimal. Cellars or garden sheds with damp atmospheres should not be used as these encourage rotting off.

Berries and fleshy fruits such as Whitebeam, Holly, Crab Apples, Rose and Barberry require quite different treatment after collection. If large fruits are placed into a tin or jar they can be gently crushed into a pulp, but care must be taken not to crush the seeds themselves. Seed is then separated from the pulp by washing it through a sieve with water under pressure from a tap or hose-pipe. The sieve must have a mesh size which retains seed but allows pulp to wash through. Flotation is an alternative method of separation. Here, pulp and seed are placed in a jar partly filled with water. After settling, good seed will sink to the bottom, débris and empty seed will float to the top; this is then creamed off and the remaining seed washed clean.

Seeds of this kind are best stored moist, by mixing the clean seed with at least three parts of moist, fine grade sand; this is then placed in sealed tins or polythene bags until sowing time. Small fleshy fruits like Cotoneaster berries can be mixed directly into sand without cleaning. This prevents fermentation and keeps the seed moist. This method of storage is also preferable for large seeded trees like Oak, Chestnuts, Beech and Walnut, and it is the best way to prevent moisture loss and subsequent loss of viability from the seed of Maples and Ash. Seed which is moist-stored should be labelled with waterproof ink. Store the containers in a cool place, free of temperature fluctuations.

Dormancy in seeds

Seeds of many trees and shrubs remain dormant even when given ideal germination conditions. This is because nature has devised various mechanisms to prevent seed from germinating at the wrong time of year, when natural conditions would be unsuitable. Some of these dormancy problems are easily solved, for example, seeds which have hard seed coats can be germinated more quickly if the seed coat is softened by soaking in clean water for two or three days. Very hard seed can be scarified by gently rubbing it between two layers of sandpaper to wear down the seed coat, but care must be taken not to damage the embryo.

In some cases there are more complex physiological reasons why seeds will not germinate immediately. Sometimes embryos are immature; in other cases chemicals present in fruits or on the seed coat inhibit germination; yet others need a period of after-ripening before growth will begin. A number of plants in the Rose family, *e.g.* Rose, Hawthorn, Whitebeam and Flowering Crab Apple, are affected in these ways and their seed normally has to be stratified for periods varying from three to twelve months before sowing.

Stratification involves placing seeds between layers of moist sand. Deep wooden boxes can be used, and these should be lined and covered with 1 cm (½ in) mesh wire netting to exclude vermin. After filling with sand and seed, place the boxes outside so that they are exposed to the elements until sowing time.

Because of dormancy factors, not all tree and shrub seed can be expected to germinate in the first year after sowing. It is therefore advisable to keep batches of sown seed for a period of at least two years before discarding them.

Sowing seeds

Sowing can begin under glass in February and March but most hardy subjects are sown outdoors or in frames between March and May. Later sowings tend to produce smaller seedlings which are more difficult to over-winter. Small batches are sown in shallow pots, seed pans or boxes made of wood or plastic. Trees and shrubs in the seedling stage are sensitive to 'damping off', a fungal disease that causes seedlings to collapse, and it is therefore sensible to take the precaution of using sterilised containers and seed compost. John Innes, Levington or one of the various proprietary seed composts available from your garden sundriesman are suitable. Peat-based composts are excellent for plants which prefer acid soils, and in particular plants in the *Erica* family, *e.g. Rhododendron*, *Gaultheria*, *Pieris* and *Pernettya*.

A simple procedure for filling a container is to slightly overfill it with compost, strike it off level using a straight-edged piece of wood and then tap the container firmly on the bench; finally, gently firm the levelled surface with a presser board made from pieces of plywood cut to the shape of your containers. Then thoroughly water the prepared containers, using a watering can fitted with an upturned fine rose. Give several light sprayings to ensure that all compost in the container is moistened without disturbing the prepared surface.

When sowing, seed should be evenly distributed on the compost. This is no problem when handling large seeds which are readily spaced out, but finer seeds, such as *Rhododendron* and *Hypericum*, need a steady hand; I like to take a pinch of seed between thumb and first forefinger and gently rub this over the container to scatter it uniformly, but some gardeners prefer to mix small seed with a more easily seen carrier such as fine sand. A common error is to sow too thickly; this results in over-crowding and weak, drawn seedlings. For guidance, I would suggest small seeds are sown at approximately 0·5 cm (¼ in) spacings, large seeds at 1 cm (½ in), and very large seeds at 2·5 cm (1 in).

When several types of seeds are being sown at the same time, and especially if there are different species of the same genus, place each container on to a sheet of newspaper as it is sown, to prevent seed accidentally spilling into compost or other containers on the bench. Mixed batches can be infuriating, especially when the aliens germinate first! All but the very smallest seeds need a covering of compost. Seeds up to 2 mm ($\frac{1}{16}$ in) diameter require a light 'sugaring' over, which can be done by tapping compost through a fine sieve. Seeds between 2 and 6 mm ($\frac{1}{16}$ and $\frac{1}{4}$ in) diameter require a covering about one and a half times deeper than the thickness of the seed, *i.e.* 3 to 9 mm ($\frac{3}{16}$ to $\frac{3}{8}$ in). Seeds of 6 mm ($\frac{1}{4}$ in) diameter can be gently pressed into the compost and covered with 6 mm ($\frac{1}{4}$ in) of grit. Winged seed like Maple or Ash, and hairy or fluffy seed like Clematis, are also better covered by this latter method.

Each container should be clearly labelled using an indelible ink. Plant names can either be written directly on to the side of plastic containers or on to a label. As birds may be inclined to pull labels out of pots, my preference is for the first method. Other useful information to note on a label is the sowing date, and a symbol to indicate the origin of the seed, *e.g.* T/M (Thompson and Morgan), NHS (Northern Horticultural Society).

Germination

After sowing, the containers should be placed in a suitable environment to initiate germination. One of the most critical requirements for successful germination is correct temperature, but the optimum requirement varies from species to species. Most hardy trees and shrubs do not require glasshouse temperatures to initiate germination and therefore spring-sown seeds can be placed directly either in a cold frame or in a sheltered position in the garden. Containers should be kept moist but not too wet and to avoid the need for frequent watering a sheet of black polythene can be placed on top of a batch of containers. A twice-weekly inspection should be made to ensure that germinated seeds are not left for more than three or four days in the dark. It is wise to protect uncovered seed containers, and for that matter germinated seedlings, from birds with wire or nylon netting.

After germination

Germinated seedlings benefit from light shading. This can be provided by an open mesh of wooden lathes, open-weave fibre mats or polypropylene netting supported on a framework about 30 cm (12 in) above the seedlings. When seedlings are large enough to handle, pricking-off takes place. This is the process of carefully transplanting seedlings to give them more room for development and transferring them into a slightly richer growing medium. In some cases this is only a matter of a few weeks after germination; in others, several months later. Seedlings can be pricked off into boxes or individual pots made from plastic, clay, paper or compressed peat. This latter type is especially suitable for plants which do not transplant well, *e.g. Eucalyptus* and *Cupressus*. A more satisfactory method for most tree and shrub seedlings is to prick them off directly into an open ground bed or frame. Prepare a 1 m (39 in) wide bed large enough in area to accommodate all your seedlings. A 2·5 to 5 cm (1 to 2 in) layer of peat is thoroughly mixed into the top 15 cm (6 in) of soil with a digging fork. A dressing of John Innes base fertiliser at the rate of 35 g/m^2 (1 oz/yd^2) can also be applied and forked in. Seedlings are then pricked out into this prepared bed, at a spacing of between 10 and 30 cm (4 and 12 in) depending on the vigour of the plant. A dibber will suffice for pricking off most seedlings, but if root systems cannot be accommodated in the dibber hole, then use a trowel. Immediately after pricking off, water the seedlings to settle soil around their roots and apply light overhead shading to prevent desiccation by strong sunshine. The shading can be removed when the seedlings are established. Continue watering as necessary and keep the bed free from weeds.

Vegetative propagation

Because forms, hybrids and cultivars are likely not to come true from seed, vegetative propagation is the only way that stock of these plants can be multiplied or prolongated. Plants which are propagated vegetatively are always genetically identical to the parent plant.

Cuttings

One of the remarkable, almost magical, things about plants is the fact that many of them can regenerate from detached stems or roots. This is possible because cells of mature plants are capable of returning to a meristematic condition. In other words, cells can actively divide to produce new tissues which have a specific function, *e.g.* new root and shoot systems. Some gardeners are blessed with 'green fingers' and their cuttings always seem to root without difficulty, but for those less fortunate let us apply a little science to the question of rooting cuttings. Woody plants can be propagated by cuttings made either from detached pieces of stem or root, and in either case success or failure can depend on several interrelated factors.

Time to take cuttings

Many plants will root at almost any time of year, but timing becomes critical with more difficult rooting subjects. Unfortunately, there is no simple answer to the question of the optimum time to take cuttings. There is obvious variation from species to species, and more difficult subjects have been known to vary from one year to the next. A useful guide is the condition of the shoot.

In spring, as young shoots extend, they are soft and succulent, and when the first-formed leaves on the bases of these new growths are fully extended (usually in May and June), softwood cuttings can be taken from them. A few examples of plants propagated by this method include Shrubby Maples, Lilacs, Hypericum, Mock Orange, Smoke Sumach and Clematis.

As the growing season progresses, shoots become firmer and from July to September semi-ripe wood cuttings can be taken. This is a satisfactory method of propagating Hebe, Senecio, Lavender, Santolina, Laurel, some Hollies, Privet, Weigela and a number of conifers, notably False Cypresses (*Chamaecyparis*) and their cultivars.

By November the shoots are fully ripened and this is the time to take hardwood cuttings. This is an excellent way of propagating trees like Poplar, Willow and London Plane and shrubs like Flowering Currant, Mock Orange, some Roses, Forsythia, Deutzia, Spiraea, Buddleias and ornamental Elderberries.

Root cuttings are best taken when plants are completely dormant in December and January.

Selection of material

Cuttings should come from the best forms of plants and from those that are in good health. As a general rule, cuttings taken from young plants root much better than those from fully mature ones. This phenomenon of juvenility is quite important in woody plant propagation and especially in certain conifers. A number of woody plants exhibit distinct juvenile and adult growth phases; for example, some Cypresses have short, needle-like leaves in their juvenile phase and flat, scale leaves in their adult phase. It is a fact that cuttings taken from shoots in a juvenile phase root very much better than those taken from shoots in the adult phase.

Generally, shoots of only moderate vigour will root much better than very vigorous shoots; likewise, lateral growths are preferable to terminal shoots. In both cases this is because the more vigorous stems have low reserves of the stored food that provides the energy necessary for root production.

Preparation of the cuttings

All types of cuttings, whether leafy or non-leafy, begin to lose moisture once they are detached from the parent plant. If this drying-out continues to the point beyond which the tissues can recover, then the cutting dies. One of the propagator's aims is to minimise this water-loss until a cutting is capable of replenishing its needs with a new root system. On collection, therefore, cuttings should be placed into moistened polythene bags or wrapped in some moisture-retentive material, *e.g.* moss, or damp hessian. If necessary, cuttings can be kept in reasonable condition for a couple of weeks in a polythene bag retained in a cool place. This is a small point worth remembering if you are offered cuttings of interesting plants during your holiday travels in this country.

Normally, cuttings should be prepared immediately after they are collected. Leafy cuttings, *i.e.* softwood and semi-ripe wood cuttings, require similar treatment. Their shoots should be trimmed with a sharp knife to a length suitable for the subject. The longest will be 10 to 15 cm (4 to 6 in), *e.g.* large-leaved Rhododendrons, Laurels, Hollies and Leyland Cypress; but most cuttings will be 7·5 to 10 cm (3 to 4 in) in length, *e.g.* Philadelphus, Shrubby Maples, Hebe, Lavender and Lawson's Cypress cultivars. Cuttings 2·5 to 5 cm (1 to 2 in) in length are adequate for Heaths, Heathers, Cassiope and several dwarf Rhododendrons and conifers.

Cuttings should be trimmed cleanly with a sharp knife at a point where there is likely to be most cellular activity for the regeneration of roots. This is either just below a node (leaf joint), or, in the case of heel cuttings, at the junction of the main stem (see Figs. 3 and 4). A few basal leaves are then trimmed off to enable the cutting to be inserted into the rooting medium. Better root systems can be developed on difficult subjects by wounding at the base of the cutting. This is done by splitting the bark about 1 cm (½ in) from the base; a heavier wound is achieved by removing a thin sliver of bark, again about 1 cm (½ in), from the base. The latter method is preferable for conifers.

Treatment of cuttings

Rooting can be further stimulated by dipping freshly prepared cuttings into a growth-regulating compound containing either IBA (indole-butyric acid), IAA (indole-acetic acid), or NAA (naphthalene-acetic acid). These are frequently erroneously called hormones and are available from garden sundries suppliers as powder or liquid formulations. Various concentrations are used, the higher ones being suitable for more difficult rooting subjects.

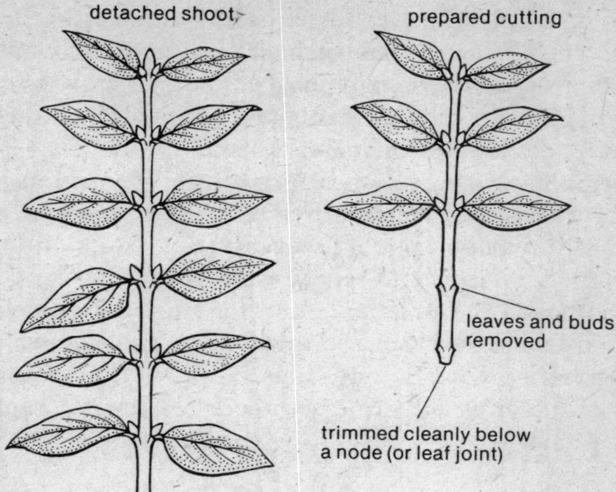

Figure 3 Stem cutting.

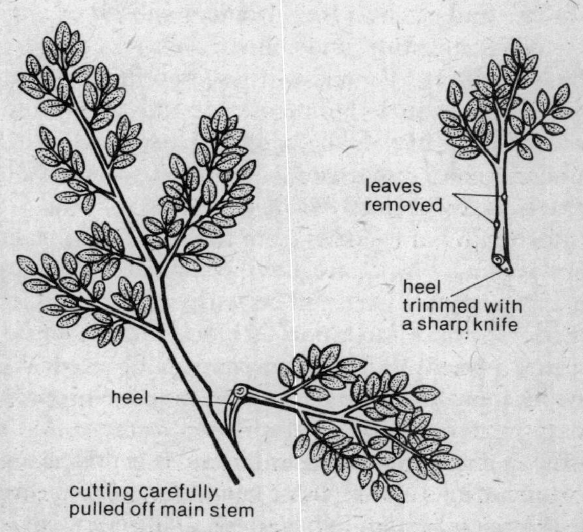

Figure 4 Stem cutting with heel.

Should the concentration be too high the treated base of a cutting will be injured and will usually die back. Some powder formulations also contain fungicides such as Captan, which minimises rotting off at the basal end of a cutting. Use of a growth regulator will often speed up rooting, and generally treated cuttings have more roots, which helps their establishment.

Another innovation of recent years is the use of anti-transpirants. Cuttings are immersed in a prepared solution of polyvinyl acetate, such as S-600. The purpose of this material is to put a thin plastic film over the leaf surface to reduce water-loss from the detached cutting. Although the effect only lasts for a few days, this is often sufficient to extend the life of a cutting until new roots can replenish the life-sustaining water supply. This treatment is obviously of no benefit to cuttings which are to be rooted in a mist propagation unit (see p. 27).

Insertion of cuttings

Prepared cuttings should be inserted into a suitable rooting medium. This needs to be a free-draining substance which at the same time holds moisture and allows plenty of air around the cutting base. A useful general-purpose rooting medium can be made by mixing an equal volume of peat and sharp sand, or grit, with a particle size of 1·5 to 3 mm ($\frac{1}{16}$ to $\frac{1}{8}$ in). For conifers and Rhododendrons a mixture of two parts of peat to one of sand or grit is more suitable. It is advisable to ensure that the peat is well moistened before mixing. Apart from these conventional materials proprietary rooting blocks are now available. These are simply placed in a plastic tray partly filled with water, and cuttings are then pushed into the wetted, porous block. After rooting they are separated and potted off. Jiffy Sevens can be used in a similar way for many tree and shrub cuttings. These are proprietary containers made from compressed peat-based compost that swells up when wetted to make mini compost blocks. It is preferable to insert each batch of cuttings into separate containers. This prevents mixtures and allows each batch to be moved to different environments when rooted.

Containers for cuttings should drain freely and be sterile – plastic pots or seed trays are ideal. These are over-filled with rooting medium, tapped firmly on the bench to settle the medium uniformly, and levelled off. Cuttings are inserted by gently pushing them deep enough into this prepared surface to enable them to stand upright. A thorough watering will settle the material to hold the cuttings firmly and no other firming should be necessary. Small or weak-stemmed cuttings such as Ericas may have to be inserted by making a hole for each cutting with a small dibber. Each batch should be labelled with the plant's full name and the date of insertion. It is also useful to record any special treatment on the back of the label, *e.g.* type and strength of growth regulator.

Conditions for rooting

Leafy cuttings will very soon wilt and die if left in an open atmosphere during bright, sunny weather. They must therefore be placed into a suitable rooting environment immediately after preparation and insertion. A mist unit, which sprays water intermittently on to the cuttings so that their leaf surface does not dry out, provides the ideal environment for leafy cuttings. Small mist units are usually controlled from a sensing element which is activated when water is evaporated from its surface. Thus, in bright sunny conditions misting occurs every few minutes, whereas in dull weather or during the night, misting takes place much less frequently. The cooling effect of evaporation prevents leaves from wilting and this allows them to function normally. Food materials produced by the physiological processes in the leaves provide energy for rooting and tissue development, and this helps to explain why cuttings root more quickly in a mist unit. Small mist units offer other advantages for gardeners in that, being electrically controlled, they can be left unattended during the day.

If possible a mist unit should be equipped with soil-warming cables. Base temperatures of 18° to 24°C (65° to 75°F) encourage a higher growth rate at the bottom of cuttings, and consequently root growth is stimulated ahead of shoot growth. This principle of 'warm bottoms and cool tops' is one whose advantages have been recognised by propagators for many years.

The only disadvantage of mist units is their initial cost, since not many gardeners can justify capital outlay for small-scale propagation. An acceptable alternative is to place cuttings in a humid environment, where the principle is to minimise water-loss from the leaves by creating a high vapour pressure in the surrounding air, and so to balance the high vapour pressure normally found inside a leaf. Old-fashioned bell jars, propagation cases, frames and modern propagators all work on this principle. A simple but effective propagation case can be made by filling a 30 cm (12 in) deep wooden box with about 7·5 cm (3 in) of moist peat, and covering it with a tight-fitting pane of glass or sheet of clear polythene. Pans or pots of cuttings can then be bedded into the peat and occasionally sprayed over to maintain a high humidity. This box can either be placed in a glasshouse or kept outdoors.

Damp conditions favour the development of moulds and rots and also encourage slugs; a fortnightly spray with Captan will minimise this first problem and a few slug pellets should eliminate the second. It is also advisable to shade newly-inserted cuttings from strong sunshine. Cuttings may also be placed in outdoor frames, preferably fitted with soil-warming cables. Newly-inserted cuttings, after being watered in, can be covered by laying a clear polythene sheet directly on top of them before closing the glass lights. This has a similar effect to double-glazing and reduces both temperature and humidity fluctuations around the cuttings.

Semi-ripe wood cuttings

Many semi-ripe wood cuttings can easily be rooted in a small polythene tunnel. Choose a sheltered site and begin by preparing a bed about 50 cm (20 in) wide. Clear the site of weeds and thoroughly fork in a 7·5 cm (3 in) layer of peat and grit to improve the soil. After raking the bed level, cuttings may be inserted with a dibber at appropriate spacings – which for most semi-ripe cuttings is about 10 cm (4 in) apart. Water the cuttings and then erect your polythene tunnel.

This needs to be no more than 50 cm (20 in) high, with the polythene supported on wire hoops and secured by strong garden twine. Bury the polythene at the sides and ends so that the cuttings are completely enclosed (see Fig. 5). Beds of cuttings can be prepared in this way during August and September and virtually left until the following spring. Because the environment is sealed, very little watering should be necessary although an occasional check is advisable to ensure that everything is in order.

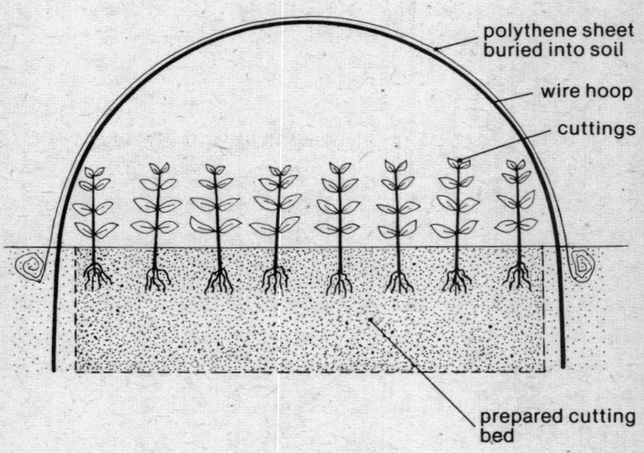

Figure 5 Semi-ripe wood cuttings in polythene tunnel.

Most cuttings begin to root, in spring when the temperature rises, and after roots are established the polythene is removed to allow the young plants to continue to grow. One note of caution: some quick-rooting plants, such as Hebe, Senecio, Lavender, Santolina and some Berberis, root so quickly that if left in closed tunnels over the winter, losses can occur because of the damp conditions. Cuttings of these plants can be taken in July, so that by September they are at a stage when the polythene can be removed and the young plants left in an outdoor bed for the winter.

Hardwood cuttings

Taking hardwood cuttings of deciduous trees and shrubs is one of the easiest methods of propagation, since no special facilities are needed. These cuttings should be taken as soon as possible after leaf fall, because at this time a woody stem contains a high level of stored food materials and natural root-inducing growth regulators.

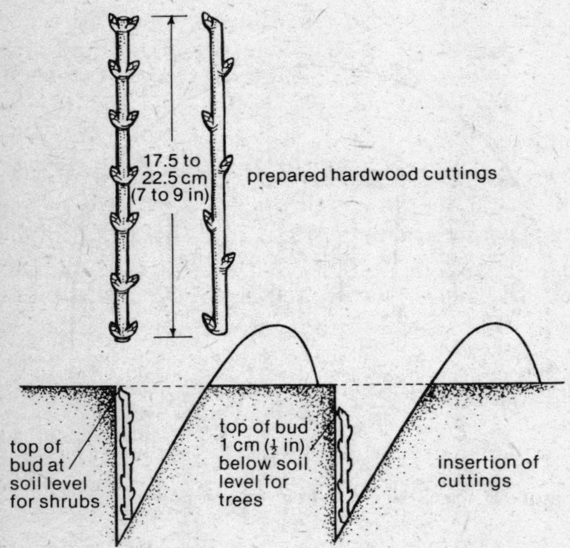

Figure 6 Hardwood cuttings.

Fully-ripened shoots of the current growing season should be selected, preferably those of moderate vigour. These are trimmed with secateurs into lengths of between 17·5 and 22·5 cm (7 and 9 in), and a straight cut at the base of a cutting is made just below a bud, whilst the top cut is slightly angled and made above a bud (see Fig. 6). Prepared cuttings can be tied into bundles and labelled. As with other cuttings, the freshly-cut bases can be dipped into a root-promoting growth regulator, but this is not necessary with easy-rooting plants like many of the Poplars and Willows.

After preparation, bundles of cuttings can be stored by plunging them in fine damp sand in a deep box or a small freely-drained pit. The aim is to keep the cuttings moist and in good condition until the following March. At this time, as soil becomes workable, the bundles should be lifted and cuttings inserted singly in short rows in the open ground. Soil should previously have been dug and forked down to a reasonable tilth.

Cuttings are inserted vertically against the side wall of a carefully dug trench. Space them 10 to 20 cm (4 to 8 in) apart with 30 cm (12 in) between rows. Insert shrub cuttings at full depth, with the top bud set at soil level. Tree cuttings need to be slightly deeper with the top bud set 1 cm (½ in) below soil level, as this produces a straight stem. Buried cuttings, being surrounded by moist, gently-firmed soil, do not dry out. As cuttings begin to grow, a dressing of high nitrogen compound fertiliser (2.1.1. NPK ratio) applied at the rate of 70 to 100 g/m² (2 to 3 oz/yd²) will encourage growth, so that by the end of the growing season excellent planting material will be ready for transfer to the garden.

Root cuttings

A great number of trees and shrubs can be increased from root cuttings. As a guide, plants which sucker, *i.e.* send up new stems from the roots, can generally be relied upon to regenerate from detached pieces of root. In this case, energy needed for new root and shoot initiation comes from stored food reserves and consequently roots selected for cuttings need to be 1 to 2 cm (½ to ¾ in) in thickness. Roots should only be detached when the plant is fully dormant. They can be dug out of the ground or, preferably, cut off lifted plants; this ensures that only young roots are used and that the roots originate from the plant you intend to propagate.

Normally, a straight cut is made at the top of each cutting with a slanting cut at the base; this is merely to differentiate the top from the bottom and ensure that they are inserted the right way up. Each cutting should be about 10 to 12·5 cm (4 to 5 in) long but their length can be varied slightly to make the most use of each detached root. Root-promoting substances are not used for this type of cutting, but dipping them in Captan fungicide will help to prevent rotting-off after insertion. A simple way of coating them with this fungicide is to place a couple of tablespoonfuls of Captan into a polythene bag containing a dozen or so cuttings, and give the bag a thorough shake.

Cuttings should be inserted vertically into suitable containers (pots or boxes) filled with potting compost. Alternatively, they may be directly lined out into open ground, where they are likewise inserted vertically against the sidewall of a trench. The top of each cutting should be 1 cm (½ in) below soil level and spaced 10 cm (4 in) in rows 30 cm (12 in) apart.

A short list of plants which can readily be increased from root cuttings includes Indian Bean Tree (Catalpa), Stag's Horn Sumach (Rhus), Tree Poppy (Romneya), Japanese Angelica Tree (Aralia) and Tree of Heaven (Ailanthus).

Layering

Not all trees and shrubs can be rooted successfully from detached stems or roots, and a useful alternative is the practice of layering. This frequently occurs naturally when stems or branches come into contact with the ground. The principle of layering is to partly sever or constrict a stem about 10 to 15 cm (4 to 6 in) from its tip. Food materials and root-inducing growth-regulators accumulate at this point, and very often, if the stem is embedded into a growing medium rooting will occur. Unlike a detached stem, a layered shoot is kept supplied with water and nutrients from its parent; as a result speed of rooting is less important. Simple layering of shrubs is achieved by bending a suitable branch down and securing it to a stake so that the tips of the branches are in contact with the soil. At this point the soil should be cultivated and ameliorated to make a good rooting medium by incorporating some peat and grit. Now constrict the shoots at about 10 to 15 cm (4 to 6 in) from the branch tips; this can be done by carefully bending the shoots, or by partly cutting through them with a knife or removing a ring of bark. Shoots are then pegged into the prepared rooting area either with short wire pins bent into a U shape, or wooden pegs (see Figs. 7 and 8). There is some benefit in putting rooting powder over any freshly cut surfaces before pegging down. Where a shrub is growing in a border, it is advisable to secure the emerging shoot tips to short canes as this ensures that they grow straight and also enables you to see clearly where layers are, and so prevent accidental damage during cultivation.

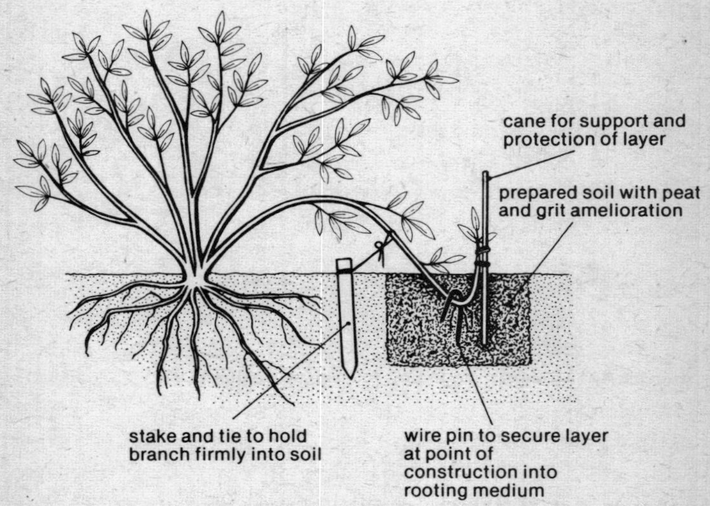

Figure 7 Simple layering.

When layers are well rooted, sever their connection to the parent plant and once they are sufficiently established, lift and transfer them to the planting site, preferably during the dormant period. With young Rhododendrons it is possible to keel the entire plant over on one side in order to bring shoots into contact with the ground. After layers have been detached, the plant is then restored to its normal growing position.

With tall-growing shrubs and trees it is often impossible to bring the branches into contact with the soil. Nurserymen layer such plants from special 'stooled' or coppiced plants, which are regularly cut back so that short flexible stems can be easily pegged down. An alternative is air layering. In this method the rooting medium is taken up to the branch and secured into position around the point of constriction with a small sheet of polythene (see Fig. 9). If clear polythene is used it becomes possible to see when the roots have formed. Do not detach the layer until it is well rooted and again, do this when the plant is dormant to avoid hindering growth.

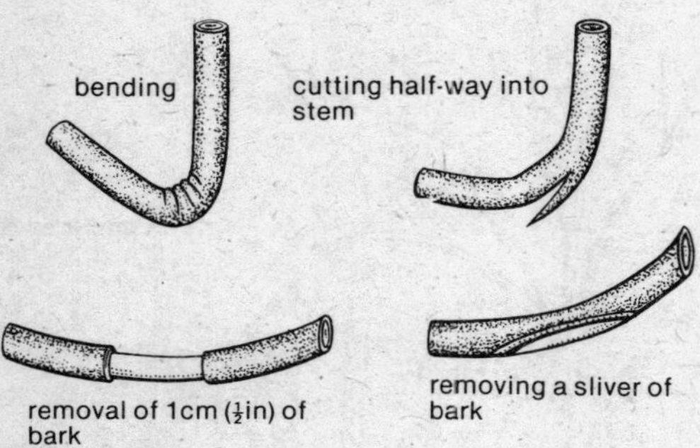

Figure 8 Method of inducing rooting at the point of layering a stem.

Grafting and budding

The final method of propagating woody plants is by grafting, a term which also embraces bud grafting, or budding, as it is more commonly known. Grafting is the art of joining parts of different plants together so that they unite and continue growing together. Plants that will not come true from seed, and which cannot be rooted from cuttings or layers, have to be grafted if they are to regenerate. Grafting requires a fairly high degree of manual skill or knifesmanship, but this can be acquired with a little practice.

The plant to be propagated is referred to as the scion, and the

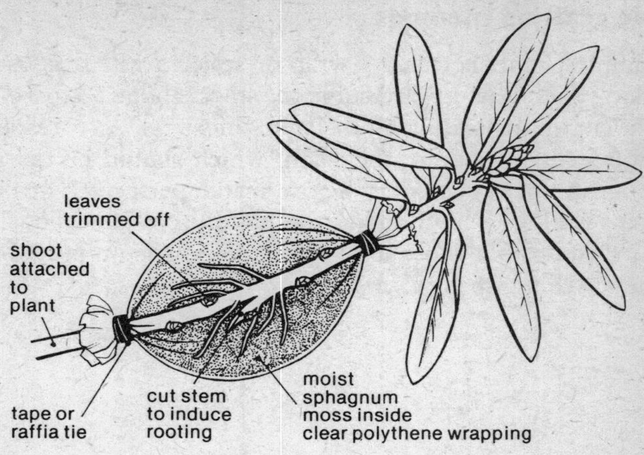

Figure 9 Air layering.

root system on to which it is placed is referred to as the stock. The first requirement for success is compatibility between stock and scion, and in most cases they must be very closely related botanically; thus, scions from dwarf forms of Scots Pine would be grafted on to Scots Pine stocks, and scions from cut leaved or weeping forms of Silver Birch would be grafted on to normal Silver Birch stocks. Stocks used are generally one- to three-year-old seedlings, but some weeping and slow growing trees may be grafted on to trees from three- to five-years-old. In these cases the grafts are placed 2 m (6 ft) up the main stem.

As with other methods of propagation, grafting is only successful at certain times of year; timing therefore has to be adapted to the particular subject you are dealing with. Volumes have been written about the various techniques of carpentry used to join the stock and scion together, but all have one aim in common, and that is to bring the exposed cambium tissue of each part into close contact. This tissue, situated just beneath the bark, then actively divides and intermingles to produce new tissues which continue growing together.

Simple grafting methods

The simplest graft is called a whip or splice graft. It is executed by making a slanting upward cut in the stock, about 2·5 to 5 cm (1 to 2 in) in length, depending on the stem thickness. A corresponding downward cut is made in the scion, which should be the mirror image of the stock cut so that the two match perfectly when placed together (see Fig. 10). Outdoor grafts require scions about 10 cm (4 in) in length, but those used on indoor grafts on potted stocks may be anything up to 25 cm (10 in) long.

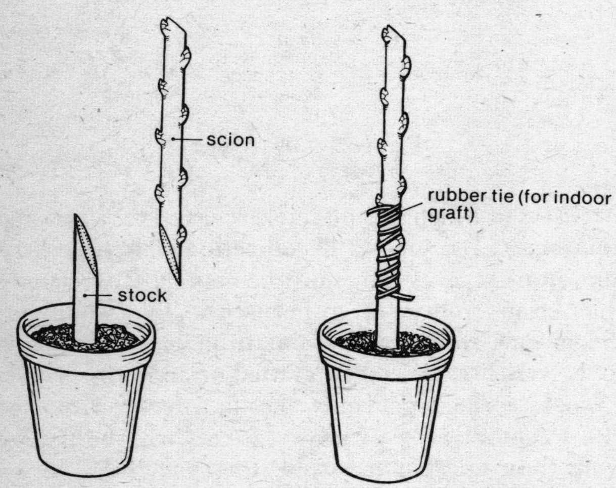

Figure 10 Whip or splice graft.

Another easy grafting technique, and perhaps the best method for conifers, is the side or veneer graft. A downward-facing nick no deeper than one third of the stem thickness is made into the stem, close to the base of the stock plant. A second downward cut is made, starting 2·5 to 5 cm (1 to 2 in) above the first, and aimed to meet the point of the nick; this removes a veneer of wood sufficient to expose the cambium. The scion is prepared by cutting

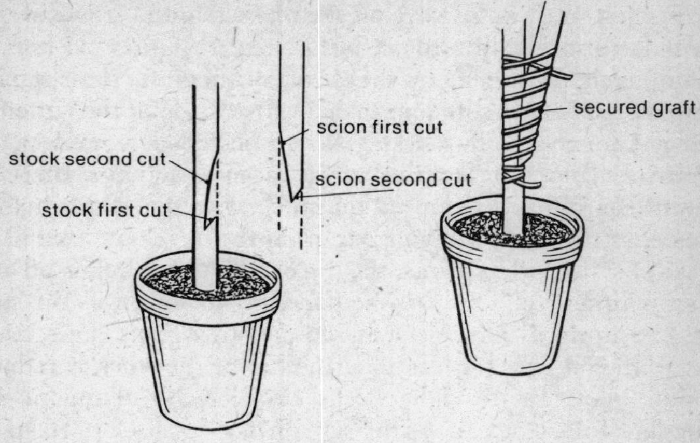

Figure 11 Side or veneer graft.

off a sliver of wood on one side, the length of which should correspond to that already made on the stock and whose depth should be such that the cambium on each side of the cut face matches the cambium already exposed on the stock. At the bottom of this cut a small oblique cut is made, so that the scion sits snugly into place against the stock (see Fig. 11).

Both types of graft must be secured with a firm binding of raffia or soft rubber tape. A large elastic band cut to form a rubber strip is ideal. The union of outdoor grafts is prevented from drying out by binding with 2·5 cm (1 in) wide polythene tape. Alternatively, the union can be sealed with proprietary grafting wax, waterproof tree-wound paint or petroleum jelly. Indoor grafted plants should be placed in a humid environment, such as a closed glass case or beneath a polythene tent, which removes the need for sealing.

After grafting

After grafting keep a close eye on the plants. Potted stocks should be kept fairly dry at the roots, but ensure that they do not dry out completely. Within a few weeks successful grafts show signs of healing by producing soft spongy new growth along the cut edges which is known as callus tissue. When healing is complete, cut away any remaining ties to prevent future constriction of the stem. Any growths which develop on the stock after this stage must be removed, as they take away vigour from the developing scion. In the case of side-grafted plants, the top of the stock is removed after healing is complete. This may be done in two stages, as the stock assists the upward movement of sap and this helps the scion to grow. With conifers, for example, the top of the stock is reduced half way, about six to eight weeks after successful union. The remainder of the stock above the scion is not cut back to the point above the graft until one full year after grafting.

Budding

Budding is preferred by nurserymen for the multiplication of many woody plants, particularly Roses, Maple, Ash, Sorbus, Malus, Crataegus, Pyrus and Prunus. This is because it is a very successful method and one that is economical on scion material: each lateral bud on a stem is potentially a new plant.

A method called 'T' budding can be used during the summer months of July and August, when the rind or bark readily comes away from the sapwood to expose the cambium tissue. The procedure is to make a 'T' shaped incision into the rind of the stock with a sharp knife. The horizontal cut is made first, followed by an upward vertical cut about 2·5 to 4 cm (1 to $1\frac{1}{2}$ in) long. As the blade point reaches the horizontal cut, make a sideways flick to the left and right; this lifts the bark and enables a bud to be inserted between the two lifted flaps (see Fig. 12). A budding knife usually has a spatula-shaped end on the handle and this is used to open the flaps further if necessary.

To collect budwood of the desired scion variety, trim off leaves to expose a short piece of leaf stalk. Keep this moist in polythene or immersed in a bucket of water until needed. Detach each scion bud by scooping underneath a bud with a knife, starting 1 cm ($\frac{1}{2}$ in) below the bud and finishing the same distance above it. Then carefully remove the thin sliver of wood beneath the bark before slipping the piece of bark containing the bud between the opened flaps of bark on the root stock. Finally, trim off any bark protruding from the inserted bud above the opened flaps and secure the bud firmly into position with raffia or a rubber tie (see Fig. 12).

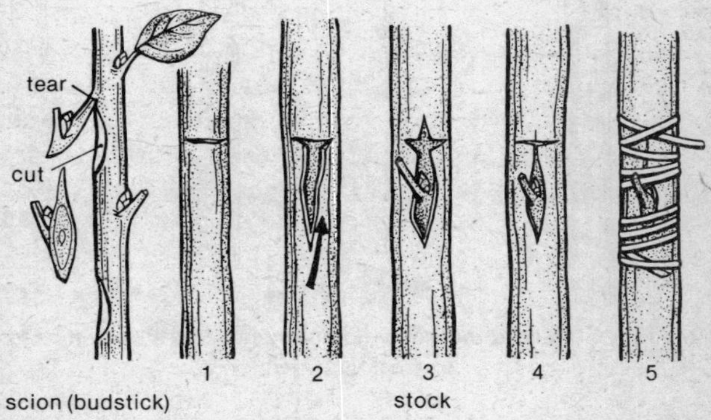

Figure 12 T-budding, showing bud, first cut, second cut, bud inserted, bud trimmed ready for tying and tied bud.

Chip budding of woody ornamentals such as Malus, Sorbus, Crataegus, Acer and Ash has increased in popularity among nurserymen in recent years. The technique is similar to side veneer grafting except that each scion carries a single bud. A downward cut roughly 0·5 cm ($\frac{1}{4}$ in) deep is made in the stock about 10 cm (4 in) above soil level. A second downward cut is made starting 3 cm ($1\frac{1}{4}$ in) above the first and aimed to meet the deepest point of the first cut. This removes a thin sliver of wood. Budsticks for chip budding are prepared by carefully cutting off both leaf and leaf stalks. Buds are removed by making cuts identical to those already made on the stock; a downward cut 0·5 cm ($\frac{1}{4}$ in) deep is made 1·5 cm ($\frac{5}{8}$ in) below the bud; and the final cut starts 1·5 cm ($\frac{5}{8}$ in) above the bud; with a slight scooping action the knife is pushed downwards to meet the first cut, and in so doing removes a sliver of wood containing the scion bud. This 'chip' is immediately placed into the stock cut and tied into position, care being taken to apply gentle pressure just above and below the bud (see Fig. 13).

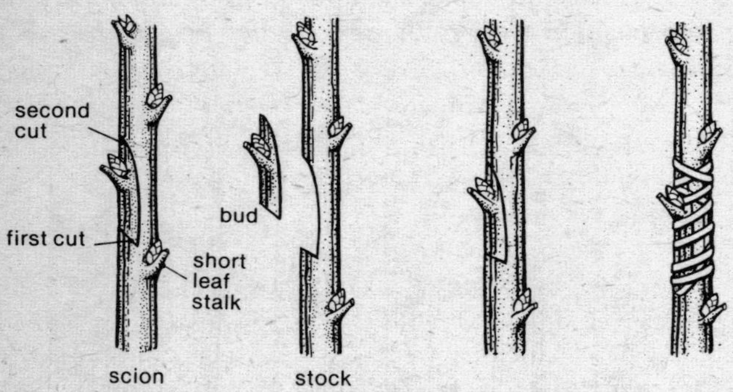

Figure 13 Chip budding, showing bud removed from scion, inserted in stock and tied.

The first spring after budding, just before growth commences, stock plants are headed back, which involves cutting them back with secateurs to a point just above the newly inserted bud. This directs the vigour from the established root system into the developing bud of the required scion variety.

4

Planting and Establishment

Choice and arrangement of plants; buying trees and shrubs; preparing the planting site – drainage, clearing the ground, cultivating the soil; planting time; planting procedure; establishing newly planted trees and shrubs – watering, applying nutrients, controlling weeds, checking supports, formative training, replacement.

Before planting it is helpful to prepare a sketch plan of your intentions. The purpose of this is to make you carefully think out your choice of plants and to consider their arrangement.

Choice of plant

The first requirement is to choose plants that will grow well in your garden. The two main limiting factors to growth are soil and climate. Fortunately, the vast majority of trees and shrubs are not fastidious about soil and consequently grow successfully on a wide range of soils. (See Chapter 16 for description of the more extreme soil conditions, where choice is likely to be restricted.)

Climate, and more specifically, the micro-climate of your planting site may limit choice. Temperature extremes vary considerably in Britain between the north and south, the east and west, and between inland and coastal districts; therefore make sure that the plants you choose are sufficiently hardy for your locality.

The best guide to what plants grow well locally is to study the trees and shrubs growing in gardens in your neighbourhood. These can be used for the main plantings. At the same time, be prepared to try out other plants which appeal to you, providing that there is no obvious reason why they might fail.

Arranging plants

Here we must take account of the size, shape, colour and texture of the plants.

Scale – scale is the size and proportion of plant mass in relation to its surrounding features. For example, it would be ineffective in a group arrangement to have a small, low-growing shrub dominated by a tall, spreading shrub. Likewise in borders, it would be pointless to have small shrubs obscured by taller-growing ones planted directly in front of them.

Timescale – Plants, and especially trees, will increase in size with the passage of time. The growth-rate and eventual size of a plant should therefore be considered when deciding on their relative positions. If your main plants are already arranged in permanent positions, use fillers, *i.e.* trees and shrubs that will eventually be removed for short term effect.

Visual characteristics – The differing shapes, colours and textures offer endless possible arrangements and here artistic flair can be given free rein. In Part Two of this book, the visual characteristics are discussed in detail to assist your selection.

Buying trees and shrubs

Success with your planting schemes begins with good-quality planting material. If at all possible, choose the trees or shrubs yourself so that you can actually see what you are paying for, and bear in mind the following points.

First you need to think about plant size. In some cases your choice may be limited to the range available from your local nursery or garden centre. The smallest plants are usually less costly than the larger specimens because they involve lower production costs for the nurseryman. Small plants also take less of a shock when transplanted from the nursery into your garden. They therefore recover quickly and for the first few years grow more vigorously than large plants. However, if you are choosing plants to fill a new garden, there is some justification for spending a bit extra on a few larger specimens which will soften the stark appearance of a sparsely-vegetated site.

The root system is the next important consideration. Ideally it should be well-balanced, compact and fibrous. A well-balanced root system is of special importance when selecting trees, as those that are one-sided tend to continue growing in that way; consequently, your trees become unstable as they increase in size and may eventually blow over. The advantage of a compact fibrous root system is that it transplants better, with less check to growth, since the roots continue to function normally – always providing they do not dry out between lifting and planting. I should point out, though, that not all woody plants have fibrous roots, and that some, such as *Ailanthus altissima* (Tree of Heaven), are thick and fleshy.

Trees and shrubs are sold as either bare root, root-balled or container-grown plants. The first type are lifted from the field and all soil is shaken off, and it is only these types of root systems which can be inspected. Root-balled subjects have a ball of soil or peat bound to the roots in a hessian or similar open type of wrapping. Most evergreen conifers, Rhododendrons, Azaleas and Magnolias are sold as root-balled specimens. Container-grown woody plants are now common: convenient for garden centres, they have the added advantage that they can be planted at any time of year. If possible, avoid container-grown trees which have constricted root systems as these result in poor growth and develop problems of instability later on.

Choose plants which look healthy. Deciduous shrubs should have several strong basal growths and a nice bushy growth habit; avoid weak, leggy-looking specimens. Trees may be purchased as seedlings, feathered trees or standards. Two- to three-year-old seedlings with only a few centimetres of top growth are the best size for planting out Pine, Spruce, Larch, Thuja, Silver Fir and Douglas Fir, and are ideal for establishing a windbreak or small copse in a larger garden. Feathered trees are young trees which have not had their side branches removed to form a clean trunk. These are quite useful for screen planting.

Standards have had their young side branches removed to produce a clean stem with an elevated branch framework which eventually becomes the crown of the tree. When choosing trees in this category select those with stems strong enough to support the head of the tree. Check that there are no stem weaknesses caused by constriction of ties or labels. Most trees should have a good central leading shoot which develops into the main trunk. Exceptions are trees such as Japanese Cherries, Flowering Crabs and Stag's Horn Sumach which develop a bush head; these form multi-branched crowns with no definite leading shoot. All trees should have a well formed and balanced framework of branches.

It may not always be possible to buy all the species you require from your local nurseryman, but he should be able to tell you where to obtain those he cannot supply. Selections can be made from catalogues, and although this means that you cannot actually see the plants before you buy, most nurserymen are reliable and will do their best to meet your needs. To assist the nurseryman and to be sure of getting the stock you want, place your orders as soon as you can. When orders are delivered check the contents of your packages to see if the plants are in good condition. If for any reason they are dry, plunge them into a tank of water to soak for one or two hours. Desiccated plants should not be accepted.

If you are not going to plant immediately, open the bundles and heel the plants into a spare piece of ground. Do this by digging a trench, laying the plants on their sides with roots in the trench and covering the roots with soil. Plants can be held like this without harm for several weeks during the dormant season. If you are not familiar with the species you are dealing with, make sure that each plant is kept labelled until planting time.

Preparation of the planting site

(*a*) Drainage

Thorough preparation of your planting site always pays dividends in the success and speed with which your plants establish; and the first essential of site preparation is drainage. A few trees and shrubs will tolerate wet sites, but if you are unfortunate enough to have a badly drained soil then it is always wise to try and improve the drainage. Many builders now install land drains into new developments, so if you are buying a new house, find out if drains have already been laid and if so, where.

Laying drains is a job which needs to be done properly, and you may wish to employ a garden contractor to do it for you. But should you decide to tackle the job yourself, start by locating a suitable outfall for the drainage water, such as a ditch, pond, stream or an existing main drain. Remember that permission must be sought before running land drains into a local authority drainage system. Also bear in mind that the local drainage authority usually requires the installation of a silt trap before drainage water flows into a main drain.

A scale plan of your proposed drainage system will be helpful in working out the materials you will need. Ideally, the plan should indicate levels, so that you have appropriate reference points and are able to set drains at the correct depth. An even gradient is needed to carry drainage water to the outfall, which should not be less than 1 in 100.

Trenches should be dug from the outfall in a simple herringbone or grid pattern. Piped drainage systems using either porous unglazed tile pipes or perforated plastic pipes are preferable for gardens. The main drain must be of sufficient diameter to cope with the normal volume of drainage water, and this will depend on the extent of the area being drained. For a garden of approximately one hectare (2·5 acres) a main drain of 15 cm (6 in) diameter with laterals 10 cm (4 in) diameter should be satisfactory.

Lateral drains need to be spaced anything from 4 to 20 m (13 to

65 ft) apart, depending on soil type. The closest spacings are for heavy clay soils and the widest for light sandy soils which rarely need a drainage system. When trenches have been dug and the fall levels set with a few marker pegs at intervals along the trench base, pipes can be laid.

Ideally, the trenches should be no less than 50 cm (20 in) in depth, and no more than 75 cm (30 in) deep at any point in the system. Gravel of 2 cm ($\frac{3}{4}$ in) diameter is placed along the trench bottom to a depth of 5 cm (2 in) to form an even bed for the pipes. A further covering of gravel is placed on top and around the pipe to give a 10 cm (4 in) covering. Finally, backfill the trenches with the previously excavated topsoil.

(*b*) Clearing the ground

After ensuring proper drainage, ground can be cleared and cultivated. Borders, and the position of other features, can be marked out on the ground with canes and garden lines according to your plan. It may be that the shape or line of a border is not quite to your liking when viewed from different vantage points on the ground – this is the appropriate time to make any necessary adjustments. When your setting-out is finalised, the border is ready for digging.

If there is a perennial weed problem, you would be well advised to use herbicides to kill off weeds before you start digging. Choice of chemicals will be determined by the nature of your weed problem; for Couch Grass use Dalapon; for broad-leaved weeds such as thistles, docks and nettles, use herbicides containing 2,4-D, repeating the application if necessary; for woody weeds like brambles, herbicides containing 2,4,5T, commonly known as brushwood killers, can be used. As new chemicals are constantly being developed, it is advisable to obtain a copy of the current weed control handbook from your public library and check up on new materials. The herbicides I have mentioned are all applied to the weed foliage, and best results are achieved when weeds are growing vigorously, as in spring and summer.

Always read labels and handle chemicals as directed by the

manufacturer and take note of any hazards, such as effects on fish or neighbouring plants. Eradicating weeds first may delay planting, but your patience will be rewarded in later years.

(*c*) Cultivating the soil

In most cases single digging will be adequate soil cultivation, but on new sites you may have to contend with compaction caused by heavy mechanical equipment working on wet soil. When imported topsoil is spread on top of soil compacted in this way, deeper-rooting plants such as trees and shrubs have difficulty in rooting down and subsequent growth is poor. In this case double-digging, although a more strenuous task, is advisable – unless the area is large enough to use a mechanical subsoiler. Double-digging means digging two spade depths. Excavate a trench one spade depth and 50 cm (20 in) wide across the width of your border. Then dig or fork over the bottom of this trench and add a bulky organic matter such as farmyard manure to this bottom layer to improve soil structure. A second trench is then marked and dug over on top of the first, and the bottom of the trench treated in the same way. This process continues until the final trench, which is then filled with soil dug from the first trench (see Fig 14).

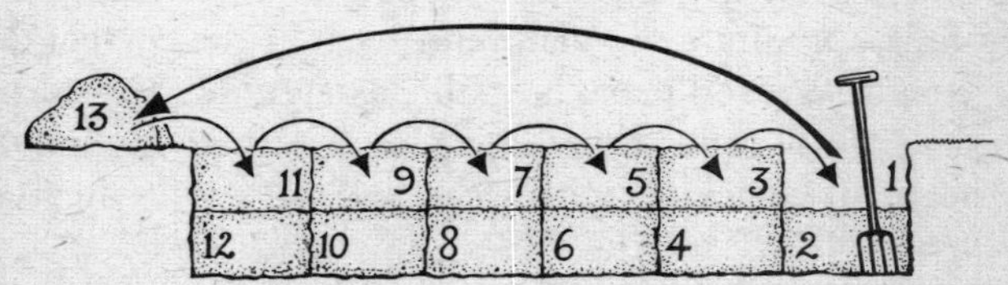

Figure 14 Double digging – even numbered sections forked over, odd numbered sections turned over.

Digging is a task for the autumn, when the ground is soft and winter frost action can break down the soil and settle it ready for planting. Personally, I prefer autumn planting and so I have to do my digging earlier in the season.

Planting time

Autumn is regarded as the best time for planting trees and shrubs because this is when their roots are least active. By the time ground conditions are suitable for spring planting, roots and sometimes buds are in active growth and consequently the plant's growth is checked. The best time for planting evergreens and conifers is September or April. In Britain both these months have damp, misty or showery weather conditions which minimise water-loss from leaves and consequently favour plant establishment.

Planting procedure

If you are planting from a prepared plan it is helpful to set out plant positions with marker canes beforehand, so that any adjustments can be made as you go along. It is preferable to lift and plant each group separately, so that plants are not left lying around for any undue length of time with their roots exposed.

Planting is done by digging a hole large enough to accommodate the roots. In poor soils, the immediate planting area can be improved by forking in a 4 cm (1½ in) deep dressing of peat and mixing this thoroughly through the soil before digging out the planting hole. Orientate the plant and set it at the correct depth – usually the nursery soil mark is visible as a guide. Spread out the roots and carefully refill the planting hole with good, friable soil. Shake the plant and gently firm the soil with your heel as you proceed.

Sometimes the soil is dry at planting time and in such conditions the planting hole should be flooded with water before refilling with its final layer of soil. After planting, apply a sprinkling of fertiliser around the base of the plant. To encourage growth, use a high nitrogen compound fertiliser, one with a nitrogen, phosphate, potash ratio of 2:1:1, at the rate of 100 g/m² (3 oz/sq yd). Take care to keep fertiliser off foliage, and lightly fork over the soil to leave a neat, tidy finish.

Trees can be planted into borders in a similar manner but will need to be supported with a suitable stake. When specimen trees are planted into lawns or grass verges, or places where the site is not going to receive overall ground preparation, the following technique of pit planting is recommended. Scribe on the ground a circle of no less than 1 m (39 in) around the planting position. Skim off surface vegetation with a spade, place it to one side, and dig the hole out to one spade depth. Surface vegetation, or other suitable bulky organic material, is then dug or forked into the pit bottom; this deeper cultivation relieves sub-surface compaction and facilitates deeper rooting. Ensure that the roots of your tree are not being exposed to drying sun or wind while you prepare the pit, and if several trees are being planted, keep their roots moist in a polythene bag or cover them with a wet sack.

A stake should be driven into the pit to support larger trees such as standards, but this may not be necessary for whips or feathered trees (see Fig. 15). Stakes should be long enough to reach the head of the tree and strong enough to provide support. For normal standards stakes 2 to 3 m (6 to 10 ft) long, with a minimum butt diameter of 10 cm (4 in) are suitable. If possible, stakes should be peeled of bark and the bottom metre treated with wood preservative. To mark the best position for the stake, hold your tree in the centre of the prepared pit. A crowbar can be used to put down a lead hole, and this is most helpful on stony ground where the stake is easily deflected. You may need some assistance in holding the stake upright as it is driven down with a large mallet or sledge hammer – and remember that the stake should be firm in the pit bottom before planting.

Before planting, check over the root system: occasionally there are damaged or broken roots which need trimming back with secateurs or a sharp knife. Also look for girdle roots which coil around the base of the stem and cause constriction in later years; these are sometimes found on old container-grown plants. Old woody girdle roots should be pruned back, but those that are still flexible can be spread out.

When planting, set the tree at the correct level and hold it 2 to 3 cm (1 to 1¼ in) from the stake. After spreading out the roots,

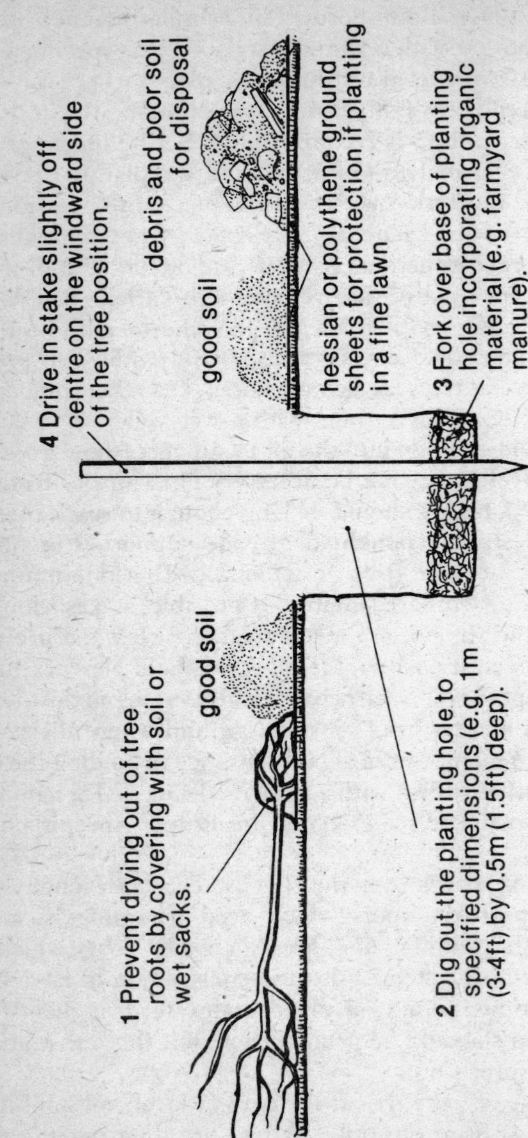

Figure 15 Tree planting – preparation of the planting site.

backfill with friable topsoil enriched with peat. Shake the tree gently to settle soil amongst the roots and firm with your foot as you fill in the hole.

A standard tree normally requires two ties to secure it to the stake, one placed at the top of the stake, and one halfway down. Proprietary rubber or plastic ties can be bought in the shops, but any durable material 2·5 to 4 cm (1 to 1½ in) wide can be used. Cord, twine or wire are not very suitable, and if you do use them, make sure that the trunk is protected with a hessian bandage to prevent chafing and injury. Proprietary ties are nailed to the stake. Remember to leave adequate space between the tie and the tree to allow for one year's increase in girth. (I allow the thickness of my finger.)

After planting, the head of the tree may benefit from light pruning. Damaged branches should be cleanly cut back to buds or lateral shoots to prevent the damage spreading. Trees which normally have a single leading shoot should have any double or competing leaders reduced to leave only one main stem. This can be done either by completely removing one shoot, or less drastically by shortening back one shoot to a suitable bud so that it develops as a lateral. Uneven crowns can be balanced by reducing growth from the heavy side of the crown. Finally, low branches or feathers arising from the trunk can be cut off if they are no longer required and might become a nuisance. This latter treatment is not necessary on specimens that are normally furnished to the ground with branches, such as Holly and Cypress.

Pruning cuts and any accidental bark wounds should now be painted with a suitable tree wound sealant. A high nitrogen fertiliser at the rate of 100 g/m^2 (3 oz/yd^2) is lightly forked into the soil and the planting is completed by adding a mulch of moist peat or well rotted farmyard manure over the root area (see Fig. 16). If possible, keep the 1 m (39 in) circle at the base of your specimen free from vegetation for a few years to minimise competition for water and nutrients.

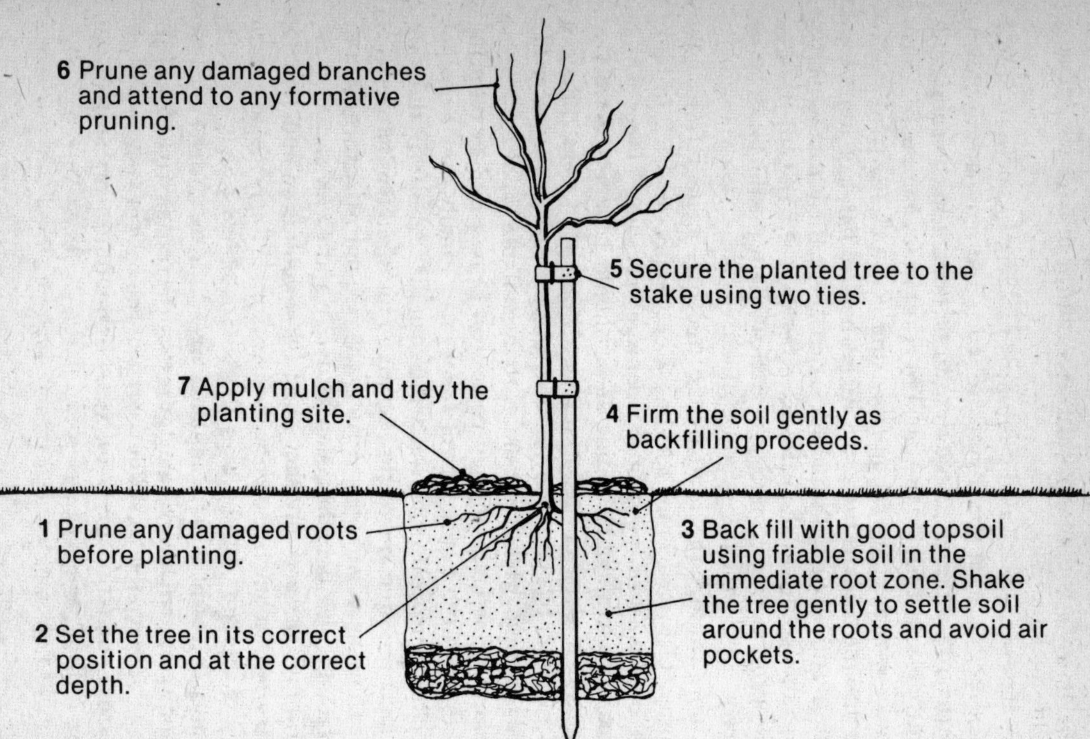

Figure 16 Tree planting – planting the tree.

Establishing newly planted trees and shrubs

Thorough preparation and careful planting are a good foundation for success, but continued vigilance during the formative years is necessary if your plants are to establish properly. Your aim is to make your plantings thrive, not merely survive.

Root systems of newly planted stock are often reduced in the process of lifting, and this, coupled with the shock of disturbance, obviously makes them function less efficiently; consequently newly planted subjects have smaller leaves, sparse foliage and shorter shoot growth. It is therefore important for growth to keep the root environment in the best possible condition.

(*a*) Watering

Water is the most urgent need, for without it plants cannot function; lack of water is the most common cause of failure. Check the soil frequently (and during dry, summer months this means at least once a week), and when soil in the root area is drying out, water it thoroughly. All soil in the immediate root area should be returned to 'field capacity' – in other words, the maximum amount of water held by a free-draining soil against the pull of gravity. In practical terms, a single shrub will require approximately 25 l ($5\frac{1}{2}$ gall) of water, and a standard tree 50 l (11 gall) at each watering. At these volumes water penetrates down to the root area. A light forking over before watering will assist penetration and prevent water running off the surface.

Regular light sprayings of water may seem a good idea, but they can be harmful. This is because much water is lost through surface evaporation and shallow penetration leads to the development of surface root systems. These become particularly vulnerable in times of drought. Mulches of bulky organic material applied to moist ground in springtime will help to conserve moisture, but these will not obviate the need for water during a dry summer.

(*b*) Applying nutrients

Nutrients are also needed by the developing plant, and a late winter or early spring application of compound fertiliser at the rate of 100 to 140 g/m² (3 to 4 oz/yd²) is sufficient to keep plants growing satisfactorily. Nitrogen, phosphate and potash are essentials for growth, and either balanced mixtures or those with a higher nitrogen content should be given during the formative years. Fertilisers which release nitrogen slowly are preferable. Other nutrients such as calcium, magnesium and iron are also needed by the plant and these are often included in proprietary fertilisers for trees, shrubs and roses.

(*c*) Weed control

Quite apart from the neglected and untidy appearance they give to borders, weeds tend to deprive new plantings of water and nutrients. You can remove them either manually or with chemicals, depending on the scale of the operation and the costs involved. Surface treatment with a garden hoe can be effective, if the weeds are caught at the seedling stage on a bright sunny day, but perennial weeds with deep root-stocks are more of a problem, and hoeing merely aggravates the situation. The aim during the establishment period should be to prevent weeds from getting out of hand. This can be achieved by regular cultivation or by using contact herbicides such as Paraquat or Diquat. These are sprayed or watered through a dribble bar on to the seedling weeds, but great care must be taken not to splash any on to the leaves of your developing plants.

(*d*) Checking supports

Trees which have been staked will need their ties checked and probably adjusted at intervals during the growing season, to prevent stem constriction. Stakes help to allow time for the root system to re-establish and also anchor the tree firmly; but the sooner a tree is self-supporting, the better. This is because as the tree grows it produces strengthening tissue to withstand the normal stresses of wind. The stakes should therefore be removed as soon as the tree is firmly rooted. Unfortunately, it is impossible to advise exactly when to do this as much depends on the species, planting size, root condition and degree of exposure. In some cases stakes can be removed after one year's growth, whilst others, especially weak-rooted trees such as Hawthorn, may still need stakes seven or eight years after planting.

(*e*) Formative training

Branch systems often need some attention in the first few years after planting. Dead or dying shoots caused by checks to growth during planting should be pruned back to live lateral shoots or buds. This improves their appearance, but more important, it keeps plants in good health by preventing the spread of decay and the development of fungal diseases such as Coral Spot.

Some formative pruning may also be needed to encourage the plant to develop a good shape. Keep the leader going on centre-leader trees and prune back any double or competing shoots which appear as the tree grows. Certain weeping trees require a support for the leading shoot, such as a cane tied on top of the stake, but once the stem becomes woody it will continue to grow straight on its own. Occasionally the leader dies back completely after planting, and if so a suitably placed lateral shoot has to be trained to take over.

(*f*) Replacement

Should you be unfortunate enough to lose any plants, clear them out and replant. If plants persistently fail on the site, replace them with something different. Similarly, if plants are still showing signs of obvious poor growth after a few years, either scrap them or, less drastically, transplant them to a different site. Fortunately, although you may encounter a fastidious subject from time to time, the vast majority of trees and shrubs are not problematical.

5

Maintenance of Shrubs and Established Borders

Pruning shrubs – reasons for pruning, pruning tools, making cuts, when and how to prune, after pruning; nutrition; adjustment of original plans; replacement planting; weed control in shrub borders.

One of the advantages of having areas permanently planted with trees and shrubs is that, once established, they do not require a great deal of maintenance. There are a few basic tasks, however, that keep borders looking at their very best.

Pruning

Pruning of shrubs is a skilful job which needs to be done regularly, and unfortunately it is often badly done. Good common sense and a basic understanding of plant growth are all that is needed to prune correctly. Let me stress that many shrubs do not need any regular pruning; after all, they manage themselves perfectly well in their natural habitat.

(*a*) Reasons for pruning

As a starting point it is useful to consider the reasons for pruning, the first of which is to maintain plant health. This is achieved by regularly cutting out dead, dying and diseased shoots back to live lateral shoots or buds to prevent further dieback and to contain stem diseases.

Secondly, pruning helps to train plants and maintain their good shape. Hedge-clipping and topiary work are severe forms of training, in which architectural shapes are imposed on the plant, but normal training aims to allow the plant to develop its natural shape; all pruning is done towards this end.

Sometimes pruning is carried out to contain a plant which has grown too large for its position – for example, one that is suppressing neighbouring plants, or one that is growing out and obstructing a path. Cutting back can be done for a few years, but ultimately the best solution is to replace it with a less vigorous subject or perhaps to realign the path.

Thinning out of the branch canopy is a third justifiable reason for pruning certain shrubs; here, the aim is to reduce the density of a thicket, thus allowing more light and air into the plant and creating a healthier micro-climate.

A fourth reason is to encourage flower production and in some cases to improve the quality of individual blooms. This is achieved by stimulating the growth of flower-bearing shoots, and the method depends on whether flowers are borne on the current year's growth or on wood made in previous seasons.

A final reason for pruning is to stimulate the growth of colourful stems by coppice treatment. This involves cutting the shoots hard back to the base of the plant each spring.

(*b*) Pruning tools

A good pair of secateurs is the best tool for shrub pruning, and it is worthwhile buying a quality tool which will be efficient and dependable in the long term. A well-sharpened pruning knife, which usually will have a strong, curved blade, may also be used. Undoubtedly, you will need more skill and effort to use the knife correctly, but it will do a good job. For cutting through thicker branches a pair of long-arm shears, or loppers, is ideal; the long handles give leverage and the 'parrot nose' of the shears makes light work of branches 2·5 to 3·5 cm (1 to 1½ in) in diameter.

Heavier branches are best dealt with by using a saw. There are two patterns suitable for shrubs; the lightweight pruning saw and the Grecian saw. The lightweight pruning saw has a narrow blade which facilitates cutting in confined or narrow-angled branch crotches. Some of these saws have cutting teeth on both sides of the blade, one side with coarse teeth, the other with fine. I have never found this arrangement very practical, as there are positions where it is impossible to cut from the top of one branch without accidentally cutting the underneath of another. To overcome this difficulty there are pruning saws with one-sided, interchangeable blades.

The 'Grecian' saw is an excellent tool for shrub pruning. It has a thin curved blade, tapering to a point to facilitate cutting in narrow crotches. The teeth are only sharpened on one side so that the saw only cuts as it is drawn towards the cutter.

All cutting tools should be kept sharp. This not only makes the job much easier but sharp tools produce clean, tidy cuts which look more professional and heal more quickly.

(*c*) Making cuts

Pruning cuts should always be made into live wood so that the wound can heal over with callus tissue. Try to avoid leaving snags and where possible make your cuts at a branch junction or to a suitably-placed lateral bud. Cuts are best made to outward facing buds *i.e.* those which point away from the centre of the plant – this keeps the centre of your bush open. When cutting to buds make a slightly angled cut on the opposite side to the bud, taking care not to cut at too steep an angle or too close to the bud as this dries out tissue immediately behind it and endangers the bud. Shrubs which have opposite pairs of buds are best cut at right angles to the shoot just above the tips of buds (see Fig 17). When cutting out is completed, wounds over 1 cm (½ in) in diameter can be treated with a fungicidal tree wound sealant.

(*d*) When and how to prune

These are important questions which depend very much on the particular subject and on your reason for pruning. The following examples are for guidance. Shrubs which flower in spring on shoots of the previous growing season should be pruned in late spring or early summer, immediately after the flowers have faded. Flowered shoots should be cut back to encourage new growth to bear the next crop of flowers. Flowering Quince (*Chaenomeles speciosa*),

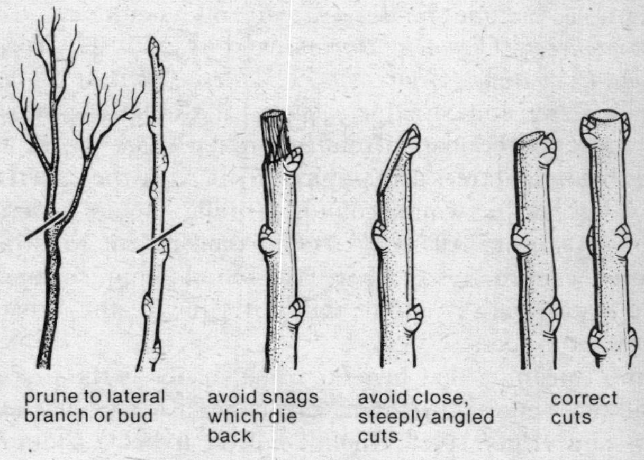

Figure 17 Making pruning cuts.

Winter Jasmine (*Jasminum nudiflorum*), evergreen Ceanothus (*Ceanothus dentatus*), *Clematis montana* and *Wisteria* can be treated in this way. *Forsythia*, *Berberis darwinii* and its hybrid *Berberis x stenophylla* can be treated likewise, but these plants all make large free-flowering specimens if left unpruned.

The next group comprises shrubs that flower in late spring and summer, again on shoots of the previous growing season. These are pruned after flowering by cutting out approximately one third of the oldest wood back to the base. The aim is to encourage vigorous new basal shoots and so to allow the plant to be constantly renewed. Flowering Currant (*Ribes sanguineum*), Mock Orange (*Philadelphus virginal*), Bridal Wreath (*Spiraea x arguta*), *Kerria japonica*, *Weigela* and *Deutzia* are examples of shrubs which benefit from this treatment.

The third group flowers during spring and summer on shoots of the current growing season. This means that as the new shoots extend, flowers are borne either in the leaf axils or at the end of the shoot. In these cases pruning is carried out in January and February, and the previous year's flowered shoots are cut hard back, in some cases to buds within a few centimetres of the shoot base. Examples include *Buddleia davidii* and its cultivars, *Caryopteris x clandonensis*, *Clematis jackmanii* and its cultivars, *Hypericum calycinum*, *Ceanothus 'Gloire de Versailles'*, *Spiraea x bumalda 'Anthony Waterer'* and *Spartium junceum*. In this latter case, regular pruning prevents the plants from becoming 'leggy' at the base.

When shrubs and trees are coppiced to increase the effectiveness of their stems, or for winter colour, pruning should be left until bud-break in spring. All stems should then be cut hard back to within a few centimetres of their base. On old coppice stools it is advisable from time to time to thin out a few of the older stubs with a pair of loppers.

A form of pruning that benefits some shrubs is the practice of dead heading. Young, developing plants of Lilac (*Syringa vulgaris* cultivars) and large-leaved Rhododendron hybrids should have their spent flower-heads carefully cut off soon after flowering, so that energy is directed into new growth, and not unwanted seed production.

(*e*) After pruning

After a pruning session clean, re-sharpen and oil your tools so that they will be in good order on the next occasion you need them. Prunings should be gathered up and disposed of; if possible, burn them so that they are not left around harbouring pest and disease organisms which can infect growing plants. Fires should be lit well away from trees to avoid heat scorch, which, although causing no outward sign of injury, kills the underlying tissue. Heat scorch will not be revealed until several months later, when a section of bark will flake off, exposing the heartwood to decay organisms.

Nutrition

Pruning is not simply a matter of cutting back plants and waiting for the right response; to achieve satisfactory results pruning should always be done in conjunction with the application of nutrients. Even when pruning is not carried out, shrubs will respond to the application of fertiliser. This is especially true in the case of long-established borders, where soil nutrient levels have been reduced by the continual uptake by plants and losses caused by the process of leaching.

It is often difficult to decide how much fertiliser to apply. Initially it depends on the existing levels of soil nutrients, and these can only be determined accurately by chemical analysis. There are inexpensive soil testing kits available from horticultural sundriesmen which give a useful indication of the nutrient status of your soil. A general recommendation is to apply a compound fertiliser containing the main plant nutrients of nitrogen, phosphate and potash in the ratios $1\frac{1}{2}:1:1$ or $1:1:1$ at the rate of 100 to 140 g/m^2 (3 to 4 oz/yd^2). There are several proprietary compound fertilisers in garden shops that are specifically formulated for trees and shrubs, and these contain other nutrients which are beneficial to growth. A number of slow-release fertilisers are also available; these release nutrients over a longer period, which is beneficial to plant growth.

Not all nutritional problems are related to the three main plant foods; for example, many soils are deficient in magnesium, others are short of iron, or in some cases the iron cannot be obtained chemically by the plant. These and other minor nutrients are not, however, needed in large quantities and many are contained in sufficient quantity in farmyard manure. Alternatively, plants can be watered with liquid fertilisers containing trace elements. Iron deficiency, for example, can be overcome by watering with sequestrene. The general health of your plants should always be a prime consideration and if you look at them regularly you should detect early symptoms of nutritional, or pest and disease problems. Prompt action to correct the problem will ensure that the plant is not seriously weakened.

Adjusting original plans

It is very satisfying to watch your planting schemes develop and your plants increase in size and spread with each passing growing season. Foliage, flower and fruit displays become more and more prolific, and give increasing pleasure as time goes on. Whilst many good compositions of plants originate as ideas on a planting plan, there are equally many which evolve while the garden grows and while you learn more about the plants or perhaps have more cash available. Sometimes ideas in your original plan do not materialise as intended; a plant may grow faster or larger than was expected, or its flower colour may not harmonise with the colour of a neighbouring plant.

It is for this kind of reason that changes and adjustments to your original plans have to be made. You should always be looking critically at your borders and planting schemes; good gardeners are rarely satisfied with what they have and will always look for ways to make improvements. Sometimes, for instance, where borders were initially well stocked, you need to remove filler plants to make room for those which are to grow on to full maturity. This is a job that needs to be done sooner rather than later, to avoid the final plants becoming suppressed or bare at the base through over-crowding.

Filler plants can often be made use of by transplanting them to fill up gaps in a border or by using them to provide some immediate effect in new borders. Likewise, if you have taken over a matured garden you may well find suitable established trees and shrubs that can be transplanted to different positions in the garden. Obviously, not all trees and shrubs will stand transplanting once they are established, but *Rhododendron*, *Syringa*, *Ilex*, *Forsythia*,

Ribes and *Hydrangea* are but a few of the many that can be successfully moved. My attitude is that when removing fillers or redeveloping a matured garden, you have nothing to lose, apart from the physical effort involved.

Replacement planting

Apart from thinning out and transplanting specimens in borders, some replacement planting is worthwhile from time to time. Plants sometimes tend to degenerate and become untidy, and if pruning and feeding achieve little result, dig them out and re-plant them. The same applies if you take over a garden with neglected borders; some plants can doubtless be integrated into your design, but clear out the poor specimens to make room for replacements.

A portable hand winch such as the Tirfor TU16 or T35 is an excellent piece of equipment for grubbing out unwanted shrubs. A chain or wire rope sling with a safe working load of 5 tonne is slung round the base of the shrub and the winch cable is hooked on. The winch will tear the plant and most of its roots out of the ground with comparative ease. In such cases soil is likely to be impoverished, and liberal application of farmyard manure is advisable before you begin re-planting, followed by a top dressing with fertiliser. Crop rotation is a sound, basic principle of plant husbandry and woody plants are no exception; therefore always re-plant the area with genera that are different from the ones removed.

Weed control in shrub borders

Shrub borders that have become infested with weeds soon give a garden a neglected and untidy appearance. There are three ways of controlling weeds in this situation: firstly, by regular soil cultivation; secondly, by using ground-covering plants; and thirdly, by using herbicides (weedkillers).

Regular soil cultivation involves forking over in spring to begin the season with ground free of weeds. This initial cultivation is followed by further forking or hoeing throughout the growing season. The second method, using ground-covering plants, is dealt with in Chapter 15.

The use of herbicides is highly effective and less time-consuming, but it does involve the added expense of chemicals. Before using herbicides, ensure that you have selected the right chemical for your particular weed. New materials are continually being developed, and it is advisable to consult a current edition of the weed control handbook at your public library first, or alternatively, seek the advice of your local horticultural sundriesman. Apply the herbicide in a safe and sensible manner as directed by the manufacturer (see further notes on the safe use of pesticides in Chapter 7).

There are three basic types of herbicide used in shrub borders:

(*a*) Foliage-applied contact herbicides

These are non-selective, and will kill off any foliage that they come into contact with; they must therefore be applied carefully, ensuring that the herbicide only contacts the leaves of weeds and not the shrubs. Normally, a hand sprayer directed at the weeds can be used, or alternatively, a dribble bar attached to a watering can. This latter method has the advantage of producing larger droplets which are less likely to drift on to adjacent lawns or herbaceous plants.

Paraquat and Diquat are two commonly used examples of contact herbicides that are excellent for killing off annual weeds and grasses, but are less effective on deep-rooted perennials which can re-grow from the root-stock.

(*b*) Foliage-applied translocated herbicides

These are absorbed through the leaves into the sap stream of the weed, and are then translocated to the roots. Examples used in shrub borders include 2.4-D, used for the spot treatment of ground Elder, nettles, docks and thistles. Dalapon is another example that is used more specifically for eradicating couch grass.

(*c*) Soil-applied residual herbicides

These are applied to weed-free ground in spring and subsequently kill off germinating weed seedlings. It is important with these materials not to cultivate the ground after treatment, as this breaks through the weed-suppressing layer. It is also important to restrict their use to established planted areas, because newly-planted shrubs can be adversely affected. In addition to liquid formulations that are watered or sprayed on to the soil, some materials are available in the form of granules, which makes for safe and accurate application.

Some of these materials, *e.g.* simazine and atrazine, persist in the soil and consequently new plantings should not be undertaken for nine months after treatment. It is also essential with these materials to check that there are no susceptible plants growing in the border being treated, by consulting the lists of plants given on the product label.

In addition to simazine and atrazine, there are also herbicides based on dichlorbenil, chloramben, chloroxuron and propachlor, which are suitable for use in shrub borders and Rose beds.

6

Maintenance of Garden Trees

Safety; tree pruning – reasons for pruning, time of pruning, tools, making cuts, sealing wounds, pruning procedures; bark wounds; structural weakness; bracing weak limbs; nutrition.

Many problems which arise with garden trees are the result of neglect or poor maintenance, and this is often due to ignorance or lack of understanding on the part of the tree owner.

Safety

Before considering maintenance let me stress the importance of safety. Working in large trees is a highly skilled job and one which has obvious dangers for untrained people, and especially for those who lack the necessary equipment. For a tree worker, safety harnesses, climbing ropes, strops, karabiners, helmets, goggles, ear protectors, safety boots and gloves are regarded as basic safety equipment. It is imperative, therefore, to know your own limitations and to refrain from attempting tree jobs for which you are not equipped and which you cannot manage competently and safely. Jobs such as these, and especially work at heights, should be delegated to a qualified tree surgeon.

Tree pruning

Trees that are planted for ornamental purposes, unlike fruit trees, do not require an annual pruning programme and generally pruning should be kept to a minimum to allow them to develop their natural character.

(*a*) Reasons for pruning

I consider that there are five basic reasons for pruning. Firstly, pruning during the formative years helps a young tree to develop a crown that is structurally safe and well balanced. Secondly, pruning is done to obtain a clean trunk and an elevated crown. (Not all trees should be treated this way, though: Holly and Cypress, for instance, are normally open grown trees, clothed to the ground with foliage.) Thirdly, pruning will keep a tree in good health, by regularly removing dead, dying and diseased branches and thus preventing eventual heartwood decay. A fourth valid reason is to reduce the density of foliage by thinning the crown. This process allows more light and air into a crown and at the same time, by reducing wind resistance, eases demands on the root system. Crown thinning is a useful treatment for large trees which are restricting light and casting a heavy shadow over nearby buildings. A final reason for pruning is to re-shape the crown of a tree, but if trees have been carefully selected this should rarely be necessary in a garden. Occasionally, a crown can be reduced successfully or a lop-sided crown can be balanced, but re-shaping is a very skilled operation, and should not be confused with the crude lopping so frequently seen on trees.

(*b*) Time of pruning

If your trees come into any of the above categories, the next question is when to prune. Most trees can be pruned at any time of the year, and precisely when will depend on the specific task and on factors such as minimising damage to neighbouring plants. Dead wood is more easily seen when trees are in leaf; similarly, crown density can be assessed more accurately if trees are thinned during the growing season.

There are several exceptions to year-round pruning; Birch, Hornbeam, Sycamore and several other Maples tend to 'bleed', *i.e.* exude sap from the pruning wound, if cut between January and the end of May. This does not mean that they will die, but in the course of bleeding sealants are washed from the wound surface and continually oozing sap disfigures the tree and can lead to bark injury. Walnut trees bleed heavily if cut while they are dormant and during early spring, so in this case pruning is best done when trees are in full leaf. Finally, the normal time for pruning Cherries is after flowering in May or June.

(*c*) Pruning tools

Saws used for cutting off branches need to be sharp and correctly set, and of the right type. The type of handsaws used by joiners and handymen usually have fine teeth and are designed for cutting through dried timber. Sawing growing timber with one of these is a slow, strenuous task and frequently the saw will jam in the kerf, or cutting groove. Ideally, a handsaw for green timber should have no more than five teeth to each 2·5 cm (1 in) of blade length.

Tubular-framed bow saws, which have replaceable blades, cut easily through branches up to 15 cm (6 in) in diameter. The full bow saw is of limited use for sawing trees, but the type with a bow tapering towards the blade at one end is ideal. For training and thinning out small branches in narrow-angled crotches, Grecian saws and small pruning saws are suitable.

Small lightweight chainsaws with guide bar lengths of 30 to 37 cm (12 to 15 in) are fast and take the toil out of sawing through larger branches. A word of caution, however: get to know your saw and become fully competent with it before using it for pruning, and under no circumstances use it in a tree without proper training.

(*d*) Making cuts

Whatever tool is used it is most important that cuts are made

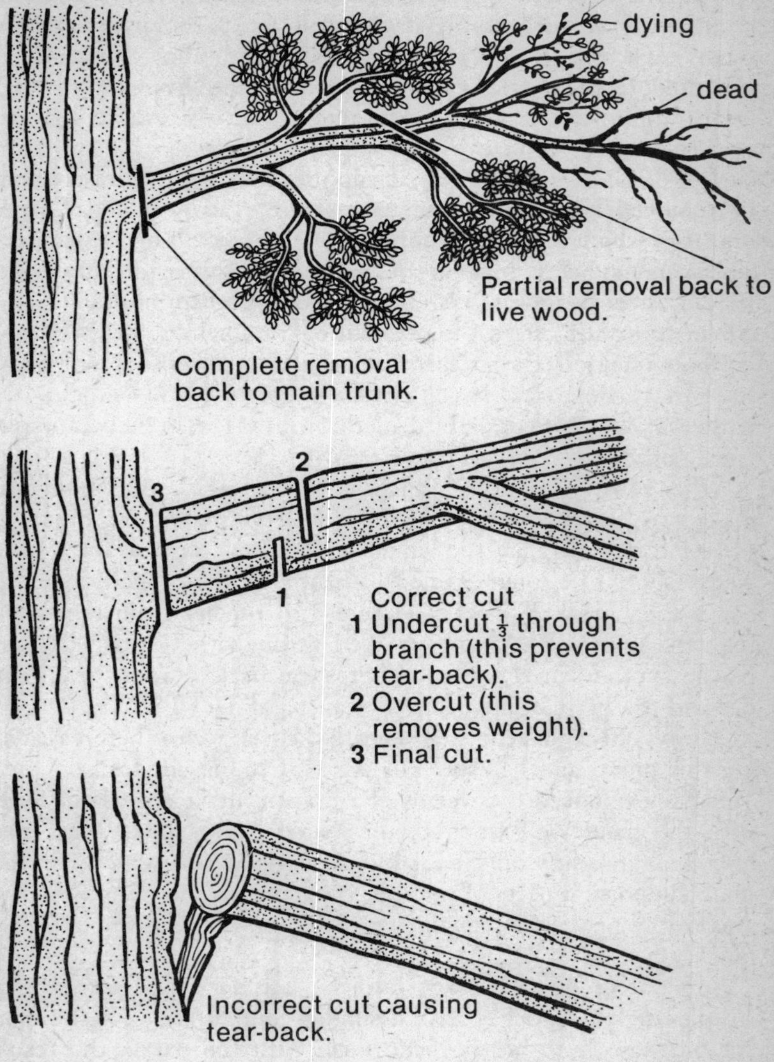

Figure 18 Removing a branch.

correctly and in the right place. Pruning may involve removing branches right back to the main trunk or in some cases partly removing a branch back to a suitable lateral branch. Wherever it is located, the final cut must always be made into live wood, so that the cambium can produce callus tissue that will eventually heal over the wound surface.

Small branches which can be supported as they are cut off can be removed in one piece at the point of the final cut. Larger branches which cannot be supported should be cut off in manageable sections; before making the final cut, always remove the main weight of the branch. This is done by making an undercut 15 to 20 cm (6 to 8 in) from the position of the final cut. This should be about one third through the branch and its purpose is to prevent the bark tearing back. If you cut too deeply the saw will jam, but if the cut is less than a third of the width, the branch can split back, so be fairly precise (see Fig. 18).

When sawing through a branch growing upright, you should first make two cuts and remove a wedge of wood facing the intended direction of fall. Like the single undercut described above, the wedge should be roughly one third through the branch. The top cut is then made 2 to 3 cm (1 to 1½ in) further from the trunk than the undercut. As you proceed through the branch the cut reaches a point where the wood fibres tear back to meet the undercut and the branch falls from a clean break (see Fig. 19).

Always check that the area beneath the tree is clear before reaching this point, and be especially wary of young children.

Having removed the weight of a branch, make a final cut flush with the trunk or branch union. Never leave stubs; these not only look unsightly but invariably die back and cause decay in the main supporting parts of the tree. The aim should be to keep the area of the final cut as small as possible, so that the wound heals quickly.

Some trees develop large branch shoulders, and those with steeply-angled branches have a similar configuration. If the final cut on these branches is made flush with the trunk, the result is a pruning wound which will be excessively large relative to the branch diameter. In such cases the cut should start flush at the top and slope away from the trunk to form a slight shoulder (see Fig. 20).

There is no need to pare the final cut with a knife, and this can be detrimental, especially if the bark is chamfered too steeply. The result is that protective bark dries out and dies back, callus tissue has further to grow, and therefore the wound takes longer to heal.

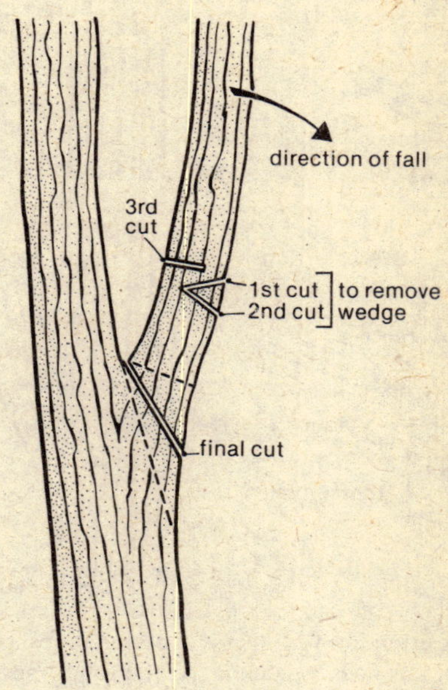

Figure 19 Making cuts to remove a vertical branch.

(*e*) Sealing wounds

When the final cut has been made, the exposed wood should be treated with a suitable tree wound sealant. These are intended to prevent infection of the wound surface by decay organisms, and some modern sealants penetrate the tissue and act as wood preservatives. If possible the sealant should be waterproof. A dry wound is less likely to decay than a wet one.

Materials currently used include Arbrex 805, which is a black, bituminous paint containing fungicide. Lac Balsam is a greenish-grey latex-like paint that forms an elastic, weatherproof coat over

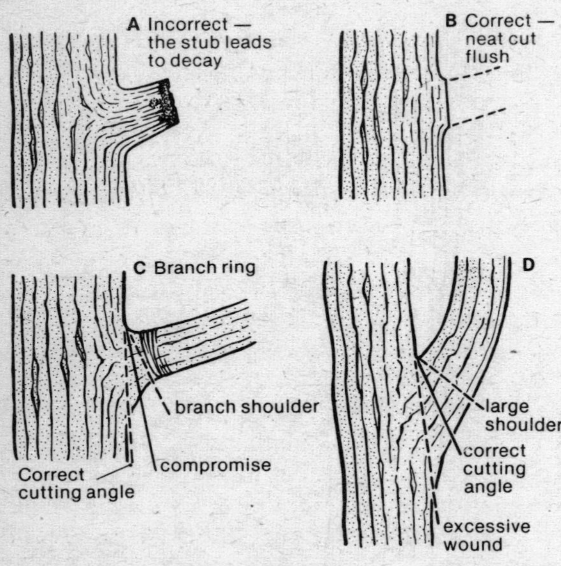

Figure 20 Position of final cuts – dotted lines result in either excessive wounds or large shoulders; the solid lines are correct.

the wound. Visually it is less obtrusive than bitumen-based sealants as its colour blends in with bark. This product also contains a plant growth regulator to stimulate callus development. On large wounds only the sapwood area need be treated; exposed heartwood is better treated with a wood preservative such as Xylamon Arbor. Piol and Tree 3 are aerosol formulations of wound sealant that are convenient to apply and effective, in that they penetrate the wood fibre and therefore give greater protection. AVR 650 is another product with similar penetrative properties and adequate fungicidal effect. It is a liquid formulation that can either be brushed or sprayed over the exposed wound.

(*f*) Pruning procedures

The art of pruning lies in knowing precisely where to make cuts and in having the ability to visualise the effects of cutting out a branch before you actually do so. Remember, the process is irreversible: once a branch is removed there is no way of putting it back. Therefore be sure of your objective before taking action.

To thin the crown of a tree, start by removing all the dead, diseased or damaged wood from the centre of the tree. Likewise, cut out weak, spindly, crossing and rubbing branches. Having gone this far, stand back and look at the tree from various vantage points to decide what further branches need to be removed.

Sometimes complete removal of branches is justified, but usually it is the twiggy growth on the outer canopy which needs to be thinned out further. On small trees this can be done from the ground with a pair of long-arm pruners, or from within the crown using a pole saw. Continue cutting out these sound branches until your objective is reached. A well-thinned crown should still retain its natural shape and remain an attractive specimen.

Lopping of garden trees is not a practice I approve of, because of the rather ugly, mutilated appearance which persists for so long afterwards. In addition, the vigorous regrowth produces a dense, congested crown, and often cavities develop in the sawn-off stubs; as a result structural weakness develops as the regenerated branches increase in size.

If a crown has to be reduced arrange for a tree surgeon to shorten back the main limbs to suitably-placed lateral branches. This less drastic treatment is aimed at reducing the crown whilst retaining the overall shape of the tree and avoiding excessive regrowth. Trees such as Lime, London Plane and Elm are remarkably responsive to this kind of treatment. Generally however, crown reduction should be kept to the minimum and removal and replacement with a more suitable species should always be the preferred option.

If the crown has been made lop-sided by wind or suppression by neighbouring trees, it is possible to balance it. This is done by shortening branch leaders on the heavy side of the tree back to suitable lateral branches and leaving the light side unpruned. Ideally, balancing should be done as the tree develops its branch framework. Problems sometimes occur in exposed gardens when branches on the windward side bend over and grow towards the leeward side. In such cases it becomes necessary to prune back to either a lateral shoot or a bud heading into the wind. This problem is extreme in exposed coastal gardens where salt damage on the windward side of a tree also retards growth. In these severe cases pruning will not resolve the problem, and perhaps the planting of enough trees and shrubs to make a shelter belt is a better solution.

Bark wounds

Bark injuries to trees, if they occur, should be dealt with as soon as possible to prevent infection of exposed wood by decay organisms. Neglect eventually leads to the formation of cavities and structural weakness. Some injuries may be quite small, such as basal wounds caused by careless use of a lawnmower, whilst others – such as injury resulting from heat scorch from a badly-sited bonfire – can be extensive.

In either case, treatment involves removing all damaged bark and

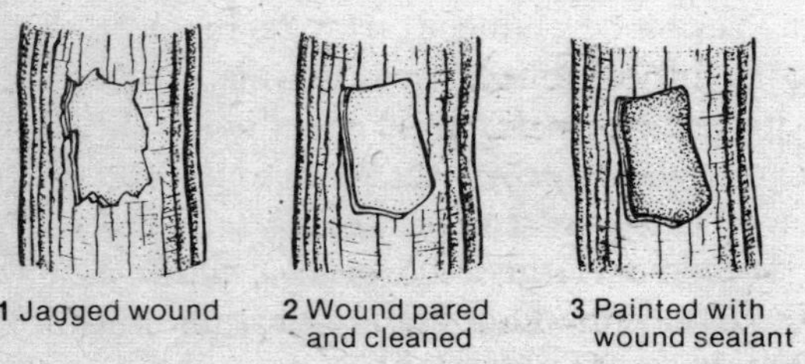

Figure 21 Repairing a bark wound.

any splintered wood back to sound tissue, and keeping the wound area as small as possible. This can be done with a 5 cm (2 in) flat wood chisel and mallet. After being cleaned, the wound is treated with at least two coats of fungicidal tree wound sealant (see Fig. 21).

Both bark wounds and pruning cuts need a yearly examination to check that they are sound. It is very often necessary to apply further protective coats of wound sealant or preservative to ensure continued protection of the heartwood until callus tissue finally closes over the wound.

Structural weakness

Cavities may already have developed in your trees as a result of several years of decay, but these need not necessarily be a cause for alarm. A tree owner, however, has a duty to act as a good estate manager, because you are responsible for your trees in the eyes of the law. It is well to remember that a tree owner can be liable for any damage to adjoining property, or persons on adjoining property or highways, caused by falling trees or branches. Quite apart from this, it is undesirable to have trees in your garden that are likely to damage your *own* property or person.

The owner of large or mature trees is advised to have them inspected by a qualified tree consultant who has expert knowledge and experience.

Bracing weak limbs

Tree-bracing with flexible cables is a technique of tree surgery used mainly to prevent weak forks from splitting by restricting the outward flexing of branches. Occasionally braces are also used to give additional support to large horizontal branches. This can, for example, prevent damage to Cedar trees when heavy snowfalls overload their large, plate-like branches. Cables should only be installed on the advice of a tree consultant, and their fitting should be a job strictly for the qualified tree surgeon.

Nutrition

I have already indicated that developing trees and shrubs respond to the application of nutrients; mature trees do likewise. Under normal circumstances, however, mature trees are only supplied with additional nutrients when they are in poor health and under growth stress or when you anticipate growth stress from, say, impending surgery or nearby building development. Symptoms of growth stress often begin with the death of branches furthest from the roots. In addition, smaller leaves, a thin canopy of foliage, early defoliation in late summer, shorter shoot extension and poor callus growth over wounds are indications that all is not well. If there are no obvious signs of disease, soil improvement and the application of nutrients will be of benefit.

The best method of applying nutrients is to make holes 3·5 cm (1½ in) in diameter, 45 to 60 cm (18 to 24 in) deep and spaced 45 cm (18 in) apart in a 3 m (10 ft) wide band centred on the drip line of your tree. The drip line follows the furthermost extension of the branches and it is along and outside this line that a tree's feeder roots are located. Ideally, these holes should be drilled out with a powered auger, but in your garden they can be 'punched' in with a crowbar. The holes are then filled with a porous, open compost to which nutrients are added – for example, 5 parts peat to 10 parts grit plus 1 part of compound fertiliser containing Nitrogen, Phosphate and Potash.

This compound can be made by mixing 5 parts Sulphate of Ammonia, 5 parts Superphosphate and 1½ parts Sulphate of Potash. If possible, do this task in late autumn or spring whilst the ground is moist and soft. Apart from providing a supply of nutrients, this method aerates the soil and considerably improves the supply of oxygen to roots and also improves water penetration, particularly in areas where the soil beneath a tree is compacted.

7

Pests, Diseases and Disorders

Leaf problems – insect infestation, disease infection, symptoms of nutritional problems; shoot problems – insect infestation, disease infection, animal damage; trunk and branch problems – insect infestation, disease infections, animal damage, frost damage; root problems – disease infection, compaction, waterlogging, drought; flower and fruit problems – insect infestation, disease infection, bird damage, physiological problems; safe use of pesticides.

The gardener's task is to keep a collection of plants in the very best of health, but plants are living things and inevitably suffer from pathological problems. At times these are serious and apparently uncontrollable, such as the recent outbreak of Dutch Elm disease; but fortunately, most problems are less serious and can be effectively managed.

It is essential to recognise problems early and to deal with them before serious epidemics occur and before remedial action is too late. Having identified a problem, the next essential is knowing how best to solve it. The following notes briefly review the common problems and state the preventative or remedial measures that can be taken.

Leaf problems

Examining the foliage of your plants is an immediate way of locating problems. Any symptoms of insect infestation, fungal, bacterial or viral infection, and nutritional or physiological disorders may be visible in the leaves of your plants.

Insect infestation

Caterpillars

The first obvious symptoms occur when leaves are eaten by caterpillars, which are the larval stages of moths, butterflies and sawflies. Caterpillars are too numerous to identify individually, but most trees, shrubs and conifers are attacked by at least one species (in many cases several kinds) of caterpillar. In serious outbreaks their voracious feeding can defoliate young plants, and for that matter mature trees, causing serious hindrance to growth. Early recognition of an outbreak is therefore essential if control measures are to be effective. On a small scale, hand-picking of the caterpillars is feasible; but a potentially serious outbreak should be treated by spraying or dusting with insecticides containing either carbaryl, DDT, gamma-HCH, derris, malathion or pyrethrum.

Other biting insects

Sometimes you may discover chewed leaves but no visible evidence of caterpillars. This is often a symptom of beetles, weevils or earwigs, which, being nocturnal feeders, are rarely seen. Damage is often confined to the lower leaves and as such is unimportant, but serious damage to young or especially valuable plants can be prevented by spraying with insecticides containing either DDT or gamma-HCH as soon as the pest is detected.

Sucking insects

Aphids (greenfly and blackfly) and several related insects, such as capsid bugs and suckers, feed by sucking the sap from succulent young leaves and stems. The first symptoms of their presence will probably be distortion or puckering, and in some cases curling, of the leaves. Later the sucking insects may appear in such numbers that their presence can hardly be missed. Their sticky secretion (Honeydew) also coats the leaf surface, which becomes further disfigured by the growth of unsightly black sooty moulds.

Many plants are afflicted by aphids, and it is remarkable how an initial infestation can soon reach epidemic proportions, as any rose grower knows too well. Immediately an outbreak is noticed, apply an insecticide based on malathion, demeton-S-methyl or dimethoate.

Leaf miners

Several trees and shrubs, notably Holly and Lilac, are attacked by small flies which lay their eggs in the leaf tissue. The resultant grubs tunnel their way through the leaf, causing either blisters or disfiguring markings. With mature plants control is unnecessary, as the insects cause no apparent loss of vigour. Serious infestations on young plants can, however, be dealt with by spraying with insecticides based on gamma-HCH or diazinon. Three sprays at fourteen-day intervals are recommended.

Mites

During hot, dry summers there are occasional outbreaks of red spider mites. These usually infest lime trees, crab apples and some shrubs, and are first noticed when they cause a bronzing of the green foliage; closer examination reveals a film of gossamer webbing. With the aid of a ×10 hand lens (most useful when detecting pests) you can actually see the small red spiders. Control, when a practical proposition, can be effected by spraying with either malathion, dimethoate or diazinon.

Gall formers

Many woody plants develop abnormal growths on their leaves, notably Oak, Willow, Lime, Sycamore and Mountain Ash. These are sometimes large structures like the 'marble' galls often seen on Oak leaves; conversely, they can be small pimples like those seen on Sycamore leaves. Most galls are caused by insects or mites which, by their feeding, stimulate abnormal cell growth. Rarely do these impair vigour and control measures are not necessary.

Disease infection

Mildew

The familiar white powdery mould which spreads over the leaves of several plants, notably Roses, Crab Apples, Oaks, Hawthorns and Mahonia, is caused by various powdery mildew fungi. They can be crippling to the foliage of susceptible plants, for example, the old-fashioned roses. Generally, in the early stages of development, powdery mildews can be controlled by spraying with fungicides based on either dinocap, benomyl or sulphur. These sprayings will probably have to be repeated at ten to fourteen day intervals during the main growing season.

Rust

Various trees and shrubs, notably Roses, Birches, Willows, Barberries and Mahonia, suffer from infection with rust. This is a fungal disease that produces orange-coloured pustules on the leaves, usually in late summer and autumn. Control is often unnecessary, but minor infections can be dealt with by hand-picking and burning the infected leaves. With more serious outbreaks, spraying with fungicides based on either thiram or zineb will be effective.

Leaf spot

There are various reasons for discoloured spots on leaves, but the most conspicuous are those caused by fungal infection, such as black spot of Rose and tar spot of Sycamore. The sickly leaves of black-spotted roses detract considerably from the beauty of the plant and gradually impair its vigour. Leaf spot can be controlled by spraying with fungicides based on captan; repeated spraying at fourteen day intervals throughout the growing season is necessary to eradicate serious outbreaks. Control for tar spot on Sycamore is unnecessary.

Peach leaf curl

This fungal disease is confined mainly to Almonds, Peaches and Nectarines. It appears in the form of conspicuous red blisters which seriously distort the leaves and generally weaken the tree, causing the branches to die off. Serious cases can be controlled by spraying dormant trees in January and February with Bordeaux mixture, a copper and lime-based fungicide.

Virus diseases

Several broad-leaved trees and shrubs are affected by virus diseases, notably Camellia, Daphne, Prunus and Malus. Viruses are minute organisms, only visible under the power of an electron microscope, that parasitise plant cells and interfere with normal growth. Whilst virus symptoms vary, many infections show as a mottling or streaky variegation of the leaves. Unfortunately, there is little that a gardener can do for affected plants. Scientists are endeavouring to eradicate them from selected woody ornamentals, but this is a slow and painstaking process. Fortunately, only a few virus diseases are destructive, such as the mosaic of *Daphne mezereum*.

Secondary symptoms

Several diseases produce leaf symptoms which indicate problems in other parts of the plant, usually in the conducting tissue.

Silver leaf

When the normally green foliage of ornamental Cherries or Plums takes on a silvered appearance, the suspicion is that the plants are infected with the fungus disease called silver leaf. Its presence can be confirmed by examining a cross-section from an infected stem, which will normally be stained in an irregular patch. Small flattened brackets (fungal fruiting bodies), sometimes purple in colour, may also be seen on the stems or on nearby pruning wounds. The silvering is only a reaction to the fungus; the serious problem is the gradual dieback of branches. The fungus enters through pruning wounds, and the best method of control is to prevent infection by treating pruning cuts and other wounds with a fungicidal sealant such as santar. Badly infected plants are best cut down and burned.

Dutch Elm disease

This disease has ravaged the elm population in Britain since the unfortunate importation of a new virulent strain of the responsible fungus. Yellowing of the leaves of elm trees is one of the earliest signs, and it becomes evident in mid- to late summer, usually in the form of small patches on the canopy. This should not be confused with normal autumn leaf colouring. An examination of the cross-section of a suspected shoot will confirm the infection, if dark-stained patches in the outermost annual rings are visible. The fungus causes a breakdown in the upward movement of water and the foliage of the infected part soon dies; this is followed by death of the branches, and progressively the whole tree succumbs.

Sadly, there is no effective cure for this disease, and trees should be felled, de-barked and burned as soon as possible (except for the timber, which, if sound, may be of value to a local timber merchant).

Should you be unfortunate enough to have trees affected or suspected of having this disease, it is advisable to seek confirmation from your local council and ascertain their requirements, if any, for felling and disposal. Some authorities offer financial assistance towards the costs involved.

Fire Blight

This is a bacterial disease that is prevalent to the south and east of a line from the Wash, through Oxford to Southampton. It is also a notifiable disease – which means that any suspected outbreak should be reported to your local Plant Health Branch of the Ministry of Agriculture, Fisheries and Food.

It appears as patches of browned or scorched leaves on certain plants in the Rose family, notably Hawthorn, Cotoneaster, Pyracantha, Pear and Whitebeam. Suspected outbreaks can be further investigated by exposing the outer wood with a knife; infected shoots usually show reddish-brown staining. Seriously infected plants should be destroyed by grubbing-out and burning. Initial outbreaks can be dealt with by pruning infected branches 60 cm (24 in) back from the stained wood. It is essential to disinfect cutting tools after each cut with a solution of 3 per cent Lysol to prevent spreading the disease. Furthermore, prunings should be immediately burned.

Symptoms of nutritional problems

Plants growing in poor soil often show signs of nutrient deficiencies in the leaves. Yellowing, and in some cases a slight reddening, can indicate nitrogen shortage. Marginal leaf scorch is symptomatic of potash shortage, whilst lack of phosphates has varying effects but often shows as a slight blueing of the leaf surface. The application of compound fertilisers or foliar feeds containing these three main plant foods will soon correct any shortage.

Lime-induced chlorosis is another common nutritional problem, particularly when acid-loving plants like Rhododendrons and Camellias are grown in limestone soils which turn their leaves sickly yellow. This problem can be resolved in mild cases by watering the plants with iron sequestrene. If this has no effect, re-planting into a specially prepared acid peat bed is necessary. Such problems can of course be avoided in the first instance by choosing plants tolerant to chalk or limestone soils.

Magnesium is another element that is deficient in most soils. In trees and shrubs magnesium deficiency shows itself in a yellowing and browning of the leaf tissue between the veins. A teaspoonful of Epsom salts dissolved in a can of water and applied to the plants will usually remedy the problem.

Shoot problems

Insect infestation

Woolly aphids

These appear as tufts of white wool on the stems of ornamental crab apple and pear trees. This white wool is a protective covering secreted by the aphids, which gives the stems an unsightly appearance. Their feeding sites can also be infected by other diseases such as canker. Serious outbreaks can be controlled by drenching with insecticide sprays based on either malathion or dimethoate. This is best tackled in June.

Scale insects
There are various kinds of scale insects which infest the stems of trees and shrubs, notably Yew, Willow, Ash, Horse Chestnut and Rose. They are sucking insects which attach themselves to the stem and have a hard protective covering which makes them difficult to eradicate. Deciduous plants can be sprayed with either a DNOC petroleum or tar oil winter wash during their dormant period. Alternatively, a spray of malathion can be applied in May.

Boring insects
Occasionally, stems are tunnelled out by caterpillars, notably those of goat moth and leopard moth. Visible signs are rarely noticed until a shoot weakened by their activity snaps off. If you come across them, prune out the infected stems.

Disease infection

Damping off
This is a fungal disease which causes young seedlings to collapse and die by rotting them off at their base. It occurs soon after germination and will quickly spread through a batch of closely spaced seedlings. It can be prevented in the first instance by using a sterilised growing medium. When an outbreak does occur, water the seedlings as soon as possible with either Captan or cheshunt compound.

Clematis wilt
A fungal disease confined specifically to certain forms of Clematis which causes the sudden collapse of infected stems. The regular removal of dead wood will help to prevent the disease, as will the spraying of developing shoots with copper-based fungicides such as Bordeaux mixture.

Coral spot
This is a common fungus disease infecting the shoots of many trees and shrubs. Infections begin in dead wood and on pruning snags,

but these can spread into sound wood and cause further dieback. If the main stem or a branch is girdled by the disease, it then dies off. The symptoms are orange to coral-pink pustules on the stems. Control is best achieved by regularly cutting out infected shoots and sealing wounds with a fungicidal sealant such as santar, or by painting wounds with a proprietary canker paint.

Abnormal growth

Fasciation

This causes thick, flattened stems and is produced by a proliferation of cells at the growing point. It can develop on most woody plants, including conifers. The causes of fasciation are not fully understood and there is no effective method of control other than the removal of affected shoots.

Witches' brooms

Occasionally, shoots proliferate in other ways to produce dense masses of twigs. These are commonly known as 'witches' brooms'. They sometimes arise as a result of insect attack or fungal infection. There are no practical preventative or remedial measures that can be taken. Several of the dwarf conifers now seen in gardens first arose from the grafted shoots of 'witches' brooms'.

Animal damage

Rabbits and hares nibble at the shoots of young trees and shrubs and stunt the plants. In severe weather they cause serious injury by gnawing at the bark. Grazing animals, such as cattle and horses, also have a fondness for the bark of certain trees. In serious cases trees can be girdled and killed. Where such damage is likely to occur, the answer is to protect your plants with rabbit or cattle guards. Bark injuries should be repaired promptly, as described in Chapter 6, and treated with a fungicidal wound sealant.

Trunk and branch problems

Insect infestation

The trunks of Beech trees often appear to be infested with woolly aphids. These are in fact related insects known as felted beech coccus, or beech scale. Heavy infestations not only weaken trees but they assist the progression of a more serious problem known as beech bark disease. With dormant trees this pest can be controlled by applying a tar oil winter wash; alternatively, apply summer sprays of insecticides containing malathion.

Disease infection

Heartwood rots

The most serious infections are the fungi that invade wounds and cause extensive heartwood decay. These can develop both in the trunk and in large branches. In either case the result is trees that are structurally unsafe. There are several fungi that cause these heartwood rots, and often they remain undetected until their conspicuous fruiting bodies appear; these are large fleshy (sometimes leathery or woody) brackets which protrude from the trunk and branches, or around the base; some fruiting bodies develop as pustules.

By the time these fruiting bodies develop, the heartwood will already be in an advanced state of decay and the tree, or parts of the tree, will probably be structurally unsafe. Unfortunately, there are no means of preventing or controlling these diseases – in all likelihood the tree will have to be felled. In such cases, I strongly recommend that the specialist advice of a tree consultant is taken without delay.

Fungal cankers

Various fungi cause cankers on ornamental trees, notably Crab Apples and Limes. These first appear as sunken patches of bark and then develop into open lesions. They become serious when several cankers unite and girdle the stem. Treat by pruning out bad cankers on branches and treating less serious ones with canker paint or fungicides based on benlate.

Bacterial cankers

These occur commonly on certain susceptible Poplars and Cherries. In the case of Poplars many lesions develop along the branches and trunk. These not only look unsightly but also considerably weaken the tree, causing progressive dieback. Unfortunately, there is no practical method of control apart from the use of canker-resistant species or clones.

Bacterial canker in ornamental Cherries causes lesions on the branches and trunk, particularly around the crotches. These weep with an unsightly gum-like exudation and the cankers cause die-back of branches. Spraying with Bordeaux mixture at the end of August or early September will cure it. Ornamental Cherries should also be grafted on to canker-resistant under-stocks.

Animal damage

Grey squirrels sometimes attack garden trees and can cause serious damage by stripping the bark off choice specimen trees. Control is not easy, and serious cases need the attention of a pest control officer or gamekeeper.

Frost damage

As a result of frost action, thin-barked trees such as young Norway Maples sometimes develop splits in the bark, usually on the south-facing side of the tree. Such splits should be repaired promptly by pinning the bark to its original position with small tacks or gimp pins, and sealing the wound with a fungicidal sealant.

Root problems

Disease infection

Honey or bootlace fungus

This is one of the most troublesome root problems affecting woody plants because it is non-selective and can invade the roots of almost any tree or shrub. Though parasitic on roots, the fungus eventually spreads beneath the bark to girdle the lower stem. This weakens a plant and inevitably brings about its premature death, particularly when plants suffer additional growth stress such as that brought on by drought. Weakened roots may be further invaded by other root-rotting fungi and trees made unstable and liable to blow over in the wind.

Often the first symptom of an infection is the appearance in autumn of honey-coloured toadstools growing around the base of a plant, or protruding from the lower stem. If you dig away the soil, you will notice black, bootlace-like strands, which are the means by which the fungus spreads to other plants; and by lifting away a section of bark from the base of plants suspected of having the disease, you will reveal masses of white fungal threads. This symptom appears before the toadstool stage, and inspecting under the bark is a useful way of checking plants known to be growing in areas affected by the disease.

The presence of honey fungus is unfortunate, but many well-known gardens are afflicted by it – so do not despair. Prevention is the best approach, and you can do this by removing sources of infection: old stumps should be grubbed out and wooden tree stakes should be carefully pulled out of the ground when they are no longer needed. If infections are confirmed early enough it may be possible to treat the plants with phenolic emulsion such as Armillatox or Bray's Emulsion. It is important to treat the plants as soon as possible and follow the dosage recommended by the manufacturers.

Other root rots

There are several root- and butt-rotting fungi that invade roots and weaken trees, and their most serious effect is loss of anchorage resulting in windblow. If your suspicions are aroused by the presence of basal brackets or other fungal fruiting bodies, seek the further advice of a tree consultant as soon as possible.

Other root problems

Compaction

Tree roots need oxygen if they are to function properly; if the soil surface becomes too heavily compacted, the oxygen supply will be restricted and the roots will begin to die back. The first symptom of compaction is a thinning of the foliage and an increase in dieback in the crown. The problem is easily solved by ground aeration:

holes can be drilled with a power auger, or punched with a crowbar, as described in Chapter 6.

Waterlogging
This also causes rotting and death of roots, partly because it reduces supplies of oxygen. The only solution is to drain the ground as described in Chapter 4, or run a series of gravel-filled trenches to a suitable outfall.

Drought
Shortage of water soon causes leaves to collapse. Many trees and shrubs are surface-rooting plants, especially in their early stages of development, and these roots must be kept moist if plants are to grow properly. The only solution to drought is adequate watering, and of course this can be difficult when water restrictions are in operation.

Flower and fruit problems

Insect infestation

Roses are sometimes disfigured by thrips or thunderflies, which distort and streak the petals. Aphids (greenfly) also look unsightly and distort the buds. Both can be controlled by regular sprays with insecticides based on either DDT/HCH or malathion.

Disease infection

Rhododendron bud blast
This is a fungal disease that invades the terminal buds of Rhododendrons causing them to turn brown or greyish in spring. The buds then rot away and never open. The disease is spread by Rhododendron leaf hopper and the most effective means of control is to spray with malathion in August. It is also helpful to remove the infected buds from young plants. Be careful not to confuse bud blast with frost-damage; buds infected with bud blast are covered in small, black, bristle-like fruiting bodies.

Scab

Crab Apples and Pyracantha berries are sometimes disfigured by scab. The symptoms are blackened sunken patches on the fruit. Both diseases are caused by fungi and can be controlled by sprays of Captan at three-weekly intervals from March to June.

Bird damage

Several birds, notably bullfinches, like to peck out the emerging buds of ornamental Cherries and occasionally other flowering plants. Strands of black threads wound amongst the shoots act as a reasonable deterrent.

Physiological problems

Sometimes flowering is disappointing or even non-existent. This can be due to various factors. The first obvious reason may be because the plants are immature: several trees and shrubs, for example, some Magnolias and Davidia, take many years before flowering.

Secondly, plants may not be suited to their particular position; plants with poor flower displays in shady places may do better where there is more sunlight.

Thirdly, there are often seasonal variations in flowering. For example, I have observed in several instances years of prolific flowering being followed by sparse displays. This may be partly because a plant needs to restore its reserves before embarking on another good crop. Sometimes it is due to climatic influences such as drought causing the buds to drop, or because of adverse weather conditions at the time of flower bud initiation and development.

Finally, it may be that you have been unfortunate and chosen a poor form of a particular plant that will never produce a prolific display. For this reason it is usually wise to stick to well-proven cultivars.

In most of these cases there is little that a gardener can do, other than adopting the best cultural practices and by trying unsuccessful plants in different positions. But when all else fails, replacement is the only option.

The safe use of pesticides

The all-embracing term 'pesticide' includes, for our purposes, insecticides, fungicides and herbicides; these are the chemicals used by gardeners to control insect pests, fungus diseases and weeds respectively. Before using pesticides a gardener should be fully aware of their limitations and their safe use. Remember that what is toxic to insects, fungi and weeds may well also be toxic to humans and pets, including fish in garden ponds. It is also worth remembering that the use of these materials can have undesirable side effects and that in controlling one pest you may kill off the predators of another and so create another problem for yourself. Pesticides can be of tremendous assistance to gardeners – but they must be used wisely as well as safely.

If you observe the following rules you should prevent mishaps:

1. Only use pesticides when they are really necessary.
2. Select the correct pesticide for the particular job.
3. Read the manufacturer's instructions carefully, and rigorously follow their recommendations. Do not add 'one for luck' and observe the time intervals specified. (*N.B.* This is essential if fruits are to be eaten or preserved, *e.g.* crab apples.)
4. Handle all pesticides with the utmost care, wear a pair of rubber gloves when handling concentrates, and generally avoid contamination of the skin. If this should accidentally occur, wash the contamination off immediately with soap and water.
5. Store full and partly-used containers of pesticides away from children and pets. Never put them into lemonade or beer bottles. If, for some unavoidable reason, chemicals are transferred to another container, make sure that it is clearly labelled with indelible ink.
6. If possible, avoid spraying plants when they are in flower; this kills bees and other beneficial pollinating insects unnecessarily.
7. Avoid applying pesticides on windy days to prevent them from drifting.

8. Wash out containers thoroughly after use, and prevent washings from draining into ponds or water-courses. (*Note:* It is advisable to use a separately labelled container, such as a watering can or sprayer, specifically for herbicides; even minute residues can be harmful.)
9. Dispose of used containers safely by washing them out and placing them in the dustbin.
10. Wash hands and face with soap and water immediately after using pesticides.

8

Legal Matters

Statute law – tree preservation orders, trees and highways; Common law – an owner's responsibilities, insurance, boundary problems, poisonous trees and shrubs.

In English law, trees and shrubs are affected by various Acts of Parliament and by decisions made in the Law Courts. These are usually referred to as Statute Law and Common Law respectively.

Legally, a land owner is responsible for any trees or shrubs growing on his or her land. The exception to this is in the case of tenanted land where the tenancy agreement transfers some of this responsibility to the tenant. If you hold such an agreement it would be wise to seek the advice of your lawyer to determine your exact responsibilities in this respect.

Statute Law

Tree preservation orders

As a tree owner, you are most likely to be affected by Statute Law when your trees come under a preservation order. This is an order made under the provisions of the Town and Country Planning Act that becomes a registerable charge against a property, with penalties for contravention. You should be notified if any of your trees are included in an order, as an owner has the right of objection before an order is approved. If you are in doubt, enquire at the local Land Charges Office of the Area Planning Authority.

The purpose of a tree preservation order is to prevent the unnecessary destruction or mutilation of trees. The existence of such orders does not mean, however, that an owner is no longer responsible for routine maintenance; nor is that person excused from his responsibilities under Common Law. Ultimately, of course, trees cannot be preserved indefinitely. They are living things that degenerate and die. But in the course of dying, trees may become dangerous objects, and as the owner of such a tree your responsibilities are clear: if proved negligent, you will be held liable for any damage or injury caused to persons or property.

Owners of trees under preservation orders must remember that any pruning or maintenance work has first to be approved by the local planning authority. This may seem tiresome, but it is necessary to ensure that the work meets a satisfactory standard and in no way constitutes an unavoidable loss of amenity to a neighbourhood. In practice, the criteria used are those of British Standard 3998 (1966), '*Recommendations For Tree Work*'. Tree owners who fail to ensure that work is undertaken by reputable firms may find themselves liable to prosecution. It is worthwhile remembering that currently the maximum fine for serious contravention of a tree preservation order is £1,000, or twice the sum which appears to the court to be the value of the tree.

When a tree becomes dangerous or dies it can be felled, but the preservation order remains in force. In fact, an owner is now obliged to plant another tree of appropriate size and species as soon as is reasonably possible. The replacement tree is then protected by the original order. In all but emergency cases it is advisable to notify the planning authority of any intended felling.

Since the 1974 Town and Country Amenities Act, trees growing in conservation areas are protected and tree owners are obliged to give at least six weeks' notice of any intended tree work, such as pruning or felling, to their local planning authority. Where such notice is not given, an owner is liable and on conviction would be subject to the same penalties as for contravention of a tree preservation order.

Trees included in preservation orders are usually of value to a local community as well as to the tree owner, and some local authorities recognise this fact by giving grants towards the cost of maintenance. Anyone wishing to obtain financial assistance should first seek the advice of their local council. Sadly, not all authorities are able to help.

Trees and highways

Under the provisions of the Highways Act, hedges, shrubs or trees must not obstruct the passage of vehicles or pedestrians, nor must they interfere with the view of drivers of vehicles or the light from a public lamp. The highway authority is empowered to serve notice on the owners of offending vegetation, giving them fourteen days to remove the cause of obstruction or interference. Owners served with such a notice have the right of appeal to a Magistrates' Court, but failure to carry out any work required after this can result in the highway authority carrying out the work and charging the owner. Under the same Highways Act, no trees or shrubs must be planted within 4·5 m (15 ft) from the centre of a made-up carriageway.

Common Law

An owner's responsibilities

The owner (or in certain cases the tenant) is responsible for the safety and maintenance of trees on his land. This involves, first of all, regular inspection to ensure that trees are not likely to cause injury or damage to persons or property on both their own or neighbouring land, regardless of whether adjoining land is publicly or privately owned.

Problems arise when dead or dying limbs collapse, as they do even on calm days. Leaning trees, or trees with imbalanced crowns, can eventually become so unstable that they topple over; rotting tree trunks can gradually lose their strength until the wind can bring them down; basal rots can weaken roots and bring about a similar fate – such problems are commonplace, and landowners must not be negligent in dealing with them.

The sensible approach for an owner of large trees is to have them inspected by a professional tree consultant, preferably twice a year; once when the trees are in leaf, and once during their dormant period.

Insurance

It is worthwhile checking household insurance policies to see if they cover damage to adjoining property caused by falling trees; also check to see if they give protection against third party liability. Although such cover is not obligatory, it is advisable for an owner of large trees.

If you employ a contractor to carry out tree work in your garden it is also worth checking their insurance cover. Firms should be covered against injury to their workmen and against accidental damage to property. The Arboricultural Association have a list of approved tree work contractors and one of several stringent conditions of approval is that contractors must currently have £250,000 public liability insurance cover. Unfortunately, accidents occasionally do happen, and it is better to be wise and protected beforehand than sorry after the event.

Boundary problems

When trees are planted in gardens they are usually entirely contained within the boundary; but as they grow, both roots and crown may trespass into neighbouring land and air space. In Common Law the owner of land is under no obligation to cut a hedge or prune the branches and roots of trees back to the boundary line. This is only necessary, as we have seen, when growth obstructs or interferes with highways. But if it can be proved that roots or branches have caused damage, such as disruption of drains or structural damage to the fabric or foundations of a building, then the tree owner is liable for that damage.

If overhanging branches or encroaching roots are a nuisance, a neighbour has the right to prune these back to the boundary line providing that the owner's land is not entered without permission, and providing that all the severed roots and branches are returned to the owner of the tree. The same applies, incidentally, to any fruit which may overhang a boundary; this *always* belongs to the tree owner, even when it has fallen from the tree.

Encroaching roots are allowed to be pruned back to a boundary, as we have seen; but if chemicals such as weedkillers are used to poison the roots, and these inadvertently kill the tree, then the person using the chemicals is liable for damages claimed by the tree owner.

It should be remembered that climbing plants can trespass on to adjoining terraced and semi-detached houses. Owners have, in the past, been held liable for damage caused by blocked gutters.

Poisonous trees and shrubs

In Part 2 I go on to mention plants such as Yew, Laburnum and Rhododendron that have poisonous fruits or foliage. If these plants trespass over the boundary into neighbouring land and are eaten by horses or cattle, the tree owner is liable if the animals die. If, on the other hand, it is the animals which trespass (and 'trespass' is held to include them putting their heads through the boundary to reach the poisonous plants) then the tree owner is not liable. A tree owner can, however, be liable for any poisonous leaves or fruits blown into adjoining land and later eaten.

A landowner is required to keep any dangerous objects under control. This includes poisonous plants: an owner could therefore be liable if unsuspecting children ate poisonous fruits growing in his garden. Horticultural chemicals such as pesticides can also be classed as dangerous objects, and an owner is bound to prevent these from drifting on to neighbouring land.

Occasionally, this kind of dispute ends up in the law courts and refines existing Common Law. In my view, court action is costly and undesirable, and should be regarded as a last resort in resolving problems. Wherever possible, give due consideration to your neighbour's point of view and endeavour to come to amicable agreement. Good neighbourliness is a *much* better solution than court action.

PART TWO
THE PLANTS

9

Flowers for all Seasons

Shrubs and trees notable for their flower displays, arranged in the following seasons: December to February, March and April, May and June, July and August, September to November.

Flowering trees and shrubs are the ones most sought after by gardeners, and quite rightly so, for it is the magnificence of floral displays which make gardens such interesting and exciting places. In your own garden you have the freedom to choose your particular favourites, but it is worthwhile choosing some plants to provide a sequence of flowering and thus create interest at all seasons. Colour is the main virtue of flowers, but many are also delightfully fragrant and a few of these should be included, especially for the summertime. For convenience, I have arranged this chapter into approximate flowering times, but because of variable factors such as locality and season some categories will inevitably overlap.

December to February

In the depths of winter, flower displays are obviously subdued, which makes colour from stems, fruits, and the foliage of evergreens and conifers all the more welcome. However a few remarkable plants ignore the elements and bravely produce their blossom.

Shrubs

Chimonanthus praecox – Winter Sweet
An aptly-named deciduous shrub with sweetly-scented yellow flowers which have unusual waxy petals. This is rarely found in northern gardens and really needs the protection of a warm south-facing wall. The cultivar '*Grandiflorus*' is superior to the type, and in favoured localities will attain a height of 1·8 to 2·4 m (6 to 8 ft).

Daphne mezereum – Mezereon
A deciduous shrub which grows from 1 to 1·5 m (3–5 ft) in height. In February, just before bud break, its purple-pink flowers cluster along the previous year's shoots. These have a powerful fragrance, no doubt to attract the few pollinating insects which venture out on colder days. By late summer, the shoots are crowded with bright scarlet berries (which incidentally are poisonous). Mezereon prefers moist, freely-drained soils and will grow well in chalk. Sadly, this plant is frequently infected with an incurable mosaic virus disease, which causes reduction in flowering and a gradual degeneration of the plant.

Erica herbacea (*syn. E. carnea*) – Winter Heath
See Chapter 15.

Garrya elliptica – Silk Tassel Bush
This unusual evergreen can either be grown as an open shrub or trained against a wall. The attraction is in the pendant, greyish-green, silky catkins. It is preferable to obtain male plants which have much longer catkins; in the south of England these may be up to 30 cm (12 in) long, but in the north they are more usually half this length. The plant itself will grow over 3·6 m (12 ft) in height, but it can be contained without difficulty by pruning soon after flowering. Container-grown plants are recommended, as it does not transplant readily.

Hamamelis mollis – Witch Hazel
An outstanding winter shrub with intensely fragrant, golden-yellow flowers borne in spidery clusters along the naked stems.

Astonishingly, these are quite unaffected by severe frost and snow. Its common name relates to the Hazel-like leaves, which turn butter-yellow in autumn. Witch Hazels like good growing conditions with plenty of organic matter around their roots; given these they grow to a height of 3 m (10 ft). Ideally, they should be positioned against a dark evergreen background, such as a Yew or Holly hedge, to provide a contrasting foil for the flowers. One of the best forms is *H. 'Pallida'*, a popular cultivar with sulphur-yellow petals.

Jasminum nudiflorum – Winter Jasmine
See Chapter 13.

Rhododendron
Most Rhododendrons flower in May and June, but two reliable early flowering species are *R. dauricum* and *R. mucronulatum*. Both originate from Russia, China and Japan, where they have adapted to bearing their bright, rosy purple flowers in January. These are borne singly along the shoots, and not in bold trusses like the more familiar hardy hybrids, but there are enough flowers to bring a surprising and pleasing cheer to the garden in winter. Good plants of *R. dauricum* grow to 2 m (6 ft) whereas *R. mucronulatum* is slightly more vigorous and will grow up to 2·5 m (8 ft).

Viburnum x bodnantense
This hybrid between two notable winter-flowering viburnums, *V. farreri* and *V. grandiflorum* is undoubtedly the best. It has vigorous upright growth and will form a bush of 1·5 to 2 m (5 to 7 ft). The naked stems bear clusters of delightfully fragrant rose-pink flowers from November through to March. Apart from garden decoration, it is excellent for cutting and bringing indoors where its perfume can be appreciated. The two named clones, *'Dawn'* and *'Deben'*, are the best forms to purchase. It is easy to grow and tolerant of most soils, including chalk.

Viburnum tinus – Laurustinus
A hardy evergreen species that flowers throughout the winter in southern gardens but remains in bud until early spring in the north. The plate-like clusters of white flowers are followed in late summer

by bluish-black fruits. Laurustinus is a tough, resilient shrub making a dense bush 2·5 m (8 ft) in height, with a spread of 2 m (6 ft). It is excellent for providing shelter, especially in coastal gardens.

Trees

Prunus subhirtella 'Autumnalis' – Autumn Cherry
This is one of the few garden trees to flower in mid-winter. Very pale pink blossom, smaller than in most Cherries, begins to open during November and continues intermittently until March. It makes a bushy-topped tree, eventually growing to a height of about 8 m (25 ft). Its flowers are more conspicuous when planted against a dark background, such as a Cypress screen. Cut stems brought into a warm room at Christmas quickly open their remaining dormant buds and provide delicate sprays for floral decoration. There is a less common cultivar *P. s. 'Autumnalis Rosea'* which has even more attractive shell-pink flowers.

March and April

Shrubs

Berberis darwinii – Darwin's Barberry
A tough, easily grown evergreen shrub that is suited to most soils, including chalk. As the spring begins to advance in April, it positively glows as its masses of small, grape-like clusters of golden-yellow flowers open. In autumn, bluish berries are conspicuous among the small, Holly-like, glossy green leaves. Like all barberries it is armed with spines, and since it also grows densely and reaches a height of 2 to 2·5 m (6 to 8 ft), it makes a useful impenetrable thicket.

Camellia japonica
This is a first-rate evergreen shrub, worth growing for its handsome, glossy foliage. Intermittently from late February to May, depending on cultivar, this shrub bears flowers that for sheer

elegance and beauty are in a class of their own. Some forms have blooms of perfect symmetry and all have distinct waxy petals. Camellias have a preference for acid or neutral soils and those containing free lime should be avoided. If the soil in your garden is unsuitable, they can be grown successfully in tubs or large containers filled with a mixture of acid soil and peat. These plants must be regularly watered, and in hard water areas, rainwater should be used to prevent bud drop.

As a shrub it is quite hardy but, alas, its flowers are easily damaged by frost, and one can have the great disappointment of finding a beautiful display ruined overnight. Frost pockets should obviously be avoided; the shelter of trees will offer some protection, but ensure that your plants are not too densely shaded. It is also feasible to train Camellias against walls, and those with a shaded northerly or west-facing aspect are best. Few plants have produced such an enormous number of cultivars, but I have limited my choice to the following:

'*Adolphe Audusson*' – semi-double, blood red.
'*Alba Simplex*' – large, single white.
'*Contessa Lavinia Maggi*' – double, white and pink with rose stripes.
'*Donckelarii*' – semi-double, pink, red marbled white.
'*Elegans*' – anemone flowered, deep pink.

Camellia x williamsii
A hybrid group named after their famous originator J. C. Williams, who crossed *C. japonica* with *C. saluenensis* at Caerhays Castle, Cornwall. They are regarded as the best group for general garden planting. Flowering is from December through to May, depending on cultivar, but they are included in this section since at this time of year most of them are at their best. Notable cultivars are:

'*Bow Bells*' – semi-double, rose.
'*Citation*' – large semi-double, blush pink.
'*Donation*' – large semi-double, pink. In my view the best.
'*J. C. Williams*' – single, phlox pink.
'*St Ewe*' – single, rose pink.

Chaenomeles speciosa – Japanese Quince

There is a good deal of confusion about the name of this plant, which is often still listed erroneously in catalogues as *Cydonia japonica*. Its scarlet to blood red, apple blossom-shaped flowers are produced in clusters along the old stems. These often open before March and continue intermittently until June, but they are at their best during March and April. Natural growth is rather untidy and, left to its own devices this plant produces a tangle of spreading, arching branches some 2 to 3 m (7 to 10 ft) in height. It does, however, respond to pruning and can be trained against a wall or over a framework such as a garden arch. These plants are not fastidious about soil, but they do grow best in full sun. In autumn they bear greenish-yellow quince-like fruits, which look like small, distorted '*Golden Delicious*' apples; these, I am told, make an excellent jelly. The following cultivars are recommended:

'*Cardinalis*' – a reliable old cultivar with large crimson scarlet flowers.

'*Nivalis*' – a vigorous grower with white flowers.

'*Simonii*' – a low growing cultivar with semi-double blood-red flowers.

Chaenomeles x superba

A hybrid group between *C. japonica* and *C. speciosa* that contains some excellent lower-growing cultivars ideal for smaller gardens.

'*Coral Sea*' – grows to 1 m (3 ft) and has coral-pink flowers.

'*Crimson and Gold*' – grows to 1 m (3 ft). It has deep red petals with contrasting golden stamens.

'*Knaphill Scarlet*' – a popular old cultivar with brilliant red flowers.

'*Rowallane*' – a spreading form with large, brilliant crimson flowers.

Corylopsis pauciflora

A deciduous shrub growing 1·5 to 2 m (5 to 6 ft) high with spreading branches. In March these bear pendant clusters of small primrose-yellow flowers. It is a plant not commonly seen in gardens which I think deserves wider recognition. Semi-shaded positions suit it best and it has a decided preference for acid soils.

Forsythia

Few shrubs enjoy the popularity of Forsythia, which is ubiquitous in suburban gardens. It can be readily propagated from hardwood cuttings, is very easy to cultivate, and it has a reliable and spectacular flower display. Towards the end of March and into April its shoots become crowded with bright yellow flowers. Cut stems brought indoors a few weeks earlier and placed in water in a warm room will also break into flower, providing useful material for indoor decoration. Forsythias are not fastidious about soil and will grow vigorously almost anywhere. Some pruning may become necessary to contain large plants but regular pruning is not advised. Occasionally, after flowering, some of the oldest flowered shoots can be shortened back to younger lateral stems. If desired, they can be pruned to form an attractive flowering hedge. There are several Forsythias listed in catalogues, but the most reliable for general planting are:

F. x Intermedia 'Spectabilis'.
F. Beatrix Farrand.
F. 'Lynwood'.

Kerria japonica

This deciduous suckering shrub bears conspicuous golden-yellow flowers in late April and continues its display into early May. It is another easily grown plant that rarely demands attention apart from occasional thinning-out of its stems. The stems themselves are an attractive bright green colour and show up well in winter sunshine. The double-flowered cultivar *K. j. 'Pleniflora'* is the most impressive and the one usually seen in gardens. It grows from 1·5 to 2 m (5 to 6 ft) in height.

Magnolia stellata

A much admired shrub and the best Magnolia for small gardens. During March and April established plants bear a great profusion of pure white, star-like flowers that are 7·5 to 10 cm (3 to 4 in) across. Unfortunately, they are easily damaged by frost. Like other Magnolias, it needs good growing conditions and prefers a sheltered, sunny position and a lime-free soil, rich in humus. Annual mulches of peat or leaf mould are beneficial. In very rare cases this plant will reach 2 m (6 ft) in height, but usually it forms a low, spreading bush.

Magnolia x soulangiana

This is a shrub of rare quality and exceptional beauty. In April, before the leaves unfurl, its large goblet-shaped flowers resembling narrow tulips emerge from their protective buds. The petals are creamy-white inside with a blush of rosy purple outside. Magnolias respond to generous treatment and thorough preparation of the planting site is advisable. They also need plenty of room: mature plants will often exceed 3·5 m (12 ft) in height and have a spread of 2·5 to 3 m (8 to 10 ft).

In the north of England Magnolias need a warm, sheltered position for best results, but in the south they can be used as border plants or as lawn specimens. Be warned: you may have to wait a few years before flowering commences, but your patience will be rewarded by many subsequent years of beautiful flowers.

Magnolias are surface-rooting plants that should not be planted too deeply, and they benefit from generous annual mulches of peat or well-rotted leaf mould. With lawn specimens it is necessary to keep a 2 m (6 ft) diameter circle of cultivated ground around the base of young plants to facilitate this. In addition to mulches, regular watering during dry periods is essential. Regrettably these plants are never happy on soils containing free lime, but they do not seem to mind heavier clays. There are several splendid cultivars:

'*Alexandrina*' – a vigorous, erect grower with more richly coloured outer petals.

'*Lennei*' – both sides of its petals are rich, rosy purple.

'*Picture*' – one of the best, which I understand flowers as a young plant.

Rhododendron

Two good hybrids for this period are *R. nobleanum* and *R. praecox*. The former bears a profusion of compact trusses of scarlet to light pink flowers. These often appear first in late January, but generally they are at their peak in March. *R. nobleanum* eventually matures into a large bush or small tree like one of its parents (*R. arboreum*) 4·5 to 6 m (15 to 20 ft) in height and almost as wide. Despite its large size it is fairly slow-growing, but it flowers freely as a young plant.

R. Praecox, by comparison, is a more dainty shrub with bright rose-purple flowers borne in twos and threes at the shoot tips. It is derived from a cross between *R. ciliatum* and *R. dauricum*. It makes a dense bush 1 to 1·5 m (4 to 5 ft) high. One disadvantage is that its blooms are sensitive to frost damage and in some years flower displays are therefore likely to be short-lived.

Ribes sanguineum – Flowering Currant

A splendid free-flowering shrub that is very easy to grow in most soils and sunny situations. Its pendant clusters of rosy-red flowers open at the end of March and continue through April. These are deciduous plants that should eventually attain a height of 2 to 2·5 m (6 to 8 ft) and a spread of 1·5 to 2 m (5 to 6 ft). Flowers are confined to the one-year-old shoots and by pruning out old flowered stems in May you can encourage new growth to bear the next crop. Superior cultivars are '*King Edward VIII*', which has good crimson flowers and a more compact habit; also, '*Pulborough Scarlet*', which has deeper red flowers.

Two other species worthy of attention are *Ribes odoratum* (*Syn. R. aureum*), which has loose clusters of lemon yellow flowers with a pleasant fragrance in April. *R. speciosum* on the other hand, is more closely related to the Gooseberry than the Currant and as such is a dense, spiny shrub. Its main attraction is its delightful bright red flowers; with their protruding stamens these resemble miniature Fuchias. This species usually blooms in May, later than other flowering Currants.

Trees

Prunus – Flowering Cherry

No garden should be without a representative from this tremendous genus of marvellous flowering trees which heralds the start of a new growing season during April and May. Cherries flower and look best in open, sunny positions. They are not fastidious in their soil requirements, provided that it is reasonably fertile and has good drainage. This is a large genus containing many excellent species and cultivars; the following represent some of the better early-flowering ones (N.B. Later flowering kinds are listed under May.):

P. 'Accolade' – a fairly upright tree, with an open crown that reaches 6 m (20 ft). It has delightful semi-double flowers, rose-pink in bud, which become paler when fully open.

P. cerasifera – Myrobalan. This begins flowering in early March with masses of small pale pink to white flowers. It forms a round-headed tree with a very dense crown that grows up to 6 m (20 ft). The dark purple-leaved cultivar of this plant *P.c. 'Pissardii'* is very much overplanted in gardens, in my view. Preferable cultivars are *P.c. 'Nigra'* or *P.c. 'Rosea'*, which have more conspicuous pink flowers.

P. 'Cheal's Weeping' – Cheal's Weeping Cherry. Occasionally this plant is listed in catalogues as *P. 'Kiku Shidare Zakura'*, a romantic Japanese name that means 'weeping chrysanthemum cherry'. This is without doubt the best weeping cherry and a great favourite for small gardens; it rarely exceeds a height of 3 m (10 ft). Its arching branches hang vertically and towards the end of April and into early May these are densely, if briefly, crowded with double, rose-pink blossom.

P. dulcis – Almond. A beautiful tree at flowering time, when its shoots bear bright pink 'almond' blossom. However, I consider it a poor choice for a garden tree, as it is highly susceptible to peach leaf curl. Dieback of the branches is also frequent, and generally it is not a long-lived tree.

P. sargentii – Sargent's Cherry. Single, bright pink blossoms adorn the branches of this tree in April. In cultivation it rarely exceeds 7·5 m (25 ft) in height, and develops a small, rounded crown. This is the outstanding Cherry for giving autumn colour

– when towards the end of September the leaves turn a bright orange-scarlet. A good choice for small gardens.

P. 'Shirotae' – This beautiful Japanese Cherry has a distinct flat-topped, spreading crown with an ultimate diameter of about 9 m (30 ft). From early April it bears dazzling white, semi-double flowers which hang in crowded bunches from the boughs.

P. 'Tai Haku' – Great White Cherry. This most beautiful of flowering cherries makes a truly marvellous sight in mid-April, when its single white flowers burst from their buds. These blooms, borne in clusters, are the largest of any cherry, measuring over 5 cm (2 in) in diameter. They are delightfully set against the coppery-coloured young leaves. Overall, it is a fairly vigorous small tree with a spreading habit, which eventually attains a height and spread of about 6 m (20 ft).

Salix aegyptiaca (*Syn. S. medemii*)
Most gardeners are familiar with the free-flowering habit of the native English Pussy Willow; but this species is much more impressive and flowers earlier, in February and March. It is important to obtain male plants from your nurseryman as these bear enormous bright yellow catkins, 3 to 5 cm ($1\frac{1}{2}$ to 2 in) long. This is not one of the vigorous willows and is rarely more than 4·5 m (15 ft) in height.

May and June

These are the most spectacular months for both trees and shrubs, giving the gardener an extensive choice of colourful plants.

Shrubs

Azalea
See under *Rhododendron*.

Camellia japonica
See under March and April.

Ceanothus
There is undoubtedly a surfeit of really good blue-flowered shrubs, but several *Ceanothus* are of exceptional merit. Being natives of California, they are sun lovers, and most kinds can be damaged by frost in severe winters. Siting is therefore important, and in the north of England warm, south-facing walls give the best results. Whilst lending themselves to wall-training, they also make beautiful open grown shrubs, given a sunny, sheltered position.

They thrive in good, freely drained soil, preferably neutral in reaction, *i.e.* with a pH of 6·5 to 7·0, although they will tolerate some lime. Little pruning is necessary, except to regulate or train a specimen on a wall or framework. If frost damage occurs, wait until new growth breaks in spring, as it is a simple task then to prune dead wood back to the emerging shoots. For May and June I have selected the following:

C. 'Cascade' – A superb evergreen cultivar growing to a height of over 6 m (20 ft) when trained against a wall. It bears a mass of compact clusters, up to 7·5 cm (3 in) long, of powder-blue flowers.

C. dentatus – An evergreen species with attractive small leaves and beautiful bright blue, roundish flower clusters.

C. 'Edinburgh' – This hardy evergreen cultivar grows exceptionally well without wall support, as the original plant some 2·5 m (8 ft) in height and 3·5 m (12 ft) in width in the Royal Botanic Garden at Edinburgh testifies. With its bright, Cambridge-blue flowers virtually obscuring the small green leaves, it really is a magnificent sight.

C. impressus – This plant makes a breathtaking spectacle in May when its distinct, small evergreen leaves disappear beneath a haze of bright blue flowers. Excellent for south-facing walls.

Chaenomeles
See under March and April.

Choisya ternata – Mexican Orange Blossom
A handsome evergreen making a rounded bush 2 to 2·5 m (6 to

8 ft) tall. It has most attractive glossy green leaves that are deeply divided into three leaflets. In late April and into May its clusters of pure white flowers open, giving off a delicate fragrance. These are reminiscent of true orange blossom – hence its common name. Although its leaves are easily damaged by cold winds and severe frost, this scorching is only a temporary ailment, and new leaves soon cover the bush in spring. Nevertheless, its sensitivity to cold requires that it should be given a sunny, sheltered position.

Cistus – Sun or Rock Rose

Coming from the Mediterranean, Spain and Portugal, these plants are obvious sun worshippers. Although they re-establish well, severe frost will kill them. They need good drainage, and their remarkable tolerance to drought makes them a good choice for a dry, rocky bank. Flowering begins in June. Individual flowers are very short-lived, but there is such a succession that the overall effect of flowering continues throughout July. My two favourites are *C. x purpureus* and *C. 'Silver Pink'*. *C. x purpureus* has reddish-purple flowers 6 cm (2½ in) across and a chocolate basal blotch. It makes a rounded bush 1 to 1·2 m (3 to 4 ft) high. *C. 'Silver Pink'* is more compact, and only grows 75 cm (2½ ft) high; as its name indicates, it has most attractive silver-pink flowers.

Colutea arborescens – Common Bladder Senna

I have included this deciduous shrub here because although flowering commences in June it will continue producing its clusters of yellow, pea-like flowers until September. These are followed by unusual puffed-out pods which persist until spring. It is an easily grown shrub that needs only good drainage and a sunny position, and it is especially good on poor soils. Specimens can grow to 3·5 m (12 ft) and should only be planted where there is sufficient space. They can be contained by regular pruning and since they flower on current year's shoots, this can be done without loss of flowering.

Cotoneaster –

See Chapter 11.

Cytisus x praecox – Warminster Broom

This plant bears such masses of creamy-yellow, pea-like flowers that its stems disappear in a haze of colour during May. Its one disadvantage is its unpleasant, overbearing smell. Brooms love open, sunny positions and their stems are designed to tolerate exposure to wind. Their preference is for neutral well-drained soil. This hybrid will grow 1·2 to 1·5 m (4 to 5 ft) tall, and to prevent them from becoming leggy, flowered shoots are shortened back about two-thirds of their length immediately after flowering. Worthy of mention is the cultivar '*Allgold*' which is slightly taller and has much deeper yellow flowers.

Cytisus x kewensis

A low-growing Broom rarely exceeding 30 cm (12 in) in height and with a definite spreading habit. Flowers open creamy-white and characteristically are produced in great profusion. It is an excellent plant for open positions in the front of shrub borders, or even for the rock garden. A plant of similar habit is *C. x beanii* which has golden-yellow flowers.

Cytisus cultivars

Some colourful Brooms that can be relied on for spectacular displays during the late spring are available from nurseries.

Popular cultivars are:

'*Burkwoodii*' – a vigorous Broom with cerise and maroon-red petals.
'*Cornish Cream*' – cream and yellow flowers.
'*Dragon Fly*' – yellow and crimson.
'*Firefly*' – yellow and bronze red.

Deutzia

A genus of splendid deciduous flowering shrubs, closely akin to *Philadelphus*. They prefer good loams but will tolerate thin, chalky soils. An open, sunny aspect should be chosen for them; whilst they are perfectly hardy, their flowers are sensitive to late frost and known frost pockets should therefore be avoided. Pruning is beneficial, and immediately after flowering approximately a third of the oldest shoots can be cut hard back to provide stimulus for the growth of new, flower-bearing stems. The following species and hybrids are all exceptionally beautiful at flowering time.

D. x hybrida 'Mont Rose' – A lovely, low-growing cultivar with freely borne clusters of rose-pink flowers. Growing to 90 cm (3 ft), this is ideal for the front of mixed borders.

D. x lemoinei 'Avalanche' – The entire length of its arching branches are crowded with clusters of the purest white flowers at the end of May and into early June.

D. x magnifica – A vigorous upright hybrid up to 2 m (6 ft) in height and bearing dense bunches of dazzling white, double flowers in June and July.

D. purpurascens – Another fairly erect shrub, growing to 2 m (6 ft) and flowering in early June. The outer petals of its white flowers suffuse with purple, giving it a distinctive charm.

D. scabra – A taller species, growing to 3 m (10 ft), with a fairly erect branching habit. Its large clusters of pure white flowers are plentiful in June and often persist into July.

Enkianthus campanulatus

So many plants in this season have bold colours that it is almost refreshing to come across the more subdued but nonetheless decorative flowers of this deciduous shrub. On close inspection its pendant clusters of creamy yellow bells are seen to be veined in red. It belongs to the same family as the Rhododendron and, like them, needs an acid soil to thrive. Mature plants attain 2·5 to 3 m (8 to 10 ft) in height; they are superb in autumn, when the leaves turn rich orange and scarlet.

Genista hispanica – Spanish Gorse

A spiny, deciduous shrub growing 40 to 60 cm ($1\frac{1}{2}$ to 2 ft) in height, with a dense, almost globular habit which looks like a golden-yellow cushion in flower. It loves a sunny position and freely-drained soil. Being a member of the Pea family, it can obtain nitrogen from the atmosphere and for this reason it grows exceptionally well on impoverished soil; in fact, it does not pay to be too generous with nutrients as the plant tends to respond with vegetative growth at the expense of flowers. Spanish Gorse has such a distinct shape that these plants tend to look best as single specimens; they are also good on rock gardens.

Genista lydia
Another low-growing species 40 to 60 cm (1½ to 2 ft) in height, but with a much looser arrangement of shoots, forming a dense tangle of small, arching branches. Genistas produce masses of bright yellow, pea-shaped flowers in May and June. Their preference is for full sun and a freely-drained soil, but they are remarkably tolerant of both acid and alkali soils. This species is excellent for the front of a shrub border, and I have also seen it used to good effect in bold groups as a ground cover plant. Another species with yellow flowers and very erect stems, which can be similarly used, is *G. sagittalis*.

Kalmia latifolia – Calico Bush
This is a splendid evergreen shrub, capable of growing to 3 m (10 ft). During May and June its distinctive flowers are borne in trusses 7·5 to 10 cm (3 to 4 in) across. Each bloom is a wide, bell shape and is unusual in having its stamens pressed into the deep, rose-pink petals. It is not one of the easiest of plants to cultivate; full sun and acid, peaty soils that are always moist are vital, yet even in these conditions it sometimes fails for no apparent reason. *K. angustifolia* seems more reliable, but generally this is much smaller, and only grows to 1 to 1·2 m (3 to 4 ft). Its flowers are also miniature versions, but it lacks the elegance of *K. latifolia*.

Kolkwitzia amabilis
An unusual name but an ideal border shrub, sometimes referred to as the 'Beauty Bush'. The 'beauty' comes in May and June, when masses of pink, bell-shaped flowers open; these are just over 1·25 cm (½ in) long and have a distinct hairy throat. It is a deciduous shrub capable of growing to a height of 2·5 to 3 m (8 to 10 ft), and will grow exceptionally well in chalky soil. '*Pink Cloud*' is a superior cultivar raised at Wisley.

Magnolia sieboldii

This is a classic plant for the connoisseur with a garden which has space to accommodate a 3·5 to 4·5 m (12 to 15 ft) shrub. It is a fastidious plant needing shelter and peaty, acid soil, and it has an extreme dislike of free lime. Being shallow-rooted, it needs annual mulches and irrigation in dry periods. The best specimens I have seen are growing in fairly open, woodland gardens. It has attractive broad leaves and the most beautiful pure white, single flowers 7·5 to 10 cm (3 to 4 in) across. Each has a protruding central core surrounded by a cluster of rose-crimson stamens. In this species the flowers look downwards and emit a delicate scent. Flowering continues intermittently from May until August and by early autumn (in favourable districts) the fruits expose conspicuous scarlet seeds.

Philadelphus

Few plants can surpass the elegant beauty of this genus of deciduous shrubs. During June and July, each bough is like a bridal spray, garlanded in a profusion of the purest white flowers which perfume the surrounding air with their powerful 'orange blossom' fragrance. Moreover, this shrub is easily cultivated and comes in sizes to suit all gardens. It grows well on most soils, including chalk, and is suited to open positions in borders. There are many excellent species and cultivars, of which the following are reliable.

P. '*Avalanche*' – A cultivar with arching, spreading branches, growing to a height of 1·5 m (5 ft). It bears a mass of fragrant single white blossom.

P. '*Beauclerk*' – A more vigorous cultivar, attaining 2 to 2·5 m (6 to 8 ft) and bearing large, single white flowers with a central blush of pinkish purple.

P. '*Burfordensis*' – One of the tallest, growing vigorously up to around 3 m (10 ft) with erect branches. Its large, single white flowers have conspicuous yellow stamens.

P. coronarius – Mock Orange. A beauty, growing to over 3 m (10 ft) with arching sprays of creamy-white flowers that have the strongest fragrance.

P. 'Manteau D'Hermine' – The best one for small gardens, as it only grows to 1 m (3 ft) and has a compact habit. Flowers are creamy-white and fragrant.

P. microphyllus – A species with dense, compact growth only 1 to 1·2 m (3 to 4 ft) in height, and suitable for planting beneath a window. Its single pure white flowers are set against its unusually small leaves.

P. 'Sybille' – Another graceful cultivar, only growing to about 1·2 m (4 ft) with freely-produced large, saucer-shaped, white flowers.

P. 'Virginal' – Undoubtedly the most popular *Philadelphus* in gardens, and rightly so. It is a vigorous shrub, attaining 2·5 to 3 m (8 to 10 ft), with erect branches that bend under the weight of blossom. Flowers are of the purest white, double and lightly fragrant.

Rhododendron

This vast genus contains over 500 hardy species from which innumerable hybrids have arisen. For garden ornamentation Rhododendrons are invaluable for their exotic, colourful displays in spring and early summer, and in some gardens they provide fantastic spectacles. Apart from their flowers, many Rhododendrons have extremely decorative and handsome foliage. They also have many uses: large evergreen kinds provide shelter and screening, whilst the dwarf forms can decorate a rock or peat garden. Rhododendrons are essentially plants for well-drained, acid soils and they prefer a pH of 5·0; any trace of free lime turns the leaves a sickly yellow. In the case of growing in soil with slight traces of calcium, watering with sequestrene will help to overcome this, but as a general rule, if you do not have the right soil, then avoid this genus. The one exception is for the dwarfer kinds, which may be used to furnish specially prepared, raised peat beds.

Rhododendrons look splendid in open woodland gardens, and many benefit from semi-shaded positions; but avoid dense shade, which tends to produce plants with long spindly shoots which give a poor performance at flowering time. Most Rhododendrons are surface-rooting plants, forming dense mats of fibrous roots which enable them to be transplanted at any time of year without detriment – even when they are in full bloom. But this surface-rooting characteristic also makes them vulnerable to drought, particularly when their roots are in competition with nearby trees, and to counteract this they benefit from annual mulches of well-rotted leaves or peat, and also from thorough watering during dry periods. Within these limitations they are easy plants to cultivate. No regular pruning is necessary, but young plants of the large-leaved hybrids do respond to dead heading; this involves pinching out the spent flower heads immediately after flowering. There follows a selection of Rhododendron species:

R. augustinii – A beautiful Chinese species forming a 3 m (10 ft) shrub, which grows even taller in favoured localities. It has small leaves and in May its boughs are a cascade of delicate, pale blue flowers that sometimes have a pinkish hue. *R. augustinii* grows well in both open and semi-shaded positions, but avoid frost pockets – these will terminate its floral display prematurely.

R. cinnabarinum – A Himalayan species making a bush 2 to 3 m (6 to 10 ft) in height with elegant small leaves. It bears clusters of distinct tubular flowers that are a cinnabar red colour, hence its name. This is one of the most beautiful of Rhododendrons when at its flowering peak in May and June.

R. fastigiatum – A low-growing, dome-shaped bush rarely more than 0·6 m (2 ft) in height, making it a perfect choice for rock garden or peat bed. It has minuscule leaves about 1 cm ($\frac{1}{2}$ in) long. In late April and May its compact crown is transformed into a haze of blue-purple flowers.

R. forrestii var. repens – A creeping, mat-forming species from Yunnan, that commemorates one of our greatest plant collectors, George Forrest. Its unusual habit makes it suitable for the front of peat beds. During April and May, bright-red, bell-shaped flowers borne in ones and twos glow against the bright green leaves.

R. lepidostylum – A choice, rather rare plant with intense blue-green foliage. It makes a dense, low bush, rarely more than 1 m (3 ft) high, and is ideal for a semi-shaded peat bed. In May it bears flowers that are a delicate primrose-yellow, perfect for the blue-green foil. These are not produced in great masses, but are sufficient to catch the eye.

R. luteum – The common yellow Azalea – but what a splendid garden plant! This is a deciduous species growing up to 2·5 m (8 ft). In May its stems are crowned with clusters of bright yellow, almost honeysuckle-like flowers; these have a beautiful rich fragrance that excites the senses on a spring day. In addition, it has colourful autumn foliage. It is an absolute must for inclusion in any group of Azaleas and excellent for massing in semi-shaded woodland gardens.

R. scintillans – An excellent species for small gardens, forming a dainty bush 0·6 to 1 m (2 to 3 ft) tall. During April and May, its many twigs are crowned with lavender to purple-blue flowers. This species prefers an open position.

R. wardii – A shrub eventually making a bush up to 3 m (10 ft) high, with neat, rounded leaves. In late May, its shoots bear terminal clusters of clear yellow, cup-shaped flowers. This name also commemorates one of our great plant collectors, Frank Kingdon Ward.

R. williamsianum – This is an absolute gem for any garden with the right acid soil conditions. It makes a compact bush, densely branched and growing 1 to 1·2 m (3 to 4 ft) high. Growth is fairly slow, which means that it could be included in a peat bed. Few plants have such a neat, tidy appearance – the bushes look almost as if they have been clipped into a formal hemispherical shape. Leaves are small, almost round and have a very pleasant coppery colour when they first emerge, but turn dark green as the season progresses. The crowning glory on older plants is the delicate, clear pink, bell-shaped flowers, which leave an everlasting impression of elegant beauty.

R. yakushimanum – This is a marvellous Rhododendron for

sunny positions in small gardens. Its name derives from the island of Yakushima in southern Japan where it originates. Surprisingly, it did not arrive in Britain until 1934, but it is now widely acclaimed. Like the previous species, this also makes a very tidy hemispherical bush of dense branches. The leaves are about 7·5 cm (3 in) long, invariably rolled and, when young, covered in a whitish to brown felty covering. The original plant introductions have only grown 1·5 m (5 ft) in height with a spread of 2·1 m (7 ft), which indicates their very slow growth rate. This does not, however, prevent them from bearing equally tidy trusses of bell-shaped flowers from a very early age. These are rosy, apple-blossom pink in bud, fading to pure white. (See also *R. yakushimanum* hybrids.)

A selection of Rhododendron hybrids:

R. 'Blue Diamond' – A *R. augustinii* hybrid, making well-shaped plants 2 to 2·1 m (6 to 7 ft) in height, with deep, violet-blue flowers.

R. 'Blue Tit' – This is almost a smaller version of the above, with a more compact bush up to about 1 m (3 ft) in height. It is always very floriferous in spring, with masses of lavender-blue flowers, and makes a splendid plant for rock gardens and peat beds.

R. 'Blue Peter' – Not my favourite, but a distinctive plant with large leaves and rich cobalt-violet flowers.

R. 'Bow Bells' – A charming hybrid of *R. williamsianum* with larger, pink, bell-shaped flowers borne in loose trusses. It is generally more vigorous than *R. williamsianum*, eventually making a 2 m (6 ft) bush.

R. 'Brittania' – An old, but still one of the most popular large-leaved hybrids. It bears plentiful compact trusses of the brightest crimson-red, set against handsome green foliage. It has a fairly compact habit and is of tough constitution, suitable for exposed gardens.

R. 'Cynthia' – A vigorous large-leaved hybrid, frequently seen in gardens, and superb for open glades in woodlands or for screening. During May and June, plants are quite spectacular, crowned in their large trusses of deep rose-pink flowers. Mature plants have grown over 6 m (20 ft) in height in sheltered valleys.

R. 'Doncaster' – Neat trusses of glowing scarlet-red flowers. It has a tendency to spread, but even so will grow over 2 m (6 ft) tall.

R. 'Elizabeth' – A superb hybrid, quick-growing and with a low spreading habit, inherited no doubt from one of its parents, *R. forrestii*. Plants will eventually grow to 1 to 1·2 m (3 to 4 ft) in height, which is a good size for small gardens. From an early age, they regularly bear good crops of scarlet, funnel-shaped flowers in April and early May.

R. 'Goldsworth Yellow' – This is one of the finest yellow-flowered hardy hybrids for general planting. It opens its bold trusses of primrose-yellow flowers at the end of April.

R. loderi – A group of sensational hybrids, but essentially for large gardens able to accommodate their vigour and their 6 m (20 ft) height. Their preference is for sheltered, lightly shaded positions, in which they will bear massive trusses of large, richly-fragrant, funnel-shaped blooms. Of the several named cultivars, '*Diamond*' has white flowers, '*King George*' is blush-pink in bud, turning to white, whilst '*Venus*' is a deeper shade of pink, fading to pale pink.

R. 'Pink Pearl' – This is perhaps the most popular hybrid in gardens, bearing large trusses of soft pink flowers that fade slightly as they age. It is quite a vigorous grower reaching a height of 3 m (10 ft). This cultivar does best in full sun.

R. 'Purple Splendour' – A good cultivar if you like a plant with bold trusses of a rich, royal purple hue. It is vigorous, but only makes a medium-sized bush.

R. yakushimanum hybrids – Rhododendron enthusiasts quickly recognised the breeding potential of this species, and since its arrival in 1934, several hybrids have been produced. Recently, a new range of dwarf hybrids have been released from Waterer's nursery in Surrey, which promise to be excellent for small gardens. The following are a selection:

'*Golden Torch*' – chrome yellow.
'*Percy Wiseman*' – pink and cream.
'*Pink Cherub*' – soft pink.
'*Doc*' – rhodamine pink.
'*Dopey*' – red.
'*Grumpy*' – yellow.

Azalea
For horticultural purposes this is often listed as a separate genus, but to be botanically correct, Azaleas are now regarded as a sub-genus of *Rhododendron* – hence their inclusion here.

Deciduous Azalea hybrids need the same growing conditions as Rhododendrons, *i.e.* acid soils and semi-shaded, sheltered positions. They bear masses of colourful flowers which emerge as the new foliage is about to break in May. Many are strongly scented and most have magnificent autumn colour. These Azaleas have arisen in various hybrid groups, of which the following are a selection:

Ghent Azaleas
This is one of the oldest groups, with distinctive honeysuckle-like flowers that are extremely fragrant. Generally they grow taller than the other groups, forming bushes over 2 m (6 ft) in height.

'*Coccinea Speciosa*' – orange red.
'*Corneille*' – white flushed pink, double-flowered.
'*Gloria Mundi*' – bright orange.
'*Nancy Waterer*' – good bright yellow.
'*Narcissiflora*' – pale yellow, double-flowered.

Mollis Azaleas
Generally this group flower in early May. They usually have fiery scarlet, orange and flame flowers but regrettably they have no

fragrance. As a group they are well suited to small gardens as they only grow into 1·2 to 1·5 m (4 to 5 ft) bushes.

'*Directeur Moerlands*' – golden-yellow.
'*Dr M. Oosthoek*' – deep orange-red.
'*Mrs Peter Koster*' – scarlet.
'*Speks Orange*' – bright orange.
'*Sunbeam*' – bright yellow.

Knaphill Azaleas
This is the largest and most recent hybrid group, and is still extending. It also embraces a group known as the *Exbury Azaleas*. They have trumpet-shaped flowers, and some, but not all, are scented. Ultimate height is about 1·5 m (5 ft).

'*Ballerina*' – white with a small orange flare.
'*Cecile*' – salmon pink with a yellow flare.
'*Devon*' – blood-red and fragrant.
'*Harvest Moon*' – primrose-yellow with darker flare.
'*Homebush*' – double, carmine-pink.
'*Klondyke*' – deep golden-yellow.
'*Strawberry Ice*' – light pink with a yellow flare.

The following is a selection of evergreen Azalea Hybrids:

Indian Azaleas
These are the ones frequently seen as forced pot plants for Christmas display. They are not fully hardy and I have therefore not recommended any cultivars.

Kurume Azaleas
These originated in Japan and are sometimes referred to as *Japanese Azaleas*. They are dense, low-growing bushes, flowering in late April–early May, when the foliage disappears beneath a sea of tightly packed, colourful flowers. Sunny or semi-shaded positions suit them, but do ensure that their roots are kept moist.

'*Azuma-Kagami*' – pale carmine-rose.
'*Hatsuguri*' – crimson purple, low-growing.
'*Hindodegiri*' – bright red.

'*Hinomayo*' – phlox-pink.
'*Kure-No-Yuki*' – white, low-growing.

Modern Hybrid Azaleas

In recent years various hybrid groups have been developed in Holland, America and Japan from which I have chosen the following:

'*Beethoven*' – lilac-mauve.
'*Betty*' – salmon pink.
'*Leo*' – bright orange, low-growing.
'*Palestrina*' – white.
'*Pippa*' – purple.
'*Rose Bud*' – phlox-pink.

Rosa – Roses

Most Roses come into their own in July and August but several good shrub Roses herald this display by blooming during May and June.

R. 'Canary Bird' – A superb shrub Rose, making a bush 2 m (6 ft) across, with long arching sprays crowded with single, canary-yellow flowers set against an attractive foil of small green leaves.

R. x cantabrigiensis – A similar Rose, with small, slightly paler yellow flowers, but still borne in great profusion against delicate, ferny foliage.

R. 'Fruhlingsgold' – You need plenty of room to accommodate this vigorous but quite superb shrub Rose. It forms a tall, free-flowering mound 2·1 to 2·5 m (7 to 8 ft) across, with long, graceful branches. These bear large, almost semi-double flowers that open a pale golden-yellow and fade to creamy yellow; their fragrance is most pleasant.

R. 'Fruhlingsmorgen' – A very similar hybrid, slightly less vigorous and with unusual rose-pink petals which have a creamy-yellow base to illuminate the purple stamens. This plant often has a second fling in late autumn.

Rubus Tridel

An extremely vigorous ornamental bramble, that looks more like a single, white-flowered Rose. It has long, arching stems reaching up to 2·5 m (8 ft), and grows almost as wide. In May, its thornless stems are adorned with pure white flowers, each 3 to 5 cm ($1\frac{1}{2}$ to 2 in) across. This reliable hybrid grows well in most soils and has given me excellent results in both open and semi-shaded positions.

Spiraea x arguta – Bridal Wreath

A very apt common name for this deciduous shrub, which in late April and early May turns every slender branchlet into cascading sprays of pure white flowers. It is a very easy, undemanding shrub to cultivate. Mature plants benefit from an occasional thinning out of the oldest flowered shoots immediately after flowering.

Spiraea x vanhouttei

Flowering later in June, this vigorous hybrid with long, arching stems can grow over 2 m (6 ft) in height. It also has white flowers, but these are borne in more clearly-defined clusters. It has rather attractive foliage, similar to maidenhair.

Syringa vulgaris – Lilac

The variety of colour and fragrant blossom all contribute towards the popularity of this splendid free-flowering shrub. Lilacs are generally undemanding plants and grow well in most soils, including chalk; in fact, they thrive on it. They can grow 2·5 to 3·5 m (8 to 12 ft) tall and have a spread of 2 to 2·5 m (6 to 8 ft), which means planting them where they have adequate space for full development. Occasionally, their suckers become a nuisance; these are best removed from below ground whilst they are still young. Apart from garden display, the elegant, delightfully fragrant flowers have a good vase life and look admirable in indoor floral arrangements. The following cultivars are recommended:

Single Flowered:
'*Hugo Koster*' – purple-crimson.
'*Marechal Foch*' – bright carmine-rose.
'*Maud Notcutt*' – pure white.
'*Primrose*' – pale primrose to creamy-yellow.
'*Souvenir de Louis Spaeth*' – wine-red.

Double Flowered:
'*Charles Joly*' – dark purple-red.
'*Katherine Havemeyer*' – lavender.
'*Madame Antoine Buchner*' – rose-pink.
'*Madame Lemoine*' – pure white.
'*Mrs Edward Harding*' – claret red.

Syringa velutina (*Syn. S. palibiniana*)
If space for Lilacs is limited, this beautiful 'Korean Lilac' is a most acceptable choice. It is slow-growing, making a dense, compact bush only 1 to 1·2 m (3 to 4 ft) tall and almost globular in shape. Even in its early stages, despite its slow growth, it bears a profusion of pale pink flower-spikes through May and June.

Viburnum
This is a large genus containing some fine garden shrubs. The following produce showy spring flowers.

V. carlesii – This is a deciduous species with dull, slightly downy leaves, growing into a rounded bush 1·2 to 2 m (4 to 7 ft) in height. During April and May it bears globular clusters of white flowers that have an extremely sweet and strong fragrance. Regrettably, this beautiful shrub is often disfigured with heavy aphid infestation, and should be examined regularly from spring onwards so that remedial action can be taken as soon as an outbreak is noticed. Several excellent hybrids have arisen from crosses using *V. carlesii*, notably *V. x burkwoodii*, which flowers earlier from March to May. Its flowers form similar globular clusters, rosy-pink in bud, opening to white, and they too carry that superb fragrance. Hybrids are generally taller and have a more open habit; the cultivar '*Park Farm Hybrid*' is one of the best clones to obtain. *V. x juddii* is another *V. carlesii* hybrid with a compact growth habit and delightful fragrance. This hybrid is also less susceptible to aphids.

V. opulus – Guelder Rose. A native shrub found in hedgerows and woods, frequently where the soil is moist, which produces attractive flattened clusters of white flowers in June. The outer florets of each cluster are sterile, which gives them a strong resemblance to the Lacecap Hydrangeas. When a few plants are grouped together to improve pollination, heavy crops of succulent red berries follow in autumn. In the cultivar *V. o.* '*Sterile*' all the florets are sterile, and the result is a dense globular cluster of white flowers which give the plant its appropriate common name of Snowball Tree. This is very decorative in flower but, alas, is incapable of bearing fruit. Both plants can grow 2·5 to 3 m (8 to 10 ft) in height. For smaller gardens or positions at the edge of shrub borders, the low-growing *V. o. 'Compactum'* is limited to a height of 0·6 to 1 m (2 to 3 ft), but does not spare itself flowering and fruiting.

V. plicatum '*Lanarth*' – This is one of my favourite Viburnums, due to its distinctive shape and vigorous growth. Its branches grow out horizontally, forming layers which bear pure white flowers in June, these being flattened and arranged like those of Lacecap Hydrangeas. Plants eventually attain a height of 2·5 m (8 ft) and can spread to 3 to 3·5 m (10 to 12 ft). Less vigorous is *V. p.* '*Mariesii*', which has even more pronounced horizontal branches. This flowers profusely in June, and in autumn its leaves turn an unusual plum colour before falling.

Weigela florida

This must be one of the easiest deciduous shrubs to cultivate and grows well in any fertile soil, including chalk. *Weigela* will quickly attain a height of 1·5 to 2 m (5 to 6 ft). It is desirable to prune out a proportion of the oldest flowered shoots immediately after flowering; they will stand quite severe pruning if they need containing or regeneration. During May and June, the plants will bear prolific numbers of reddish, tubular flowers. Two distinct and less vigorous cultivars are *W. f. 'Variegata'* and *W. f. 'Foliis Purpureus'*. The former has creamy-edged leaves and pink flowers, whilst the latter has purple foliage and deeper pink flowers.

Weigela cultivars
These named cultivars are superior to the species in terms of flower quality and colour range, and the following are all worthy of inclusion in a mixed shrub border.

'*Abel Carriere*' – rose-pink.
'*Bristol Ruby*' – dark red.
'*Eva Rathke*' – crimson.
'*Mont Blanc*' – white.
'*Newport Red*' – bright red.

Trees

Aesculus hippocastanum – Horse Chestnut
This is one of the finest flowering trees, and is most impressive when illuminated with its 'candles' of creamy-white flowers in May. Essentially, it is a parkland tree which should only be planted in gardens large enough to accommodate a tree capable of growing over 21 m (70 ft) in height and over 18 m (60 ft) across. Only in spacious surroundings can its magnificent stature be attained and its full beauty appreciated. Trees such as these in small gardens are usually seen as either mutilated plants or as oppressive objects which prevent or severely limit other gardening activity. Even in large gardens, care should be taken not to place them too close to buildings, where their dense canopy will shut out the light. Mature chestnuts also yield 'conkers', except for the double-flowered, sterile cultivar, *A. h. 'Baumanii'*. Chestnuts are generally very hardy trees, which are easy to establish and grow satisfactorily in most soils, including chalk.

Aesculus x carnea – Pink Flowered Horse Chestnut
This hybrid between Horse Chestnut and American Red Chestnut is more suitable for gardens, as it is less vigorous and only grows to 9 to 14 m (30 to 45 ft) in height. It forms a distinct dome-

shaped crown with pendulous branchlets which, during May, support the erect reddish pink 'candles'. These are smaller than in Horse Chestnut, but are produced in great quantity and give a fine display. The trunk and branches of this tree often have cankerous growths, but as yet their cause is unknown, and so, therefore, is the treatment. The best cultivar of this hybrid is *A. x carnea 'Briotii'*, which has larger and more richly-coloured flowers.

If you have room to grow Chestnuts in your garden two very commendable species are *A. indica* and *A. flava*. The former is a hardy tree with the most handsome foliage of any Chestnut that I know. It has the typical compound Chestnut leaves but in this case they are smooth and slightly shiny. Its flowers are white, each with a salmon-pink blotch and protruding stamens. Flowers appear in late June and July, later than those of the common Horse Chestnut. The cultivar *A. i. 'Sydney Pearce'* is the choicest form.

A. flava (*Syn. A. octandra*), commonly known as *Sweet Buckeye* has two visual attractions. Firstly, it has unusual creamy yellow flowers which appear in May. These are smaller than those of Horse Chestnut, but nonetheless conspicuously displayed. Secondly, the leaves turn to attractive orange and yellow tints in late summer, often before the end of August.

Cercis siliquastrum – Judas Tree

This is a breathtakingly beautiful flowering tree for gardens in the south and milder parts of Britain. It is deciduous, forming a bushy headed tree about 7·5 m (25 ft) in height. It seems to grow well on most soils, including chalk, providing they are well drained. During May, its leafless branches bear clusters of slight purplish-pink, pea-like flowers. These are peculiarly borne along the entire branches and even on the trunk – in fact, the young branches are often so crowded with blossom that the overall effect is most impressive. Originating from the Mediterranean, this plant loves sunshine, but will also grow successfully in the north of England when trained against a south-facing wall. Its common name is derived from the legend that it was from one of these trees that Judas hanged himself after betraying Jesus.

Cornus nuttallii – Pacific Dogwood
A north-American plant, only suited to gardens in the milder counties, where it forms a large bush or small tree about 7·5 m (25 ft) in height. During May, each true flower is surrounded by six showy bracts, which look like large, white petals. This plant has a strong dislike of chalk. A suitable, though less impressive alternative for northern gardens is *C. kousa*. In this species, each flower has four smaller white bracts. It is also less vigorous, and only grows to 4·5 to 6 m (15 to 20 ft) with a spreading crown.

Crataegus oxyacantha – Hawthorn or May Blossom
This species and *C. monogyna* are an important constituent of agricultural hedges and if left untrimmed they can form attractive small trees with a pleasantly knarled character. Commonly seen in gardens is the cultivar *C. o. 'Paul's Scarlet'*, which yields dense masses of small, double red flowers at the end of May and early June. It grows successfully virtually anywhere in lowland Britain, and being limited to a height of 6 m (20 ft) at maturity, is the right size for small suburban gardens. But it is a weak-rooted tree, which, coupled with its very dense, mop-headed crown, often makes it unstable and easily wind-blown. Sadly, it is also highly susceptible to Fire Blight.

Crataegus is a vast genus containing some very good species and cultivars for gardens, of which I think the following are of special merit:

C. arnoldiana – In addition to its showy white flowers in May and June, this species is most impressive for a short period in autumn, when it bears a crop of large, bright red fruits.

C. x. grignonensis – Masses of white flowers in June are set against glossy green leaves, which remain on the plant until late winter, as do the bright orange-red fruits.

C. x. lavallei (*Syn. C. carrierei*) – This is one of the best, with large, glossy green leaves and orange-red fruits which persist into the winter months.

C. prunifolia – Good in flower and fruit, but at its best when glowing with its orange-red autumn leaves.

C. tanacetifolia – This is an unusual, fairly slow-growing tree with hairy, deeply cut leaves. It is quite good in flower and has conspicuous large yellow fruits.

Davidia involucrata – Pocket Handkerchief Tree

This is also known as 'Dove Tree' or 'Ghost Tree', and all these common names relate to the unequal large white bracts attached to each globular flower. The larger bracts can be 15 to 20 cm (6 to 8 in) long and on mature trees during May they are borne along the branches in such profusion that their overall effect is quite fantastic. Unfortunately, young trees are prone to have their shoots damaged by late spring frost, which makes them difficult to establish in northern gardens. Another disadvantage is that they can take many years to come into flowering. The foliage is most handsome: heart-shaped, 7·5 to 12·5 cm (3 to 5 in) long, with a slight resemblance to that of Lime. Mature trees rarely exceed 12 m (40 ft), and if you do decide to plant one, give it generous treatment at planting time to encourage its early establishment.

Embothrium coccineum – Chilean Fire Bush

Of all flowering trees that I know, nothing provides such a breath-taking spectacle as the Chilean Fire Bush. This common name could not be more appropriate, for in May and early June its stems are emblazoned with a fiery mass of bright scarlet, tubular flowers. Unfortunately, it is confined to the milder districts of the south and west, but northern gardeners can at least enjoy the flowers of the hardiest form, *E. c. 'Norquinco'*, providing they can find it a warm, sheltered corner of the garden. Essentially, these are sun-loving plants with a preference for lime-free soil.

Laburnum x watereri 'Vossii' – Golden Rain Tree

A commonly-planted garden tree of great beauty in late May and June, when its branches are adorned with cascades of bright yellow, pendulous flower spikes. Laburnums thrive in most freely-drained soils, including chalk. Normally, they grow 6 to 7·5 m (20 to 25 ft) in height, with a fairly erect branch framework. They tend to be weak-rooted and need good support until properly established. Rarely are they long-lived, but they more than make up for this by being so easily established and free-flowering from an early age. Laburnums are notorious for their poisonous seeds, which can occasionally have fatal consequences if eaten. This particular cultivar of hybrid origin fortunately produces very few seeds, but parents of young children should nonetheless be aware of the danger and if necessary gather the seeds before they fall. Laburnum can form an attractive feature by being trained over an archway or pergola.

Malus – Ornamental Crab Apples

This is an excellent group of small and medium-sized trees which are prolific in suburban gardens and readily obtainable from garden centres. Their flowering period extends from the end of April almost to June, and in several species or cultivars there is a further display of showy autumn fruits (see Chapter 11). Their extensive planting in gardens indicates how well they tolerate a great variety of soils and situations; they are, however, less suited to windy or exposed sites. Most grow well in towns, but be wary of planting them in areas affected by Fire Blight. The following selection have a prolific flowering habit.

M. baccata – Siberian Crab. One of the taller-growing species, reaching a height of 9 to 12 m (30 to 40 ft); but Siberian Crab is a tree of gnarled character and looks superb when smothered in its masses of pure white flowers.

M. floribunda – Japanese Crab. A common garden tree 6 to 9 m (20 to 30 ft) high when mature, with a spreading crown usually composed of a dense tangle of branches. As its name suggests, it bears a real abundance of blossom; there can be few plants with such crowded flowering shoots. Flowers are blushed rose-pink in bud, but open a pale pink and finish almost white.

M. x. purpurea – This is still quite popular, but has been superseded by improved forms. Young leaves have a purple hue turning to dark green as they mature and forming a harmonious foil for the rose-crimson flowers. Trees in this group generally have more open crowns.

M. 'Aldenhamensis' – A good cultivar in the *purpurea* group and rather similar in appearance, except that it flowers about a fortnight later, which makes it useful for extending the flowering season.

M. 'Lemoinei' Another from the *purpurea* group with richer flower colour and bronzy foliage.

M. 'Profusion' – Undoubtedly the best in the group with deep wine-red flowers, borne in great profusion. A superb garden tree.

M. 'Van Eseltine' – I mention this for its distinct columnar shape, which makes it a suitable choice for restricted places such as courtyards or small gardens. It bears dense clusters of rosy pink flowers.

Prunus – Flowering Cherry

May is the month when flowering Cherries dominate the tree scene with their glorious displays of blossom. There is no shortage of choice, and the following are only a selection:

P. 'Amanogowa' – A small, distinctly erect tree, making a narrow column similar to a miniature Lombardy Poplar, but rarely more than 6 m (20 ft) in height. Its narrow outline makes it perfect for the smallest gardens or for adding height to a narrow shrub border. It should always be allowed to branch from the base as a feathered tree, and not trained into a standard like other Cherries. Occasionally, branches become splayed out by wind or snow, and these are best pruned back to suitably-placed lateral branches or buds. Plants are at their best in May when the stems are crowded with clusters of fragrant, semi-double, pink flowers. It is not a long-lived tree generally, but it can soon be re-established when a replacement becomes necessary.

P. avium – Gean or Wild Cherry. A native Cherry growing over 15 m (50 ft) in height and consequently less suited to small gardens. It is, nevertheless, a beautiful tree at flowering time, and ought to be chosen more often in community tree-planting schemes. It is adorned with massed bunches of pure white blossom, followed in July by bright red cherries which, unless protected in some way, are quickly devoured by birds. In autumn, its leaves turn orange and scarlet, but this can be variable. The best Gean for ornamental planting is the cultivar *P. a 'Plena'*. As the name indicates, this has double flowers and these bloom noticeably longer than the type. However, there are few cherries to eat, as most of the flowers are sterile.

P. 'Jo-Nioi' – This is not one of the most spectacular Cherries, but I mention it briefly for its excellent fragrance. It flowers well in early May, and bears small, single white flowers; it eventually grows to 7·5 m (25 ft).

P. 'Kanzan' – A glorious flowering Cherry that has become so popular as to be regarded by some people as being vulgar. It is a tough, easily-grown tree which unfailingly flowers very profusely during May, its erect boughs wreathed in bunches of double pink blossom.

Normally, '*Kanzan*' is sold as a standard tree and develops an inverted cone-shaped crown, eventually tending to spread as it matures, by which time it will have reached a height of 7·5 to 9 m (25 to 30 ft). Plants grafted at ground level, although not readily available, are worth seeking, as they make splendid bushes for lawn or border decoration. Less well known but equally attractive is a hybrid containing Kanzan blood, called '*Pink Perfection*'. This has inherited many of Kanzan's desirable qualities, but bears bright, rosy-pink flowers.

P. 'Shirofugen' – A beautiful Japanese Cherry, aptly described by its name, which means 'White God'. It grows to 7·5 m (25 ft) and develops the usual flat-topped crown of Japanese Cherries, which can spread to 9 m (30 ft). This is one of the latest to flower, in mid-May, when its white to pale pink flowers hang in long, stalked clusters; these are set against the emerging bronze-coloured leaves.

P. 'Ukon' – This Japanese cultivar is distinguished by its unique flowers, which are pale yellow, with a hint of lime-green. These are semi-double and crowd the branches during May. This may not sound an attractive colour for a Cherry, but I can assure you that it is a very acceptable shade. The tree has an upright branching habit reaching 6 m (20 ft) and spreading with age to 9 m (30 ft).

Sorbus
Most members of this genus bear clusters of creamy-white flowers during this season, but I have included them in Chapter 11 on account of their more impressive fruit displays.

July and August

Shrubs

Buddleia davidii – Butterfly Bush
An easily-grown shrub suited to any well-drained soil, including chalk. Its adaptability can be gauged by the fact that it grows as well in exposed coastal gardens as it does in the heart of industrial towns. It prefers a sunny site in which to produce its long, flowering spikes in July and August; these are a great attraction to all kinds of butterflies, which seek the nectar from the base of the small tubular florets. Unpruned plants will make bushes up to 3 m (10 ft), but annual hard pruning, carried out before growth commences in spring, will produce superior-quality flowers and neater plants. Give them what I call coppice treatment, and cut all stems to within a few centimetres of their base. Do not forget to apply nutrients to stimulate vigorous re-growth. The following cultivars show the range of colours available.

'*Black Knight*' – rich, dark purple.
'*Empire Blue*' – violet purple.
'*Peace*' – creamy white.
'*Royal Red*' – rich red-purple.
'*White Profusion*' – pure white.

Two Buddleia species that are noteworthy are *B. alternifolia* and *B. globosa*. The first begins flowering towards the end of June, when its arching branchlets are wreathed in clusters of fragrant, lilac flowers, forming a graceful cascade. This species is less suited to smaller gardens, as it grows over 4·5 m (15 ft) high with a spread of 3 m (10 ft). *B. globosa* is better suited to gardens in mild districts, as it is easily damaged in hard winters. The common name of 'Orange Ball Tree' adequately describes its flowers, which first appear in June. Neither of these species require hard pruning, apart from an occasional thinning out to keep them tidy.

Caryopteris x clandonensis
A lovely, blue-flowered shrub perfect for the front of borders. It can grow to 1 m (3 ft) in height, but it is best to treat it like a hardy perennial and cut it back to within a few centimetres of the ground in March, just before new growth commences. *Caryopteris* grows best in full sun and well-drained soil, including chalk. The best form is the cultivar '*Arthur Simmond's*', which has bright blue flowers which are produced continuously through August and September.

Escallonia
A useful group of evergreen shrubs, growing 2 to 2·5 m (6 to 8 ft) tall, with dark green, glossy leaves; these are a perfect foil for the myriads of small saxifrage-like flowers borne through July, August and often into September. They grow in all well-drained soils, including chalk, and are fairly resistant to drought. Unfortunately, they are not all completely hardy, and can consequently be badly cut back by frost in severe winters; for this reason, they are best positioned in the warmer parts of northern gardens with a southerly aspect. They are excellent coastal shrubs and also respond to clipping, and make good hedges for seaside gardens, especially in the south and west of England. Notable forms are as follows:

E. '*Apple Blossom*' – A compact, tidy plant making a rounded bush 1·5 m (5 ft) high. Its rosy-pink flowers are truly like miniature apple blossom.

E. '*C. F. Ball*' – This is a taller cultivar, reaching 2 to 2·5 m

(7 to 8 ft) and forming a dense bush bearing masses of bold red flowers.

E. 'Donard Seedling' – A well known, vigorous cultivar named after the Irish nursery that produced several excellent hybrids. Its flower buds are pink, opening to white.

E. 'Edinensis' – Another tall-growing form, reaching to 2 m (7 ft), its carmine flower buds open shell-pink.

E. 'Iveyi' – Excellent for mild districts, but can only survive with the protection of a south-facing wall in the north. It has admirable foliage and an abundance of white flowers in late August, which continue until the onset of frosts.

Eucryphia glutinosa
An uncommon but very beautiful shrub for the plant connoisseur. It has a preference for peaty, acid soils and likes semi-shaded, sheltered woodland situations, where it can grow up to 4·5 m (15 ft). *Eucryphias* do not establish well, unless planting sites are well-prepared and young plants cared for. During July and August, single white flowers decorate the branches. Each bloom is about 5 cm (2 in) across and carries numerous stamens, giving them a resemblance to Hypericum flowers. In autumn, its deeply-divided leaves turn rich orange with a few tinges of red and scarlet. *E. glutinosa* is the hardiest species, but several others are worthy of cultivation in larger, sheltered gardens. *E. x nymansensis*, 'Nymansay', makes a small evergreen tree with a narrow columnar habit, capable of growing to 7·5 to 9 m (25 to 30 ft). This is a gem when adorned in its pure white flowers during August.

Hydrangea macrophylla – Hortensia Group
These are the familiar Hydrangeas forced as spring-flowering pot plants, and as open-ground plants they make splendid flowering shrubs. The massive round flower-heads are composed of many smaller flowers that have enlarged showy sepals around each true flower, and it is for this reason that the flowers appear to persist for so long. Hydrangeas in this group have a strong preference for acid soils, and the slightest hint of free lime will turn their

leaves a sickly yellow. If your soil is not suitable, you can grow them successfully in tubs or large pots filled with an acid-based compost. The only proviso is to keep them well watered, and in hard water areas to use only rainwater.

Hydrangeas grow equally well in both warm sunny positions and semi-shaded woodland gardens. They also thrive in coastal gardens, where their soft new shoots remain unaffected by the greater temperature extremes found in inland areas. Mature plants will normally grow to a height of 1·2 or 1·5 m (4 or 5 ft) and often have a similar spread. Pot-grown Hydrangeas are frequently planted out into gardens with success, but confusion can arise when that choice blue variety suddenly appears with pinkish flowers. The reason for this apparent change is that good blue coloration only develops in acid soil; if your soil is neutral or slightly alkaline, blueness has to be induced. This can be done by watering responsive cultivars with a proprietary Hydrangea blueing compound. These are based on alum and are usually obtainable from garden centres or shops. Shoots that are frosted back will invariably re-grow from the base; all you need to do is to remove the dead wood. Normal pruning only involves the removal of spent flower-heads, which, in northern gardens, is a task best left until the end of April, when new growth appears. Of the many cultivars the following are reliable out of doors:

'*Altona*' – pink, or mid-blue if treated.
'*Generale Vicomtesse de Vibraye*' – very hardy, pink or clear blue if treated.
'*Madame Emile Mouillière*' – a popular white-flowered cultivar.
'*Maréchal Foch*' – always free-flowering, deep pink or gentian blue.
'*Westfalen*' – deeply-coloured, rich crimson or purple blue.

Hydrangea macrophylla – Lacecap Group
In this group, the flower-heads are flattened and almost plate-like, with only the outer flowers bearing enlarged sepals; this gives them the appearance of being edged with lace – hence the group name. Their requirements are virtually the same as the Hortensias. Good cultivars are as follows:

'Blue Wave' – A marvellous plant for a semi-shaded woodland garden. The outer sepals vary from pink to blue, depending on soil acidity. It grows to 1·5 to 2 m (5 to 6 ft) in height.

'Lanarth White' – More compact, only growing to 1 m (3 ft). Outer sepals are white, set against blue to pink central flowers.

'Mariesii' – A beautiful cultivar, with pink to mauve flowers, growing up to 1·2 to 1·5 m (4 to 5 ft).

'White Wave' – A seedling of *'Mariesii'* with white outer sepals. This one prefers an open situation.

Hydrangea paniculata 'Grandiflora'
This is hardier than those of the *macrophylla* groups and can be just as impressive. From July almost through to October, it produces large cone-shaped clusters, densely packed with white flowers that gradually turn pale purplish-pink. Unpruned plants will grow to 1·5 m (5 ft), but massive flower-heads can be grown on coppiced plants. These are pruned to within a few centimetres of the ground in spring, just as growth commences. This is followed by a generous application of general fertiliser and a mulch of rotted manure. The resultant terminal flowers are superb and may be anything from 30 to 45 cm (12 to 18 in) long.

Hypericum 'Hidcote'
If you only have room for a few shrubs, at least endeavour to find room for this one, which gives good value for money. From July through to October, whenever one flower fades there is another fat bud waiting to open, and overall the bushes are always well furnished with bloom. Each flower is like a single Rose, about 5 cm (2 in) across but bright, golden-yellow in colour with a central head of protruding stamens. It is perfectly hardy, very easily grown, but best in full sun. Normally, it is a tidy rounded bush 1 to 1·2 m (3 to 4 ft) in height.

Lavandula – 'Lavender'
An old-fashioned evergreen shrub, but still deservedly very popular in modern gardens. Its silvery-grey, aromatic leaves make the perfect foil for the blue, purple flower spikes that appear in

July and continue into September. These in turn can be dried for winter flower arrangements, or used in pomanders or traditional 'lavender bags'. Lavender is of Mediterranean origin and likes sunny positions and well-drained soil. Old plants tend to become leggy, but replacements are easily raised from late summer cuttings. Alternatively, plants can be kept trimmed. This is done each spring, before growth commences, by shearing the previous year's shoots back to half their length. Botanical nomenclature of garden lavender is very confused, but *L. spica* is the name which persists in most catalogues. Two notable cultivars are *L. 'Hidcote'*, which has dark purple-blue flowers, and *L. 'Munstead'*, a deep blue; both make neat compact plants 0·4 to 0·6 m (1½ to 2 ft) tall.

Potentilla

Few plants can better the shrubby Potentillas for length of flowering. The majority are at their peak in July and August, but some begin flowering as early as May and continue through to September. Their cultivation presents no problems: they grow well in all freely-drained soils, including chalk. Whilst they tolerate partial shade, a greater freedom of flowering is shown on plants in open, sunny positions. Most are low-growing to medium-sized, and are therefore suitable for borders in small gardens. There is a great variety to choose from, and the following are merely a popular selection:

P. arbuscula – A low-growing bush, rarely exceeding 0·4 m (1½ ft), with a tendency to spread to about 1 m (3 ft). The five-petaled flowers are about 3 cm (1½ in) across and, apart from their bright yellow colour, resemble miniature wild Roses. *'Beesii'*, with its silvery foliage, is a good cultivar of this species, and an excellent hybrid is *'Elizabeth'*, which forms a mound of yellow flowers about 1 m (3 ft) tall.

P. 'Jackman's Variety' – A more vigorous shrub, growing up to 1·2 m (4 ft), with a continuation of bright yellow flowers.

P. 'Katherine Dykes' – An old favourite, growing 1 to 1·2 m

(3 to 4 ft) high. Its flowers are about 2·5 cm (1 in) across and canary-yellow.

P. 'Tangerine' – A low-growing cultivar, reaching about 0·6 m (2 ft) and spreading to 1 m (3 ft). As its name suggests, its flowers are orange-yellow on opening but fade as they mature. Their colour is generally better in semi-shade.

P. 'Red Ace' – A recent cultivar, introduced in a blaze of publicity, which disappointed me when its first, eagerly-awaited flowers opened an orange colour, and not the bright red I had seen on the garden centre posters. It has now redeemed itself, however, and produced plenty of good red flowers which fade to deep orange. It is not as strong-growing as other Potentillas.

Rosa – Roses

Throughout history, the Rose has figured prominently in gardens, art and literature, and there is no doubt that it will remain permanently crowned as the 'Queen of Flowers'. It is not difficult to understand the perpetual fascination of Roses; they come from a vast genus, containing well over a hundred wild species that have been interbred to produce many hybrid groups and innumerable cultivars. Most have singularly beautiful flowers that are generally borne in great profusion, fragrant scent, and riotous colours.

Roses are versatile, ranging from miniatures a few inches tall to climbers that can scramble to 18 m (60 ft). I doubt if any investment will repay with such interest as a Rose plant.

Species and Shrub Roses

Roses in this group usually grow into medium or large shrubs. In my view, they should be planted in association with other shrubs to extend the season of interest. They grow best in sunny, sheltered positions with their roots in fertile, freely-drained, but not acid soils. Unlike other Roses, these do not require regular pruning apart from an occasional thinning out.

R. x alba – The White Rose of York. A Rose of historical interest, with pure white, semi-double flowers that are strongly scented. Mature plants make a 1·5 m (5 ft) bush.

R. centifolia – Cabbage Rose. A 1·2 m (4 ft) bush, with full 'cabbage'-shaped flowers of the type so often seen in old paintings; these are pink in colour and have an almost intoxicating fragrance.

R. gallica 'Versicolor' – Rosa Mundi. Another fine old Rose, often portrayed in historical prints, with semi-double flowers and distinctive pink-and-white striped petals. It makes a compact bush 1 to 1·2 m (3 to 4 ft) across.

R. rubrifolia – A splendid Rose with uniquely coloured greyish-green foliage with a blush of mauve. This provides a perfect foil for its single, clear pink flowers. It is a vigorous bush up to 2 m (6 ft) high, whose persistent bright red hips also offer a good show in autumn and winter.

Rosa rugosa – Ramanas Rose. A dense, suckering shrub 1·2 to 1·5 m (4 to 5 ft) across, with distinctive roughened leaves. This is a tough, easily grown rose, which produces pleasant fragrant flowers from June to October. These are followed by large globular hips in autumn. The following are notable cultivars:

'Blanc Double De Coubert' – semi-double, white flowers.
'Frau Dagmar Hastrup' – single, pale pink flowers.
'Roserie De L'Hay' – double, velvet-textured flowers, rich crimson-purple; undoubtedly the best.
(See also Chapter 15 under Rose Hedges.)

R. 'Cardinal De Richelieu' – A splendid *R. gallica* hybrid with rich, royal purple, full-bodied flowers. It makes a bush 1·2 m (4 ft) high.

R. 'Cornelia' – A hybrid musk Rose of exceptional beauty. These are at their best in June and July, but will continue flowering late into the season. This cultivar bears a plentiful crop of showy pink flowers that have a lovely soft fragrance. It makes a fairly dense bush 1·5 to 2 m (5 to 6 ft) across.

R. 'Felicia' – Another hybrid musk with similar qualities but a more compact, bushy habit, and thus suitable for informal hedges. Flowers are salmon-pink and intensely fragrant.

R. 'Moonlight' – My favourite hybrid musk: a large, spreading shrub 2 to 2·1 m (6 to 7 ft) high and as much across. Throughout summer and well into autumn, it bears a prolific·crop of bold, semi-double flowers that open creamy white and fade to almost pure white. As with other musks, it has that characteristic scent inherited from its distant parent *R. Moschata*.

R. 'Heidelberg' – A modern shrub Rose resembling a vigorous *floribunda*, and growing 1·5 to 2 m (5 to 6 ft) in height. When flowering, it gives a spectacular display and bears plentiful trusses of vivid scarlet, scented flowers.

R. 'Nevada' – A vigorous modern shrub Rose with arching branches and 2·1 to 2·5 m (7 to 8 ft) tall. Flowering begins in June, followed by a second flush in August. Each flower is large, single and creamy white in colour. *R. 'Marguerite Hilling'* is an equally beautiful pink-flowered sort of this Rose.

Large-flowered and cluster-flowered Roses (*Hybrid Teas and Floribundas*)

These are two distinct groups of modern Roses, but for cultural purposes they can be treated together. Large-flowered (Hybrid Teas) are the popular Roses, with full-bodied blooms usually borne singly but occasionally in small groups on a stem. The cluster-flowered (floribundas) have dense clusters of flowers, usually with each flower containing fewer petals; their overall effect, however, is a mass of long-lasting colour. Both groups are popular for bedding, but unquestionably the cluster-flowered (floribundas) are superior for this purpose.

These Roses may be purchased as bushes, standards or half standards. Bush Roses are the ones most frequently used; they are budded close to the ground so that the resultant basal growth produces a low-growing bush. Standards and half standards are budded on a single stem, usually on a *R. rugosa* under-stock; standards at a height of 1 m ($3\frac{1}{2}$ ft) and half standards at 0·7 m ($2\frac{1}{2}$ ft). This produces a bush on an elevated stem, rather like a miniature tree. Such plants are ideal for giving height in Rose beds or narrow borders, provided their slender stems are firmly staked.

For good results both large-flowered and cluster-flowered Roses demand attention and are responsive to generous treatment. Pruning often causes unnecessary problems. Firstly, provide yourself with a good pair of sharp secateurs and protective gloves. If you are tackling older bushes a pair of long-handled loppers will come in useful for making light work of thicker branches. Newly planted bushes should be pruned hard back to within 15 cm (6 in) of the ground; this will encourage strong basal growth. Cuts should always be made to outward-facing buds, so that an open-centre bush develops. When pruning mature plants, picture in your mind's eye a goblet without its stem, as this is the open-centre shape you are aiming to develop. This will allow light and air into the plant and should minimise disease.

The cultivars vary in vigour, and as a general guide, vigorous cultivars need only moderate pruning compared with weaker growers which need hard pruning to stimulate more vigorous re-growth. 'Hard' pruning entails cutting shoots back to within 10 or 12·5 cm (4 or 5 in) of their base, leaving three or four buds; 'moderate' pruning means reducing shoots by half their length to an appropriately positioned bud, which should be outward-facing.

When to prune is a contentious question among rosarians; some favour autumn, others spring. My view is that these groups should be shortened back in October, leaving bushes 0·4 to 0·6 m ($1\frac{1}{2}$ to 2 ft) in height. This not only gives the plants a tidy appearance, but is also of practical importance in reducing wind rock. The main pruning then begins when the bushes show signs of breaking into growth, *i.e.* as the buds begin to swell, usually sometime in March.

To achieve the best results, you must give your roses nutrients; I recommend a proprietary Rose fertiliser that contains all the main plant foods, plus essential minor elements. Roses are gross feeders, and will benefit from two applications of fertiliser, one at pruning time and another sometime in June. Every bush should receive 50 to 80 g (2 to 3 oz) at each application, but when using proprietary fertilisers be guided by the manufacturer's recommendation. Mulches of well-rotted farmyard manure are also beneficial and these should be applied carefully and generously around the bushes immediately after pruning.

Unfortunately, some Roses are susceptible to diseases such as mildew and black spot, and most are vulnerable to the ubiquitous greenfly. Speedy control of these diseases will prevent serious epidemics. (For details see Chapter 7).

Choice of cultivar is always difficult: there are so many to choose from that ultimately one has to be guided by personal colour preferences. If at all possible, see cultivars either growing in the 'flesh', or at least as cut blooms at shows. Colour illustrations in catalogues can often be misleading, as scale is variable and colour reproduction is not always accurate. I find it useful to browse around nurseries or garden centres which stock container-grown Roses during summer, to assess the true visual qualities of the newer cultivars. The following table contains a collection of proven popular cultivars that are currently available:

Large-flowered (Hybrid Tea)

'*Alec's Red*' – cherry red, fragrant.
'*Blue Moon*' – silvery lilac, fragrant.
'*Duke of Windsor*' – orange-vermilion, fragrant.
'*Ena Harkness*' – crimson-scarlet, fragrant.
'*Ernest H. Morse*' – crimson-red, fragrant.
'*Fragrant Cloud*' – orange-red, fragrant.
'*Grandpa Dickson*' – medium yellow.
'*King's Ransom*' – rich yellow, fragrant.
'*Mischief*' – coral salmon, fragrant.
'*National Trust*' – red.
'*Pascali*' – white.
'*Peace*' – yellow suffused pink.
'*Spek's Yellow*' – golden-yellow.
'*Superstar*' – light vermilion, fragrant.
'*Wendy Cussons*' – cerise pink, fragrant.
'*Whisky Mac*' – bronze yellow and apricot, fragrant.

Cluster-flowered (Floribunda)

'Allgold' – golden-yellow.
'Anne Cocker' – bright vermilion.
'Arthur Bell' – deep yellow fragrant.
'City of Belfast' – scarlet.
'City of Leeds' – rich salmon.
'Elizabeth of Glamis' – light salmon, fragrant.
'Evelyn Fison' – bright red.
'Iceberg' – pure white.
'Lili Marlene' – scarlet-red.
'Masquerade' – a paintbox of yellow, red and pink.
'Orangeade' – orange-vermilion.
'Paddy McGredy' – carmine.
'Queen Elizabeth' – clear pink, well-shaped flowers.

Spartium junceum – Spanish Broom
Another good, value-for-money shrub that will flower from June through to September. It bears a resemblance to the Common Broom, but is much more vigorous with thick, rush-like green stems that grow to over 2·5 m (8 ft). These carry large, pea-like flowers that are rich yellow in colour. Dry, freely-drained soils and full sun are its main requirements. An excellent shrub for coastal gardens.

Spiraea x billardii 'Triumphans'
A suckering deciduous shrub with stems 1 to 1·2 m (3 to 4 ft) high, that bear erect terminal flower spikes during July and August; these are composed of dense clusters of small purplish-pink flowers. Old flowered stems should be cut hard back to the ground in February to stimulate the growth of vigorous new suckers. It grows best in a sunny position, but unfortunately does poorly on chalk.

Spiraea x bumalda 'Anthony Waterer'
An attractive little plant for the front of borders or rock gardens; it makes a compact tidy bush 0·4 to 0·6 m (1½ to 2 ft) high. In August, each shoot terminates in plate-like clusters of bright carmine, crimson flowers. It appears to grow almost anywhere

provided the soil is freely drained, and is worth trying in appropriate positions where other plants have failed.

Tamarix pentandra – 'Tamarisk'
For a light, feathery texture there is no finer plant than this. It is also one of the outstanding woody plants for exposed coastal gardens. In July and August, every branch becomes a foaming mass of light pink, formed from myriads of small flowers crowding its stems. Unpruned plants grow up to 2·5 m (8 ft) high, but to avoid legginess, prune flowered shoots hard back in March before new growth begins. Be careful not to confuse this plant with *T. tetrandra*, which is of almost identical appearance but flowers in May.

Trees

Catalpa bignonioides – Indian Bean Tree
A deciduous tree for gardens in the south and midlands, but rarely successful in the north as its succulent shoots never fully ripen before the onset of cold weather. It makes a medium-sized tree 9 to 12 m (30 to 40 ft) high, with a definite spreading crown that can extend to over 12 m (40 ft). Few trees have such large, handsome heart-shaped leaves, and these are quite spectacular in the golden-leaved cultivar *C. b. 'Aurea'*. In favourable localities it flowers during July and August. The flowers are borne in erect, open trusses, with each tubular floret sporting attractive yellow and purple throat markings. Later, trees become festooned with the characteristic bean-like fruits from which the tree derives its common name.

Koelreuteria paniculata – Golden Rain Tree
This must not be confused with Laburnum, which has the same common name. This tree is rarely found in northern gardens, where it tends to take the form of a large shrub, but in the south some trees have been known to grow to over 12 m (40 ft). It has rather fine, much-divided compound leaves that are an attraction in themselves, especially in autumn, when they turn yellow and orange before falling. During July and August, in favourable

localities, each shoot is crowned with open, branched clusters of golden-yellow flowers which are followed by bladder-like seed pods. Their main requirement is for a sheltered, sunny position and well-drained soil.

September to November

After the spectacular displays of spring and summer, flowering in woody plants becomes less prodigious; but this is compensated for by the fiery colours of foliage and fruits, which are dealt with in Chapters 10 and 11. The following are a few subjects which continue flowering, in some cases into the depths of winter.

Shrubs

Calluna – Heather
See Chapter 15.

Ceratostigma willmottianum
An attractive small shrub 0·3 to 0·6 m (1 to 2 ft) in height, with bright gentian-blue flowers produced intermittently from the end of July into late autumn. The flowers are very similar in shape to the florets of herbaceous *Phlox*. By coincidence, this plant is also best treated like a herbaceous perennial, by trimming it off close to the ground each spring before new growth begins. It is essentially a sun-loving plant that does well in most freely-drained soils, including chalk.

Erica cinerea and *E. vagans*
See Chapter 15.

Hebe – 'Autumn Glory'
Whilst 'Autumn Glory' is an apt name for this decorative low-growing shrub, do not be surprised to see it begin flowering in July; rest assured, however, that it will continue blooming into late autumn. Normally, it grows to about 0·6 m (2 ft) and displays dark blue to purple flower spikes, set against attractive evergreen

leaves. Unlike several Hebes, this one is hardy in the north. It is a sun-loving plant, which likes a well-drained soil.

Hydrangea aspera (*Syn. H. villosa*)
This deciduous shrub looks very striking during September and October, with its flattened flower-heads terminating each stem. Its flowers are in the style of the Lacecap Hydrangeas and are a very distinctive pinkish-purple colour. Unlike other Hydrangeas, this species is successful on chalk; but whatever your soil, good drainage is essential. It is an excellent plant for semi-shaded woodland gardens and generally benefits from sheltered positions. Mature plants can be 2·5 to 3 m (8 to 10 ft) in height.

Perovskia atriplicifolia – 'Blue Spire'
Erect, feathery sprays of dark, lavender-blue flowers emerge from this plant in late August, continuing into October. These are delightfully set against aromatic deeply-divided greyish-green leaves. It makes an open plant about 1 m (3 ft) in height, and is best pruned close to the ground each spring. Its preference is for warm, sunny positions and good drainage.

Romneya coulteri – Californian Tree Poppy
A sub-shrub with impressive, large, poppy-like flowers, papery-white in colour, that open from August to October. It is essentially a sun-loving plant and is not suitable for cold districts. It spreads, although not vigorously, by means of underground stems, eventually growing 1 to 1·2 m (3 to 4 ft) in height.

Mahonia x media – 'Charity'
An evergreen shrub with several erect stems which bear large pinnate leaves. During November and December, the shoot tips support several sprays of bright, lemon-yellow flower spikes, each 25 to 35 cm (10 to 14 in) long. Like several winter-flowering shrubs, these have a delicate fragrance. Mahonias grow in most soils, including chalk, and are often seen in semi-shaded woodland gardens. Apart from its winter flowers, this plant is worth growing for its majestic architectural form. Two very promising seedlings from this hybrid, '*Faith*' and '*Hope*', will no doubt soon establish themselves in gardens.

Trees

There are no trees for general planting that bear significant quantities of flowers in these months, apart from the Autumn Cherry, *Prunus subhirtella* '*Autumnalis*', which I included in the first section.

10

Decorative Foliage

Foliage for textural effect; yellow or golden foliage; grey or silver foliage; red or purple foliage; variegated foliage; autumn coloured foliage.

Leaves perform the vital function of manufacturing food materials; but in this chapter we shall be concerned mainly with the decorative value of foliage. In my view, the foliage of a plant is of greater significance than the flowers, since it is present throughout the growing season – and all year round, in the case of evergreens. With their differing shapes and sizes, leaves create a variety of textures in a mixed planting scheme; they also come in a multitude of colours which in many instances change through the seasons. In this Chapter, I have directed my choice to broad-leaved plants; conifers are covered separately in Chapter 12. For convenience, I have arranged them in groups.

Foliage for textural effect

Shrubs

Acer palmatum – 'Dissectum'
This decorative Japanese Maple makes a low, rounded bush usually 0·6 to 1 m (2 to 3 ft) high, and, in rare cases, 1·2 m (4 ft). Its drooping branchlets are covered in delicate, finely cut, fern-like

leaves, which look superb in autumn when they turn gold and orange. It is a very slow-growing plant, suited to rock gardens, and it needs a sunny, sheltered position. Though costly, it is always much admired when mature. There are also purple- and golden-leaved cultivars with the same decorative foliage, namely *A. p.* '*Dissectum-Atropurpureum*', and *A. p.* '*Dissectum-Aureum*'.

Aralia elata – 'Japanese Angelica Tree'
In the north, these are suckering shrubs with vigorous, erect stems 3 to 4·5 m (10 to 15 ft) high; but in the south-west, plants have grown to 10 m (30 ft). They have massive compound leaves often over 1 m (3 ft) long, which are much divided and look most handsome; even more impressive is the variegated cultivar *A. e.* '*Variegata*'. In August and September, feathery plumes of creamy white flowers decorate the tops of all main shoots.

Bamboos
This is a large group of plants, embracing several genera, but for the sake of brevity they are all grouped together here. Most form dense, suckering tufts of 'canes' that are decorated with evergreen, grass-like leaves. They generally grow best in moist, but not waterlogged, soils and will succeed in shade. Planting is best carried out in September or April. Bamboos belong to the grass family, and herbicides such as Dalapon or Aminotriazole, used to control grass weeds, must not be used near bamboo stools.

Arundinaria anceps – A rampant bamboo suitable for forming a screen, which grows in dense tufts 2·7 to 3 m (9 to 10 ft) in height. Be careful not to plant it where its invasive, suckering habit can become a nuisance.

A. japonica – This is perhaps the commonest bamboo in gardens, forming dense thickets of green canes and bearing glossy, dark green leaves. It is a very hardy and adaptable plant, growing 2·7 to 3·5 m (9 to 12 ft) in height.

A. murieliae – This is a highly ornamental bamboo, growing to 2·5 to 2·7 m (8 to 9 ft) in dense clumps, with narrow leaves that give the plant a rather fine texture.

A. nitida – Very similar to the above, but with slightly narrower leaves; forms a very elegant clump.

Phyllostachys aurea
These are less invasive than *Arundinaria*. This species forms dense clumps of yellowish canes 2·1 to 2·7 m (7 to 9 ft) in height, with tufts of grass-like leaves at each node.

P. viridi-glaucescens – A vigorous species growing 3·5 to 4·5 m (12 to 15 ft) and even higher in favoured localities. Its leaves have a whitish bloom, mainly on the undersides.

Fatsia japonica
An impressive evergreen shrub that grows into a large, rounded bush 2·5 to 3 m (8 to 10 ft) across. It carries large, palm-shaped, but lobed leaves which are often 30 to 37 cm (12 to 15 in) long. These are thick and leathery in texture, but with a glossy-green surface. Despite its subtropical character, this is quite a hardy plant, but it does prefer a sheltered, semi-shaded position. In October, it also bears creamy white, globular flower-heads, but these are no match for the luxuriant leaves.

Mahonia lomariifolia
Several Mahonias have excellent foliage and fall naturally into this section, but I have chosen this particular one for its most impressive leaves. These are pinnate; in other words, they have a central leaf stalk with opposite pairs of leaflets arranged along it. In this case, the total length of each leaf varies from 37 to 50 cm (15 to 20 in). They are stiff and evergreen and arise from erect stems which grow 2·5 to 3·5 m (8 to 12 ft) high. These are crowned with bright yellow, fragrant flower spikes that are borne in a cluster during the winter months. A handsome plant, but not completely hardy in cold northerly districts.

Yucca
Few plants give better foliage effect than the two hardy members of this genus, *Y. filamentosa* and *Y. gloriosa*. The first develops tufts of strong, spiky leaves from which splendid stems filled with creamy white flowers emerge during July and August. These can

be 1 m (3 ft) in height, but the plant itself rarely exceeds 0·6 m (2 ft), as new basal tufts of leaves are continually replacing the older rosettes. By comparison, *Y. gloriosa* has even stiffer sharply-pointed, almost menacing leaves. These are about 0·6 m (2 ft) in length, and radiate symmetrically from a central trunk which is very occasionally branched, but rarely more than 1·2 m (4 ft) in height. Its effect is dramatic, and perfect when strong textural contrasts are needed. *Y. gloriosa* flowers infrequently compared to *Y. filamentosa*, which flowers annually even as a very young plant. Both need a sheltered, warm, sunny position and a well-drained soil.

Trees

Ailanthus altissima – Tree of Heaven

A deciduous tree normally 15 to 18 m (50 to 60 ft) in height, with large pinnate leaves. It is fast-growing, especially in the south of England, and few trees grow better in polluted town atmospheres. Female trees are preferable for gardens, as male flowers have an unpleasant smell. For foliage effect in borders, they need to be coppiced in February by pruning all the stems back to within a few inches of the ground. Apply fertiliser after pruning, and as growth begins, thin out the new shoots to leave five or six on each stool. By summer, stems 2 to 2·5 m (6 to 8 ft) tall will be supporting magnificent leaves, often over 1 m (3 ft) long.

Alnus glutinosa '*Imperialis*'

This is the deeply cut-leaved variant of our native common Alder. Much less vigorous, it makes a very decorative tree for small gardens, and rarely exceeds 6 m (20 ft) in height. Viewed from a distance, the tree has a distinctive soft, feathery texture. Like common Alder, it grows best in moist soils and does well in waterside positions.

Fagus sylvatica '*Asplenifolia*' – Fern Leaved Beech (*Syn. F. s.* '*Heterophylla*')

Beech is one of my favourite native trees for general landscape planting. It has a majestic crown, clothed each spring with fresh, bright green leaves that turn russet-brown in autumn; even in winter, the lofty silvery trunks stand defiantly in a carpet of rustling leaves. Beech has produced many variants, but for gardens the fern-leaved Beech is a popular choice. This cultivar attains almost the same majestic stature as normal Beech, eventually reaching a height up to 21 m (76 ft), and should therefore be planted only in spacious gardens. It has distinctive linear leaves that are deeply cut or lobed and, as its name indicates, from a short distance these strongly resemble fern leaves. Like the common Beech, it thrives on chalk soils, but grows well in most fertile soils with good drainage.

Juglans regia – Common Walnut
This is a tree with handsome foliage and attractive grey bark. Walnuts grow well in most soils, but they can be difficult to establish in colder areas, where the unripened shoot tips are nipped by frost. Their handsome leaves are pinnate, with five to seven leaflets, and are often over 30 cm (12 in) long; sadly, these never colour in autumn like their American allies, the Hickories (Carya). Generally, they have a spreading crown and can grow to 18 m (60 ft). If you want a tree that will bear nuts, choose one of the named cultivars selected for this purpose.

Liriodendron tulipifera – Tulip Tree
A highly decorative tree with a unique four-lobed leaf design. Its handsome foliage is attractive from the time it emerges in spring through to the autumn, when the leaves turn bright butter yellow before falling. Its common name is derived from the green to creamy yellow tulip-shaped flowers that appear in July. Tulip trees grow into stately specimens and a number of trees in large gardens are well over the 30 m (100 ft) mark. If space is limited, opt for *L. t.* '*Fastigiatum*', which makes a narrow, columnar tree, or *L. t.* '*Aureomarginatum*', which has a decorative golden leaf variation.

Rhus typhina – Stag's Horn Sumach
This is the perfect tree for small courtyards, and can also be planted in borders. It develops a multi-branched, dome-shaped

crown 4·5 to 6 m (15 to 20 ft) in height. Its brown furry stems bear attractive pinnate leaves 30 to 45 cm (12 to 18 in) long. In autumn, these turn scarlet and orange. Shoots of female plants terminate in crimson flower plumes which persist on the plants after leaf fall. For a spectacular effect, choose the cut-leaved cultivar *R. t. 'Dissecta'* (often listed as '*Laciniata*'). This has each leaflet cut into shreds and, like the type, it colours well in autumn. These are both easy to cultivate, but give better autumn display in sheltered positions. Their one disadvantage is their undesirable suckering habit.

Yellow or golden foliage

Shrubs

Acer japonicum 'Aureum'
For a superb, dazzling, yellow-leaved shrub there is no finer plant, and it retains its brightness throughout the growing season. Each leaf is 5 to 10 cm (2 to 4 in) across, with seven to eleven pointed lobes that fan out around the edge. These give the plant a charming fine texture and a vivid colour. '*Aureum*' prefers a sheltered, sunny position and good loamy soil. I have seen it used to good effect in rock gardens and beside still water. The only disadvantage is that its growth is very slow and patience is needed before you see it in all its mature glory.

Ligustrum ovalifolium 'Aureum' – Golden Privet
This is perhaps more frequently seen as a clipped garden hedge. However, it is also an excellent golden-leaved evergreen shrub. It forms a dense rounded bush 2·5 to 3 m (8 to 10 ft) in height, which can be contained by clipping, or, in less formal situations, by pruning. Close examination shows that the leaf is variegated, although from a short distance away the plant appears to be a bright yellow bush. This cultivar is less vigorous than the normal green form, and can easily be cultivated in any reasonable garden soil.

Lonicera nitida – 'Baggesen's Gold'
Another popular evergreen hedging plant, and one that has sported this bright yellow-leaved cultivar. It forms a bush 1 to 1·2 m (3 to 4 ft) in height, and is covered in sprays of wiry shoots supporting the 1 cm ($\frac{1}{2}$ in) long oval leaves. The plant as a whole is quite dazzling when caught in bright winter sunshine. Like privet, it is an easily-grown plant, but may not prove hardy in severe winters.

Philadelphus coronarius 'Aureus' – Golden Mock Orange
I have already mentioned the flowering virtues of this plant in Chapter 9. This cultivar has bright yellow leaves in spring, which turn pale green as the season advances.

Sambucus racemosa 'Plumosa Aurea'
Few plants are more reliable than this on difficult sites; Elderberries are generally good pioneer plants, as witness the natural colonies formed by the native English golden-leaved Elderberry, *S. nigra 'Aurea'*, on railway embankments. For garden planting, this species, with its rich yellow, handsomely-cut, pinnate leaves, is superior. It is a vigorous grower, and if you prune it hard back each spring before growth begins, you will find shoots 1·2 to 2 m (4 to 6 ft) high, rocketing from the stool. This treatment produces a marvellous foliage effect, provided you sustain the plants with annual applications of fertiliser. Unpruned plants bear creamy white elderflowers in April, and these are followed by bright scarlet berries that contrast well against the yellow leaves.

Trees

Acer cappadocicum 'Aureum'
This is a choice garden tree of moderate vigour that I think resembles a smaller version of Norway Maple. Each spring sees the emergence of bright yellow maple leaves, each 5 to 7·5 cm (2 to 3 in) across. These become slightly greener by mid-summer but turn butter-yellow in autumn before falling. Trees are usually 9 to 12 m (30 to 40 ft) high, and in rare cases exceed 15 m (50 ft); their main requirement is a sheltered position on any good loam soil.

Acer negundo 'Auratum' – Golden Box Elder

An unusual Maple with uncharacteristic pinnate leaves which resemble those of Elderberry – hence its common name. This cultivar is a first-rate golden-leaved tree; when caught in bright sunshine and set against a blue sky, its brightness is almost dazzling. Unlike many golden plants, it does not lose its rich colour during summer. Normally, it makes a 6 to 9 m (20 to 30 ft) tree with a rounded crown. Like *A. negundo* it grows well on chalk and any other freely-drained soil.

Acer pseudoplatanus 'Worleii' – Golden Sycamore

This is now regarded as the best golden-leaved Sycamore, and has superseded the 'Corstorphine Plane', *A. p. 'Corstorphinense'*. Sycamore is one of the toughest trees, growing well in exposed places and tolerating most soils; the same is true for most of its cultivars. The leaves of *'Worleii'* are identical in shape and size to Sycamore, but are golden-yellow in colour and with a distinct red leaf stalk. It seems to be a vigorous grower, and I suspect that like the 'Corstorphine Plane', this cultivar will grow 18 to 21 m (60 to 70 ft) in height – in other words, a tree for spacious gardens.

Gleditsia triacanthos 'Sunburst' – Golden-Leaved Honey Locust

This much-neglected tree is at last becoming recognised as suitable for gardens, thanks to the popularity of its golden-leaved cultivar. It has small pinnate leaves 10 to 15 cm (4 to 6 in) long, giving it a fine, almost fern-like texture; these remain dazzling yellow throughout the growing season. For poor, dry soils this is an excellent choice. The normal green-leaved species makes a tree 15 to 18 m (50 to 60 ft) in height, and it seems feasible to suggest that this cultivar should attain 12 to 15 m (40 to 50 ft). Normal trees are armed with spines, but fortunately this is not the case in the cultivar *'Sunburst'*.

Robinia pseudoacacia 'Frisia' – Yellow-Leaved False Acacia

This is similar to the previous plant in having a preference for dry, freely-drained soil. It also has pinnate leaves that are bright yellow, but in this case they are 15 to 20 cm (6 to 8 in) long, and with larger leaflets. If possible, transplant only small trees; they do not re-establish easily after planting. This is an excellent tree for town gardens, but be wary of planting it in exposed corners where its brittle branches are liable to be broken. If grown in shade, it turns a sickly green colour – so do it justice, and plant it where it gets full sun.

Grey or silver foliage

Shrubs

Hippophae rhamnoides – Sea Buckthorn
A pioneer shrub of coastal sand dunes, this makes a first-class screen or windbreak in exposed seaside gardens. It is a vigorous grower, forming a dense thicket of spiny branches up to 4·5 m (15 ft) in height. If necessary, its growth can be restrained by pruning, and it even responds to being clipped into a hedge. Its leaves are long and slender, almost willow-like, and silver-grey. Plants are either male or female, and where both sexes are planted together (usually one male to eight females), the female plants bear heavy crops of bright orange berries that persist well into the winter. It grows well in most soils and is remarkably well adapted to both wet and dry sites.

Ruta graveolens – Rue
Originally, this plant was grown as a medicinal herb. It is a small evergreen shrub 0·6 to 1 m (2 to 3 ft) in height, with deeply divided silvery, blue-green leaves; in the cultivar '*Jackman's Blue*', the blue colour is even more intense. During late summer, clusters of small mustard-yellow flowers contrast with the splendid foliage. It is easily cultivated in freely-drained soil, and colours best in sunny positions. Ideally, it should be planted in groups at the front of a mixed border.

Salix lanata – Woolly Willow
Another low-growing shrub, usually 0·6 to 1 m (2 to 3 ft) in height,

that grows wild alongside Scottish mountain streams. Its bright grey leaves have a soft woolly covering, no doubt to give protection from their harsh natural micro-climate. As the leaves unfurl in spring, erect greenish-yellow catkins appear on the stems. It has a dense habit, and makes an attractive ground cover when closely grouped. It is also the perfect plant to set into crevices alongside rock garden streams. It needs only moist ground and an open position to flourish.

Santolina chamaecyparissus – Cotton Lavender

This is one of the easiest grey-leaved shrubs to cultivate. It forms hemispherical tussocks of minute, feathery silver foliage, 0·4 to 0·6 m (1½ to 2 ft) in height. These plants are not suited to wet soils and much prefer sunny positions. To prevent them from becoming leggy, rejuvenate them with hard cutting back after each year's growth. They root easily from summer cuttings, and replacing worn-out plants presents no problems. When planted in groups, they form an excellent foil for scarlet-flowered plants like *Geum 'Mrs Bradshaw'* or summer-flowering *Begonias*. In formal gardens Santolina is used for edging, and is clipped like dwarf Box. In addition to its distinctive colour and texture, its foliage is aromatic. Unpruned plants also bear yellow flowers, which stick out like yellow-headed knitting needles from a silver pin cushion.

Senecio greyii

An evergreen shrub 1 m (3 ft) in height with white-felted, oval leaves; this covering wears off the upper leaf surface, but the shrub retains a greyish appearance. In June, it bears clusters of bright yellow, daisy-like flowers that closely resemble those of common Ragwort. This is another sun-loving plant and one that grows well in seaside gardens. As well as decorating the garden, its stems make a splendid foil for indoor flower arrangements.

Trees

Populus alba – White Poplar

A vigorous deciduous tree, growing over 18 m (60 ft) in height, and with a spreading, heavily-branched crown which makes it unsuitable for planting close to buildings. Its leaves are lobed, like those of Maple, and vary from 5 to 10 cm (2 to 4 in) in width. Their white woolly covering give the tree its distinct silvery appearance, and this covering also protects the leaves and is one of the reasons why it can tolerate salt-laden winds when growing in exposed coastal gardens. It has also proved to be a good pioneer tree on poor soils. Unfortunately, it is a suckering tree and the suckers can be a nuisance on lawns. When coppiced, *i.e.* pruned hard to the ground in spring, the trees are most attractive and blend well with purple-leaved shrubs. The cultivar *P. a.* '*Pyramidalis*' (*Syn. P. a.* '*Bolleana*') is a narrow-crowned form, not unlike Lombardy Poplar in shape, but with silvery foliage.

Pyrus salicifolia – 'Willow-Leaved Pear'

An excellent deciduous garden tree, growing 6 to 7·5 m (20 to 25 ft) high and developing a pendulous crown. It is often used in foliage borders for the splendid effect of its silver-grey, willow-shaped leaves, which blend well with purple-leaved plants. It looks equally fine as an open-grown lawn specimen, with its arching branches cascading to the ground. Young trees need careful training, and it is best to cane up a leading shoot to form a trunk – otherwise, the plant will become an entanglement of sprawling branches. Periodic crown-thinning is also needed to keep it neat and tidy. During April, it bears white pear blossom, but this is scarcely noticeable against the silvery new leaves.

Salix alba – White Willow

A native deciduous tree, common along riverbanks and water meadows, where it develops a large, billowing crown 18 to 24 m (60 to 80 ft) high. It is a fast-growing tree, suitable for building up a quick screen or for providing shelter, especially in seaside gardens. Obviously it loves moisture and flourishes in waterside sites or damp areas. Avoid planting it near buildings, as it often sheds its brittle branches during gales. Its roots can also make a nuisance of themselves by entering small fissures in drains and causing blockages. From a distance, the tree has a greenish-grey colour, and for gardens a more attractive cultivar is *S. a.* '*Sericea*', commonly known as 'Silver Willow'. This has bright silvery leaves and is less vigorous than the type.

Sorbus aria – Whitebeam

This is a familiar native tree in woodlands on the chalk soils of southern England, and has conspicuous grey-felted leaves in spring. This colouring is more persistent in the cultivar *S. a.* '*Lutescens*'. Whitebeam and its various cultivars are very hardy and are well suited to gardens. They tolerate a wide range of soils and conditions, growing well in exposed, coastal or urban sites. Few trees are more easily managed, its tidy oval crown growing ultimately to a height of 9 to 12 m (30 to 40 ft), which is the ideal size for suburban gardens. In May, it bears clusters of white, hawthorn-like flowers which produce large orange fruits in September. These never last for long, as birds waste no time in stripping the fruits once they become succulent.

Tilia petiolaris – Pendant Silver Lime

Few trees have the grace and elegance of this easily-grown Lime, which forms a broad columnar crown growing to over 24 m (80 ft) when mature. Its large, rounded leaves, which are borne on long stalks, are dark green on the upper surface but white-felted underneath. A gentle breeze will expose these silvery undersides and give the tree an overall light green colour. Unlike some Limes, this species is not troubled by the honeydew secretions of aphids and the subsequent sooty moulds; the foliage is always clean. In autumn, its leaves turn an attractive bright yellow. In winter its branch tracery reveals the domed crown formed by the erect upper branches. These become pendant as they mature, whilst the lower branches grow downwards at an angle of about 45°. Normally, these trees are grafted, which makes them a little more costly; but the extra expense is negligible in the long term. Note that the nectar of this tree is toxic to bees and so should not be planted near hives.

The Silver Lime *T. tomentosa* has similar white-felted leaves, but with a more rugged texture. It, too, forms a large crown, but in my view it lacks the elegance of *T. petiolaris*.

Red or purple foliage

Shrubs

Acer palmatum 'Atropurpureum'
This attractive cultivar of the smooth-leaved Japanese Maple hovers on the borders between a large shrub and a small tree, as it matures to a height of 4·5 to 6 m (15 to 20 ft). It is readily distinguished from the type by its reddish-purple summer foliage, which turns bright red and scarlet in autumn. It thrives in sheltered positions: on exposed sites its foliage is soon disfigured and shredded.

Berberis thunbergii 'Atropurpurea'
A popular deciduous Barberry that forms a dense, prickly thicket. Once established, it is easy to grow and undemanding, and tolerates most freely-drained soils and open positions. This cultivar has reddish-purple leaves which intensify in autumn. It grows 1·2 to 1·5 m (4 to 5 ft) in height, but there is also a lower-growing cultivar, *B. t. 'Atropurpurea Nana'*, that rarely exceeds 60 cm (2 ft) and makes a dense, compact bush. In the cultivar *B. t. 'Rose Glow'*, leaves are attractively variegated, with pink and white flecks set against the reddish-purple base colour. *Berberis x ottawensis 'Purpurea'* is the most vigorous purple-leaved Barberry, and will grow up to 2 m (6 ft), with large, dark purple leaves.

Corylus maxima 'Purpurea' – Purple-Leaved Filbert
This deciduous shrub closely resembles the native English Hazel in appearance, except that this cultivar has distinct rich purple leaves and similarly-coloured catkins. It is a moderately vigorous shrub, capable of growing to 4·5 m (15 ft), but it responds very well to coppice treatment, if you require something smaller. Growth is satisfactory on most soils, including chalk.

Cotinus coggygria – 'Royal Purple' – Purple Leaved Smoke Bush
A delightful plant and my favourite purple-leaved shrub, clothed with neat, small round leaves. Its colour is first-class throughout

the growing season, which it concludes with glowing red tints. It grows quickly and soon makes a rounded bush 2·5 to 3 m (8 to 10 ft) across. The cultivar *C. c. 'Notcutt's Variety'* (*Syn. 'Rubrifolius'*) is a less intense purple colour.

Photinia x fraseri Robusta
I am sure this little-known evergreen shrub will eventually become a popular choice in gardens. It has glossy, leathery leaves which are a cheerful bronze-red when they emerge in spring, and remain so for several weeks, until the leaves have fully expanded. With its hardy new growth, this is a useful alternative to Pieris (see below), especially on chalky soils and in areas affected by late frosts. It is a vigorous grower and will eventually reach 3 to 4·5 m (10 to 15 ft) in height.

Pieris formosa – 'Wakehurst'
Its brilliant red young leaves make this the best *Pieris*. These leaves are superb during May, and outshine the creamy white flower clusters that so resemble bunches of small Lily of the Valley. *Pieris* is a vigorous evergreen growing to 4·5 m (15 ft) in height, and belongs to the *Rhododendron* family. Like Rhododendrons, it needs peaty acid soils with moisture at its roots, but with good drainage. It also prefers sheltered sites and, although semi-shaded positions are not essential, the protection of an open tree canopy minimises the effect of late frosts, which can affect the tender new shoots.

Prunus x cistena
A recent hybrid, derived partly from the popular purple-leaved tree *Prunus cerasifera 'Pissardii'*. This plant, however, is a bushy shrub, ultimately growing to 2 m (6 ft) in height. It has excellent dark purple leaves 3 to 6 cm (1½ to 2½ in) in length, and as these unfurl in April the unpruned plants bear small white flowers. For foliage effect, it may be coppiced; it also responds to clipping and will make a good hedge.

Trees

Acer platanoides – Norway Maple
Several Norway Maple cultivars have superb purple foliage. *A. p.*

'*Schwedleri*' has reddish-purple young leaves that become a duller greenish-purple in summer, and I find this less intense colouration most attractive in tree-planting schemes and far less oppressive than the following dark-leaved forms. *A. p.* '*Crimson King*' is a seedling of '*Schwedleri*', bearing darker crimson-purple leaves throughout the summer. *A. p.* '*Goldsworth Purple*' and *A. p.* '*Faasen's Black*' bear leaves which are dark purple, almost black in colour. This latter cultivar has red leaves in autumn. All are large, easily grown trees. (See further notes under this tree in the section on autumn colour.)

Fagus sylvatica '*Purpurea*' – Purple or Copper Beech
This is undoubtedly one of the finest purple-leaved trees, and attains the stately proportions of 21 to 24 m (70 to 80 ft) in height and often over 18 m (60 ft) across; these trees obviously need spacious gardens to mature majestically. This cultivar has reddish young leaves that darken in mid-summer. A good named cultivar of Purple Beech is *F. s.* '*Riversii*', which is noted for its dark purple leaves. Even more striking is the cut-leaved Purple Beech *F. s.* '*Rohanii*'.

Prunus cerasifera '*Pissardii*'
A popular purple-leaved tree for small gardens, which makes a densely-branched round head that grows 7·5 to 9 m (25 to 30 ft) in height. Although most noted for its rich purple foliage, it is also covered in attractive small white flowers in late March and early April. It is easy to grow and suited to most freely-drained soils.

Variegated foliage

Shrubs

Aucuba japonica '*Variegata*'
Few evergreen shrubs are more tolerant of shade than this one. I have successfully grown it beneath the dense canopy of a young woodland, where little else survived the competition for light and

nutrients. The variegation, however, is always much more colourful on plants grown in the open. The handsome leaves are similar to those of Laurel, being glossy and 10 to 17 cm (4 to 7 in) long, but are pointed at the ends. In this cultivar they are speckled with yellowish-white blotches. The best variegated cultivar is *A. j.* '*Crotonifolia*', whose creamy white blotches are more pronounced, and give brighter colouration overall. Aucubas are excellent plants for providing shelter and privacy and form dense evergreen thickets 2 to 2·5 m (6 to 8 ft) in height. They can also be easily restrained by pruning, where necessary. They are noted for their tolerance to smoky, town conditions.

Elaeagnus pungens '*Maculata*'

This is one of the finest variegated evergreen shrubs. It grows with moderate vigour and eventually forms a rounded bush 2 to 2·5 m (6 to 8 ft) across. Its leaves have a tough, leathery texture, enabling them to withstand exposure, even to salt-laden winds. Each leaf has a broad central splash of bright golden-yellow, and in winter, when garden colours are generally subdued, this plant is most conspicuous when caught in the sunlight. It is also an invaluable foil for indoor cut-flower arrangements as it holds its foliage well in water. It does not seem to be too fastidious about soil, and although it is not generally recommended for chalk, I have seen good plants thriving in thin chalky soil on the Yorkshire Wolds.

Another attractive variegated *Elaeagnus* is the recently-introduced cultivar of *E. x ebbingei*, called '*Gilt Edge*', whose leaves are edged with a band of lemon-yellow. It makes a compact bushy plant 1·5 to 2 m (5 to 6 ft) across and, like the type, is a first-class coastal plant.

Euonymus japonicus '*Ovatus Aureus*'

This plant could also be included in the golden-leaved group, such is the richness of its golden variegation. It is a compact evergreen shrub 1·5 to 2 m (5 to 6 ft) in height. Its highly polished leaves are oval-shaped, 5 to 7·5 cm (2 to 3 in) long, and have an irregular marginal band of rich golden-yellow, which makes them an excellent foil for indoor floral arrangements on green and yellow themes. In the garden, the plants should be grown in full sun to bring out their colour to the full. Like the previous plant, they are excellent seaside shrubs, as salt and sand do not adhere to their glossy leaves. It is not always hardy, and in northern, inland districts plants have been known to die during severe winters. Easily contained by pruning, they also respond to clipping and will form an unusual, bright yellow hedge.

Griselinia littoralis 'Variegata'
An attractive evergreen, but only completely hardy in the south and west of Britain or in coastal areas where winter temperatures are less severe. In favourable localities plants have reached a height of 6 m (20 ft), but more usually it only grows to 2·5 to 3 m (8 to 10 ft). It has oval to roundish leaves that are a distinctive pale yellow-green in the true species, and attractively margined with creamy white in this variegated cultivar. This is another shrub noted for its tolerance to seaside conditions, where it is sometimes seen as a hedge. In colder districts, it can be grown in containers to decorate patios or terraces, and given protection during the winter in a cool glasshouse or conservatory.

Trees

Acer negundo 'Elegans'
This is the best variegated Box Elder, with a broad margin of creamy yellow around each leaflet. There is also a less fine cultivar *A. n. 'Variegatum'*, which has a white margin. Both make large bushes or small trees, eventually growing to a height of 7·5 m (25 ft). They have an occasional tendency to send out normal green branches; these should be pruned out, as they are usually over-vigorous and will detract from the appearance of the plant. Both cultivars grow well in containers and are often used by nurserymen for decorating flower show stands. Equally, they can be used for display in enclosed courtyards or on patios and terraces.

Acer platanoides 'Drummondii'
A very decorative and popular cultivar of Norway Maple, with

a white variegated leaf margin. It has all the virtues of the type, but is much less vigorous.

Acer pseudoplatanus 'Brilliantissimum'
This cultivar of common Sycamore is ideal for gardens; it grows slowly and forms a dense, compact crown usually only 6 to 9 m (20 to 30 ft) in height. In spring, its leaves unfurl in an exotic coral-pink variegation, which for a few weeks remain rather garish. Unfortunately, by mid-summer the tree assumes a rather dull, sickly appearance and for this reason I prefer the less well-known cultivar *A. p. 'Nizetti'*. This has a pink and creamy white variegation that is most striking in the young leaf stage, and remains attractive until late summer. It is also a little more robust in growth, and has a more open crown. *A. p. 'Prinz Handjery'* is similar, but has a purple bloom on the underside of the leaf. Two variegated Sycamores are *A. p. 'Leopoldii'* and *A. p. 'Simon Louis Frères'*. Both have a streaky, virus variegation of creamy white and yellow, interspersed with shades of green. All these cultivars are budded or grafted on to common Sycamore stocks and grow well on all fertile and freely-drained soils.

Ilex – Holly
These marvellous evergreen trees have produced some really first-class variegated forms. When established, they are excellent trees for giving privacy and seclusion, and provide shelter at the same time. Obligingly, they grow almost anywhere in lowland Britain and though noted for their tolerance of shade, the variegated cultivars are seen to better effect in open positions.

They can be grown in mixed borders, but they look better as lawn specimens where they can be beautifully furnished to the ground. Most of these cultivars develop into medium-sized, dome-shaped or sometimes conical trees, rarely more than 9 m (30 ft) in height. In small gardens, trees that grow too large can readily be contained by pruning and, if needs be, they all respond to clipping. Good variegated forms are as follows:

Ilex x altaclarensis cultivars

'Camelliifolia Variegata' – This has large glossy leaves not unlike

those of *Camellia* in shape but darker green and, in this cultivar, irregularly marbled and margined with pale green and gold.

'*Golden King*' – A superb variegated holly and a popular favourite. It grows fairly quickly and has leaves with a broad golden margin. Some confusion must have occurred in the naming of this cultivar, as it turned out to be a female tree.

'*Lawsoniana*' – An attractive Holly with leaf centres irregularly splashed with yellow and light green.

Ilex aquifolium cultivars

'*Aurea Medio-picta*' – A lovely variegation with leaves splashed with a centre of golden-yellow. Both male and female forms are available, and are usually listed in catalogues as '*Golden Milkboy*' and '*Golden Milkmaid*'.

'*Handsworth New Silver*' – An excellent white-margined Holly that often has good crops of berries if there are male pollinators nearby.

'*Madame Briot*' – Similar in leaf to the above, but with golden-yellow margins. It also bears good berries when pollinated.

Populus candicans '*Aurora*'
A curiously variegated tree, in which the young leaves at the shoot tips are irregularly blotched with creamy white and blushed pink. Like other poplars, it is a vigorous, fast-growing tree. Quite a garish effect is created when plants are either coppiced or 'pollarded'. Pollarding involves regular hard pruning, back to a point on an elevated trunk.

Autumn coloured foliage

Chlorophyll, the green pigment of leaves, dominates leaf colour during the spring and summer, but in many deciduous plants just prior to leaf fall in autumn, chlorophyll production ceases and other pigments which are normally obscured become visible. Xanthophyll (yellows), carotenes (orange), and anthocyanins (reds) are the chemicals responsible for autumn displays. Many plants have autumn tints, and the following selection includes those that are reliable for this effect in most years.

Shrubs

Acer japonicum 'Vitifolium' – Vine Leaved Japanese Maple

This comes first in my selection because I regard it as the finest garden plant for autumn colour. Its leaves are 10 to 15 cm (4 to 6 in) across, comprising seven to eleven pointed lobes which fan out around its margin, and look rather like vine leaves. During October, green begins to merge into shades of purple, which in turn become orange and scarlet; eventually the whole plant is a blazing mass of differing shades of red, and when bathed in sunshine it creates a breathtaking spectacle.

Unfortunately, this splendid plant is rarely seen in gardens, and for good reason: propagation by grafting is difficult, and most nurseries have waiting lists for the plants. Although their scarcity makes them expensive, they are so magnificent visually that the expense is well worthwhile. Good, well-drained soils and a sheltered position are essential, and given these, large bushes or small trees 4·5 m (15 ft) across and about 6 m (20 ft) tall will slowly develop.

For a smaller and more readily-obtainable plant, *A. j. 'Aconitifolium'* is very attractive. It has delicate leaves with deeply cut and frilled lobes, which, as its name suggests, resemble the leaves of the herbaceous perennial, Monkshood (*Aconitum*). This normally grows into a rounded bush 2 to 2·5 m (6 to 8 ft) in height, and can be relied upon to turn crimson and ruby-red every autumn.

Acer palmatum – Smooth-Leaved Japanese Maple

These are excellent garden plants throughout the year, but are especially beautiful in autumn, when their delicate, palm-shaped leaves turn a variety of shades of yellow, orange, crimson and scarlet, depending on the cultivar and, to some extent, the season. Both open and semi-shaded sites suit this Maple, but sheltered positions are needed to prevent injury to their delicate leaves, which are easily scorched and shredded when exposed to cold winds. They also have a preference for good fertile soils that are moist but freely-drained. In gardens, the true species can grow into a large open bush or small tree up to 6 m (20 ft) in height.

There are several notable cultivars, including the following:

A. p. 'Atropurpureum' – See section on purple foliage.

A. p. 'Dissectum' – See section on texture.

A. p. var. heptalobum 'Osakazuki' – This is a superb shrubby Maple. Its leaves are about 12·5 cm (5 in) across, larger than other palmatum types, and normally with seven lobes. It colours a brilliant scarlet in autumn.

A. p. 'Sen-kaki' – This plant is sometimes known as the Coral Bark Maple, and if you can only accommodate one Maple, then this is the one. In winter its bright, coral-red stems make a conspicuous feature, especially if seen against a dark background in winter sunlight. In spring, delicate yellowish-green leaves burst from the buds; the summer foliage is slightly darker and, incidentally, is excellent as cut foliage for indoor decoration; by autumn, its leaves turn a fine pale orange before falling, to reveal once more the colourful stems. It grows fairly vigorously with upright branches, and eventually makes a bush about 3·5 m (12 ft) in height.

Cotinus coggygria – Smoke Bush

An easily-grown deciduous shrub, making a rounded bush 2·5 to 3 m (8 to 10 ft) in height at maturity. Its branches are decorated with small rounded leaves about 3 cm ($1\frac{1}{2}$ in) across; these are bright green during summer, and turn yellow in autumn. The common name refers to the interesting effect of its flower-heads: individually, the flowers are insignificant, but the plumes formed from the small-branched flower stalks open flesh-pink in June and July, turning ashen-grey as they mature. These give the curious effect of puffs of smoke hanging over the entire bush. This effect is less noticeable on plants growing in rich soil, which tend to produce vegetative growth at the expense of flowers. The cultivar *C. c. 'Flame'* turns orange-red in autumn. See also the cultivars *C. c. 'Royal Purple'* and *'Notcutt's Variety'* under the section on purple foliage.

Euonymus alatus
A deciduous, slow-growing shrub with a dense spreading habit, eventually growing 1·5 to 2 m (5 to 6 ft). It is rather an insignificant shrub until its moment of glory in October, when its leaves turn a distinctive rich crimson. Cultivation presents no problems, and this is a plant that is particularly suited to chalky soils.

Fothergilla major (*Syn. F. monticola*)
A close relative of *Hamamelis*, with smaller but similar-shaped leaves. It is another fairly slow-growing plant forming a rounded bush that eventually grows to around 1·5 m (5 ft) in height. Each spring, just before the leaves unfurl erect, creamy white flower clusters 2·5 to 5 cm (1 to 2 in) long are borne on the shoot tips. Its best show, however, is reserved for the autumn, when the leaves turn yellow, orange and red. Unfortunately, it only grows well in peaty, acid soils, and to get a good autumn display, choose a sunny but sheltered position.

Trees

Acer platanoides – Norway Maple
An eventual height of 18 to 21 m (60 to 70 ft) and a fairly spreading crown make this a tree which can only be realistically included in larger gardens. It has the typical 'Maple' leaves 15 to 20 cm (6 to 8 in) across, which are smooth and light green until autumn, when they turn bright butter-yellow before falling. In some localities, these autumn leaves have a blush of red or orange. In spring, just before bud break, greenish-yellow flowers are borne in plentiful clusters; no doubt, many people mistake these for the emerging leaves. Cultivation rarely presents problems, as these are extremely hardy trees and grow well in most soils.

Acer rubrum – Red Maple

It surprises me that this splendid North American tree is so rarely planted in British gardens; few trees have such marvellous autumn colours. Its small Maple leaves are 5 to 7 cm (2 to 3 in) across, and can be various shades from bright yellow to rich scarlet, and almost to blood-red in autumn. It seems to be a hardy tree in the north, if sheltered from cold north-easterly winds, which can disfigure its foliage. Moist but freely-drained soils suit it best. Its normal growth habit is a broad column, sometimes conical when young and eventually 12 to 15 m (40 to 50 ft) in height, growing occasionally to 21 m (70 ft). For small gardens, the cultivar *A. r.* '*Scanlon*' has a very narrow, upright habit, whilst *A. r.* '*Schlesingeri*' has excellent red autumn colours.

Cercidiphyllum japonicum – Katsura

A beautiful Japanese deciduous tree with distinct round, heart-shaped leaves about 5 cm (2 in) across and similar to those of the Judas tree (*Cercis*). It can easily be distinguished from this tree, however, by its leaves, which are borne in opposite pairs in *Cercidiphyllum*, and arranged alternately in *Cercis*. The overall effect of these decorative leaves is to give the tree a fine, rather delicate-looking texture. Autumn leaf colour is often variable, as in October it sometimes changes from pale green into bright yellow. At other times the leaves develop a pink blush and turn shades of salmon. In either case the result is always impressive.

Unfortunately, the young shoots are easily damaged by spring frost, and consequently, plants grown in the north tend to remain bushy and rarely develop into the stature of the 15 m (50 ft) high specimens seen in the gardens of the south and west. All the best trees I have seen are to be found in sheltered localities.

Liquidambar styraciflua – Sweet Gum

At first glance this deciduous tree can be mistaken for a Maple, as it has typical five-lobed, Maple-shaped leaves. Closer examination will reveal that these are arranged alternately on the stems and not in opposite pairs, as is the case in all Maples. In the milder districts, *Liquidambar* makes a conical tree that can grow 15 m (50 ft) in height, but it never attains anything like this in the north. Its autumn colours are quite remarkable, turning to an assortment of greens, purple, crimson and orange at first, but finishing with a blaze of orange and scarlet. It prefers moist, but not waterlogged soil.

Malus tschonoski – Pillar Apple
A vigorous Crab Apple capable of growing 12 to 15 m (40 to 50 ft) in height. It has distinctive erect branches which, when young, give it a definite diamond outline that eventually develops into a narrow, cone-shaped crown. Unlike other Crab Apples, this is not noted for its flowers or fruits, as it produces very few of them. It is, however, the best Crab for rich autumn colour.

Quercus rubra (*Syn. Q. borealis var. Maxima*) – Red Oak
This is a splendid North American Oak that forms an open-branched tree 18 to 24 m (60 to 80 ft) in height. In spring, its young leaves unfurl bright yellow and for a few weeks retain this eye-catching colour. When fully expanded, its leaves are slightly larger than our native Oaks and have pointed lobes. In autumn, the foliage turns russet brown and, in good forms, red and orange. This tree has become very popular in recent years for general landscape planting; once established, it grows well in most lime-free soils in lowland areas.

Two similar North American Oaks are Scarlet Oak, *Q. coccinea*, which also has bright yellow leaves in spring, followed by scarlet-red foliage in autumn. *Q. palustris* (Pin Oak) is a smaller tree and a good choice for moist, but not waterlogged, soil; it is not, however, well suited to chalk. Its smaller leaves turn an attractive scarlet in autumn.

Sorbus 'Embley' (*Syn. S. discolor*)
Many Sorbus colour well in autumn, but none more reliably than this. Its leaves are pinnate, like those of Mountain Ash, and never fail to become engulfed every autumn in fiery crimson and scarlet tints. It is ideal for smaller gardens, as it rarely exceeds 9 m (30 ft) in height and has fairly erect main branches. Like Mountain Ash, it grows well in most soils and situations.

Sorbus 'Joseph Rock' – This cultivar is even more impressive, and in my view the best Sorbus for gardens. It grows no more than 9 m (30 ft) in height, and has a neat, fairly upright crown. In spring, it bears flattened clusters of white flowers, but these are trivial compared to the spectacle it presents in autumn, when its leaves transform from green to fiery shades of purple, crimson, scarlet and red. Clusters of pearly-yellow fruits nestle amongst this splendid foliage and will persist long after the first frosts.

11

Ornamental Fruits, Bark and Shapes

A selection of trees and shrubs which have conspicuous fruits, followed by a selection of those with decorative bark and stems; trees with erect or narrow crowns and weeping or pendulous crowns.

Conspicuous fruits

A few plants with decorative fruits are worth including in a mixed collection, as the fruits will last beyond the normal flowering season and often into the very depths of winter. For the conservation-minded, berried plants also provide food and enrich the bird life of a garden.

Shrubs

Berberis x carminea
This hybrid group includes those cultivars that give exceptional fruit displays. They have orange and red translucent berries, that hang like pendant beads beneath the arching branches. These displays coincide with the colourful autumn leaves. These Barberries are sun-loving plants and grow in any well-drained soil. Being dense, thorny plants they are ideal for an impenetrable thicket. The reliable cultivars are *B. 'Barbarossa'*, *B. 'Buccaneer'*, and *B. 'Pirate King'*, which are vigorous and grow 1·2 to 2 m (4 to 6 ft) in height, whilst *B. 'Bountiful'* remains more compact and only grows to 1 m (3 ft).

Cotoneaster

These are one of the outstanding genera of berried plants, and are mostly easily-grown shrubs, suitable for all areas except those affected by Fire Blight.

C. conspicuus 'Decorus' – An evergreen shrub growing 1 to 1·2 m (3 to 4 ft) in height, with a spreading habit forming an irregular tangle of branches. In May, these are wreathed in small white flowers, followed by dark red, globular berries that remain crowded on the stems from October until the following spring.

C. franchetii – This has a more upright habit and grows to about 2 m (6 ft). Generally, it is a more elegant, semi-evergreen Cotoneaster. In October, its attractive orange-red berries are set off against its small pointed, oval-shaped leaves.

C. horizontalis – An easily-grown and very popular shrub with a unique herringbone branching pattern. Normally, it sprawls along the ground and rarely grows more than 0·6 to 1 m (2 to 3 ft) in height, but if given a wall to lean against, its branches scramble up to 2·5 m (8 ft). It bears a profusion of white flowers in May, which turn into myriads of bright red, globular fruits. In October, its leaves also turn orange-red, but the tremendous display of fruits persists until well after Christmas.

C. microphyllus var. cochleatus – A good choice for rock gardens or for overhanging low retaining walls, as its arching branches hug the ground. It produces a decorative cascade of dark red berries, set against small, glossy evergreen leaves.

Pernettya mucronata

An evergreen shrub growing 0·6 to 1 m (2 to 3 ft) in height, that spreads by suckers to form low, dense thickets. It belongs to the *Erica* family and, like its relatives, needs a peaty, acid soil to grow in. May brings out its small white flowers, but these are less showy than the fat, succulent berries that adorn the plant from late summer through to spring. These vary in colour from pure, glistening white to pink, and some are almost crimson. Most Pernettyas are either male or female plants, and best results occur when they are planted in groups with at least one known male to every five or six females. I have been particularly pleased with the clone *Bell's Seedling*.

Pyracantha
See Chapter 13

Rosa moyesii
Many Roses display fruits commonly known as 'hips' or 'heps', but none surpass the elegance of *R. moyesii*. It begins its summer display with attractive, five-petalled single blooms, each 5 to 6 cm (2 to 2½ in) across and blood-red in colour. By late summer, these produce showy scarlet-red, elongated, flask-shaped hips, that are individually 2·5 to 3 cm (1 to 1½ in) long. The plant itself has a fairly erect branching habit and grows 2 to 2·5 m (6 to 8 ft) high.

Skimmia japonica
An evergreen shrub, making dense, rounded bushes about 1 m (3 ft) in height. It is grown mainly for its bright red, Holly-like berries, which it bears, like the white flowers, in terminal clusters. To achieve good pollination, plant them in groups: plants are either male or female, and berries can only be produced in mixed groups. Plants will tolerate moderate but not dense shade, and have a preference for acid soils.

Stranvaesia davidiana
This is not unlike an evergreen Cotoneaster at first glance, as it bears clusters of white flowers in June, followed in autumn by dense bunches of red berries which persist until early winter. This species is a vigorous grower, soon reaching 2·5 to 3 m (8 to 10 ft) in height. Like Cotoneaster, it can be affected by Fire Blight.

Viburnum betulifolium
Several Viburnums have showy fruits in late summer and autumn, but good forms of this rank among the best berried plants. It is a tall, open-branched shrub, growing 2·5 to 3 m (8 to 10 ft) in height. Clusters of white flowers appear in June, but more noticeable are the heavy bunches of small, bright red fruits closely resembling red Elderberries.

Trees

Cotoneaster frigidus
Most Cotoneasters are shrubby, but this species can be trained into a small tree about 6 m (20 ft) in height. White flowers are seen in May, followed in autumn by prolific clusters of bright red fruits which are still plentiful at Christmas. Its hybrids also make good plants, notably *C. 'Cornubia'*. This is really a large evergreen shrub, which I have seen trained as a tree, but preferably should be allowed to retain its lower branches; eventually it grows 6 to 7·5 m (20 to 25 ft). It bears masses of bright scarlet-red fruits.

C. 'Hybridus Pendulus' is also a descendant of *C. frigidus*. This can be a perfect weeping tree for small gardens when grafted on to a standard stock, and forms a small dome 2 m (6 ft) in height. Its branches hang loosely and are heavily festooned with bunches of red berries.

Crataegus
See Chapter 9.

Ilex aquifolium – Common Holly
Our native Holly is an attractive and useful tree. Traditionally, a few berried sprigs of Holly are used for Christmas decoration, but it must be remembered that berries only develop on female trees and that at least one male tree is needed to pollinate their flowers. To determine the sex of your plants closely examine the flowers during May or June. Male flowers have a cluster of anthers in the centre, while females have a single style. Two particularly good berrying cultivars are *I. a. 'J. C. van Thol'* and *I. a. 'Pyramidalis'*; the cultivar *I. a. 'Bacciflava'* has unusual yellow fruits.

Malus 'Golden Hornet'
Having previously extolled the virtues of flowering Crab Apples, I have chosen two of several cultivars that are outstanding in fruit. This first is unquestionably the best yellow-fruited Crab, and each autumn its boughs hang heavily laden with small round apples,

each being about 1·5 cm (¾ in) across and golden-yellow. These remain on the tree into late autumn, but a few can be harvested and make delicious Crab Apple jelly. Its white flowers in spring are less decorative than many Crab Apples, but the fruits more than compensate. It is also an ideal size for smaller gardens, rarely exceeding 7·5 to 9 m (25 to 30 ft) in height.

Malus 'John Downie' – This cultivar also has white flowers, but in this case they are followed by heavy crops of orange-scarlet, conical Crab Apples in September. These give a splendid display and also make excellent preserves.

Sorbus aucuparia – Rowan or Mountain Ash

A deciduous native tree, popular in gardens on account of its easy cultivation and decorative features. It matures to a height of 9 or 12 m (30 or 40 ft), with a fairly open, upright crown. Leaves are pinnate and resemble a smaller version of Ash leaves. Each May its crown carries flattened clusters of white flowers that develop into heavy bunches of bright red berries by mid-August. Judging by the way greedy birds descend on the trees, these fruits must be a favourite delicacy – the plants are soon stripped. In Britain it is found at 915 m (3000 ft) above sea level, higher than any other native tree, and this partly explains its common name of Mountain Ash. Remarkably, it grows on both acid and alkali soils, but on chalk the Whitebeam *S. aria* is a better choice.

Interesting cultivars for gardens include *S. a. 'Asplenifolia'*, which has fern-like, cut leaves and very good autumn colour. *S. a. 'Fastigiata'* has a very narrow, erect crown which can be accommodated in the smallest of gardens. *S. a. 'Sheerwater Seedling'* is probably better, in that it has a slightly broader, oval-shaped crown and is generally more robust. Finally, *S. a. 'Xanthocarpa'* is a novel, yellow-fruited cultivar.

Sorbus cashmeriana

This is not one of the popular species, but I think it makes a splendid small garden or courtyard tree. It has decorative, small pinnate leaves and clusters of pale pink flowers in spring, followed by bunches of white, bead-like berries. Unlike the red fruited forms, these persist long after leaf fall, often until after Christmas.

Sorbus hupehensis
A tree almost identical in growth habit and leaf-shape to our native Mountain Ash, though this species originates from China. It is easily recognised by its almost glaucous (*i.e.* blue-green) leaves. During June, it bears profuse bunches of creamy white flowers, followed in September by hanging bunches of pure white berries that form a delightful contrast with its crimson stalks. Like other white-fruited Sorbus, these persist well into winter and their abundance makes an impressive sight. In addition to this visual extravaganza, the leaves turn red in autumn. There can be few other trees that offer such year-round interest.

Sorbus hybrida 'Gibbsii'
An excellent fruiting Sorbus carrying bunches of large orange-red berries. It has a compact, rounded crown and is a reliable tree in most situations.

Sorbus intermedia – Swedish Whitebeam
This is an attractive and very useful deciduous tree, that develops a dense, dome-topped crown and matures to 9 to 12 m (30 to 40 ft) in height. Its leaves are halfway between those of *S. aucuparia* and *S. aria*, in that they are deeply lobed but not completely pinnate. In May, it bears plentiful white flower-clusters, followed by good crops of orange-red fruits in October. In some seasons, the leaves turn orange and scarlet at the same time. Swedish Whitebeam is a tough, wind-hardy tree, that tolerates exposure and the more extreme conditions of coastal gardens. It is also remarkably tolerant of both acid and alkali soils.

Sorbus pohuashanensis
A Chinese species, always heavily laden in early autumn with large bunches of bright red berries which in October are vividly contrasted against the bright orange foliage. In leaf and habit it closely resembles Mountain Ash.

Sorbus sargentiana
Not commonly seen in gardens, but an excellent species with

large pinnate leaves and much larger bunches of red berries than other Sorbus. It is also noted for its superb autumn colour. Normally, it grows into a round-headed tree 6 to 9 m (20 to 30 ft) in height.

Decorative bark and stems

The configuration of tree trunks and stems is a worthy but often neglected aspect of plant composition. Multiple-stemmed plants sometimes bring a delightful 'sculptured' quality to a focal point in a garden, and plants with coloured or textured bark are decorative in their own right. The following selection has been made with these features in mind.

Shrubs

Acer palmatum 'Sen-Kaki'
See Chapter 10.

Cornus alba 'Sibirica'
On a sunny winter's day, this shrubby Dogwood looks splendid, its shiny red stems cheering the subdued colours of the dormant season. It is a moisture-loving plant that thrives if planted beside a pond. To produce stem effect in winter, it is best to coppice plants each spring just as the new growth commences; otherwise, it grows into a 2 m (6 ft) high rounded bush that only has brightly coloured young shoots. Newly imported plants from Holland always have vivid scarlet stems, which turn a disappointing dull red after a season's growth. I can only conclude that nutritional factors in the soil have influenced stem-colour – perhaps I have been too generous to my plants.

Cornus stolonifera 'Flaviramea' is a vigorous suckering Dogwood, that forms an interesting contrast with its yellowish green stems.

Corylus avellana 'Contorta' – Corkscrew Hazel
This remarkable shrub, sometimes quaintly referred to as 'Harry Lauder's Walking Stick', has curiously twisted and spiralled stems.

It is a contorted aberration of our native Hazel and naturally grows much slower – although I have seen plants 3·5 to 4·5 m (12 to 15 ft) in height. It looks especially attractive in spring, when bearing Hazel catkins or 'lambs' tails'. If possible, it should be planted where its silhouette can be seen, as its beauty is easily lost in the background of other plants. Cut stems are always much in demand for floral art work.

Rubus cockburnianus
This is a vivid contrast to red-stemmed Dogwood, with erect purplish stems which are densely covered in a pure white bloom in the dormant season, giving the plant a ghostly white appearance. The best effect is created when a few of the older stems are pruned back to the ground in spring, to stimulate basal re-growth.

If clumps become sparse, new plants can be readily propagated by bending the shoots and burying the tip 7·5 to 10 cm (3 to 4 in) into the ground (a technique known as tip layering). If this is done in June, it should be possible to lift and detach a new crown from the stem by September.

Trees

Acer davidii – Père David's Maple
An interesting tree originating from China and unquestionably one of the finest 'snake bark Maples'. This description refers to the attractive green-and-white striated pattern of the bark; a feature of several Maples grouped under this name. Apart from the bark, other visual delights of this tree are the pendant flower spikes in May and, in some forms, highly colourful orange and red autumn leaves. It grows 9 to 12 m (30 to 40 ft) in height on good soil. Two notable cultivars named after great plant collectors are *A. d.* '*George Forrest*' and *A. d.* '*Ernest Wilson*'; the latter forms a more spreading tree.

Acer griseum – Paper Bark Maple
Attractive bark is but one feature of this lovely tree. Mature trees in good growing conditions reach 9 to 12 m (30 to 40 ft) in height, though more usually 6 to 9 m (20 to 30 ft), and develop round,

spreading crowns. Leaves are unusual in being composed of three leaflets that turn shades of orange and scarlet in autumn. It is the stems, however, that really attract attention, with their papery-thin, peeling bark that sloughs away to reveal the rich cinnamon-coloured trunk. The young branches are often garlanded with hanging, flakey strips of old bark, which fall away as they mature.

If you have room, a small copse or grove of these lovely stems makes a desirable feature. Single specimens should always be planted beside a path or at the front of borders, where their stems can be seen. This tree will thrive in most soils, including chalk, but though quite hardy, it prefers a sheltered site.

Arbutus x andrachnoides

With its richly coloured, cinnamon-red flaking bark, this is a rare and beautiful tree for the plant connoisseur, and worth encouraging in its multi-stemmed form. This plant belongs to the *Erica* family, but uncharacteristically will grow on soils containing lime. Older plants have slowly grown to 9 m (30 ft) in height, with wide-spreading crowns.

Betula pendula – Silver Birch

This is truly one of our finest garden trees, and few others share its elegance and its year-round beauty. In winter, we can admire the delicate tracery of its graceful pendulous branchlets and the charm of its silvery white bark. In spring, there are fresh green leaves and catkins; and in the autumn the leaves are golden. If you have room for a grove of Silver Birch, this creates the ideal setting for a peat bed or underplanted Rhododendrons, or can be used simply as a grass area for naturalising daffodils.

Birch is also an excellent pioneer tree for difficult sites and grows well in almost any soil. Normally, it attains 12 to 18 m (40 to 60 ft) in height, but its light branches prevent it from being an oppressive tree. As a young tree, it grows rapidly and soon makes an impact on new gardens that are devoid of vegetation.

One of my favourites is the Swedish Birch *B. p. 'Dalecarlica'*. This is a cut-leaved cultivar which has a finer texture than *B. pendula* and makes an elegant columnar tree over 15 m (50 ft) in height. Two contrasting cultivars are *B. p. 'Youngii'* and *B. p.*

'*Fastigiata*'. The former is a strongly pendulous tree that makes a low sprawling bush unless its leader is caned up during its initial development. *B. p.* '*Fastigiata*' is a very narrow, erect form that is rather weak and ineffective.

Apart from our native Birch and its cultivars, there are many other species with exceptionally good visual qualities, from which I have selected the following:

B. albo-sinensis var. septentrionalis – A beautiful Chinese Birch that is distinguished in good forms by its creamy orange bark.

B. ermanii – A fairly vigorous Asian species with attractive creamy and pinkish-white bark and bright yellow autumn leaves.

B. jacqemontii – A Himalayan birch of outstanding merit; some forms have bark that is superior in colour and texture to any other species. Its white bark extends into the very young branches, and in winter give the tree a ghostly skeleton.

B. nigra – River Birch. An American species that, as its common name suggests, grows well beside ponds or streams where its roots can get to water. No other birch has bark quite like this one; it is blackish in colour and drapes from the trunk and branches in thin, papery flakes. The stems look almost as if they have been scratched by a mob of wild cats.

B. papyrifera – Paper Birch. Another North American birch. As a garden tree, it has attractive stems and branches, covered in papery-thin bark that peels away in strips to reveal silky-textured pure white new bark. It is also magnificent before leaf fall, when its leaves turn bright yellow.

Eucalyptus niphophila – Snow Gum

Being an Alpine species, this Australian tree is proving to be one of the hardiest Eucalypts for British gardens. It also happens to be one of the most beautiful, with silvery-green leaves that sparkle in sunlight. In addition, it has the most extraordinary stem markings: these result from the exfoliation of the bark, which comes off in irregular flakes to reveal new, silvery-white patches. These undergo a gradual transition from cream, grey and finally to green shades, but all may be present on a trunk at any one time. Eucalypts do not transplant well, and initially small container-grown plants should be purchased. This particular species grows quickly for the first few years but eventually settles down, rarely exceeding 6 m (20 ft) in height. Coppiced Eucalypts also make decorative foliage plants.

Platanus acerifolia – London Plane
A stately tree that grows to 24 to 30 m (80 to 100 ft) in height, and obviously can only be accommodated in spacious gardens. It is included in this section because of its unusual marbled stem, which is caused by old patches of bark flaking off and revealing a light creamy patch of new bark. Its striking leaves are like those of a large Maple, but are easily distinguished by their alternate arrangement; this tree also bears distinct globular fruits.

The magnificent specimens in London's parks and squares prove how tolerant it is of town conditions. Young trees grow rapidly, establish themselves quickly, and are capable of growing on for at least 200 years. Few other trees respond so well to pruning and even badly pruned and lopped trees will successfully regenerate their crowns. It is a hardy tree that grows well on most soils.

Prunus serrula
Unlike most Cherries, this is never a spectacular tree at flowering time, but it does have the most impressive bark which never fails to attract attention. This is mahogany-coloured and looks highly polished. The paper-thin bark peels in narrow strips around the trunk to reveal yet more highly polished young bark. It is not a difficult tree to cultivate and as it rarely exceeds 7·5 m (25 ft) in height, it is not out of place in small gardens.

Salix alba 'Chermesina' (*Syn. S. a. Britzensis*)
This cultivar of White Willow has bright orange to scarlet stems that are most colourful in winter sunlight. A splendid effect is achieved by planting a group beside a pond and coppicing a few plants in alternate years. Its counterpart, *S. a. 'Vitellina'*, has rich golden-yellow stems and looks well in association with '*Chermesina*'.

Salix matsudana 'Tortuosa' – Pekin Willow
A fast-growing Willow, which eventually forms a medium-sized tree up to 15 m (50 ft) in height. It has curious spiralled stems, arising from contorted, fairly erect branches, and looks particularly effective in winter, if planted where its silhouette can be seen.

Trees with distinct shape

Trees come in all shapes and sizes, but occasionally, where space is limited, there is a need for trees with narrow crowns. I am also sometimes asked to recommend pendulous or weeping trees. For the sake of brevity, I have confined my choice to these two categories, although there are many other shapes already included in other chapters.

Trees with erect or narrow crowns

Acer lobelii – Lobel's Maple
A tree that closely resembles Norway Maple in the character of its foliage, but with a distinct narrow crown formed of erect growing branches. This is a splendid tree for gardens; it grows with reasonable vigour when young and eventually reaches 18 m (60 ft) in height.

Carpinus betulus 'Fastigiata' (*Syn. C. b. 'Pyramidalis'*)
This is a form of our native Hornbeam with a narrow, erect-branched crown that broadens slightly as it matures. Young trees have a rather formal appearance, but are ideal for adding height where space is limited. Like the type, it has yellow leaves in autumn and grows naturally on chalk. Trees mature to a height of 12 to 15 m (40 to 50 ft).

Corylus colurna – Turkish Hazel
This much-neglected tree has a narrow, conical outline, with a structure of light branches not too unlike the Wheatley Elm, although the branches of Turkish Hazel are more horizontal and slightly pendulous. It has Hazel-like foliage but, unlike our native

plant, this grows into a tree 18 to 21 m (60 to 70 ft) in height.

Fagus sylvatica 'Dawyck' – Dawyck Beech
This splendid Beech is virtually identical to Lombardy Poplar in outline, and forms an erect column of branches. In all other respects, it is like the normal Beech, with identical silvery-grey bark and foliage that has russet autumn tints.

Populus nigra 'Italica' – Lombardy Poplar
This is perhaps the most commonly planted narrow-crowned tree, with its distinctive erect branches. The male trees tend to be narrower than the females, which develop a slender diamond outline. Visually, Lombardy Poplar looks best planted in groups, where its strong vertical lines can be used to contrast with the horizontal lines of, for example, buildings or a distant skyline. They never look right when planted in straight lines, or as a screen to hide objects from view.

This is a vigorous tree that establishes itself quickly; no doubt this is one of several reasons for its popularity. However, it can be too vigorous for positions near buildings. Its roots have been known to contribute to soil shrinkage, by extracting water from certain types of clay soil and so causing foundation damage. The same vigorous growth can be troublesome when the roots invade small fissures in drains and cause blockages. It is also worth remembering that these trees can grow to 27 m (90 ft), and so would be hopelessly out of scale in small gardens. Despite these drawbacks, Lombardy Poplar is a fine tree if planted in the right place.

Prunus 'Amanagowa'
See Chapter 9.

Pyrus calleryana 'Chanticleer'
This cultivar is a promising tree, fairly recently introduced to Britain from the United States of America. It makes a compact, narrow cone-shaped crown of formal appearance, which is densely packed with white pear blossom in spring. It is reported to do well on dry sites.

Trees with weeping or pendulous crowns

Fraxinus excelsior 'Pendula' – Weeping Ash
This is a common tree in churchyards and public parks, and one that is occasionally planted in gardens to create a shaded arbour. It has stiff, strongly pendant branches bearing typical Ash leaves in the growing season. Plants have to be grafted on to a standard common Ash stem, usually at a height of 2 to 2·5 m (6 to 8 ft). Mature trees have a dome-shaped crown of contorted branches. Like common Ash, it grows well on most soils and is especially happy on chalk and limestone. It has also proved remarkably tolerant of smoky, town atmospheres.

Prunus 'Cheal's Weeping'
See Chapter 9.

Salix caprea 'Pendula' – Kilmarnock Willow
The perfect weeping tree for a small garden, as it rarely grows more than 2·5 to 3 m (8 to 10 ft). It forms a neat, round-topped column of slender pendulous branches that cascade to the ground. In fact, this tree is an abnormal variant of Goat or Pussy Willow, but, being a female clone, it bears only the less showy female catkins.

Salix x chrysocoma – Weeping Willow
There is a good deal of confusion about the naming of this tree and you may find it referred to in catalogues as *S. babylonica*, *S. alba 'Vitellina Pendula'*, or *S. alba 'Tristis'*. It is now, however, regarded as a hybrid between *S. alba 'Vitellina'*, the golden-stemmed Willow, and *S. babylonica*, the original Weeping Willow. Perhaps the thing to do is simply to ask for a Weeping Willow.

This is a superb tree for waterside planting, where its broad crown and elegant hanging branchlets sweep gracefully down to the waterline. With its distinct tracery and bright, golden stems glinting in the sunlight, it is equally effective in winter. Unfortunately, this tree is all too often planted in the wrong place, for example, as a centrepiece for a small front garden, where its vigorous growth soon takes over and dominates the entire area until it is either removed or mutilated to reduce its spread. When deciding where to plant a Weeping Willow, it should always be remembered that they can quickly grow 15 to 18 m (50 to 60 ft) in height and have an equally large spread. They thrive in moist ground and often their vigorous roots can cause problems by invading small fissures in drains in their search for water; once inside pipes, they soon produce masses of absorbant root fibre which inevitably causes blockages. This tree is also unfortunately susceptible to Willow scab, which disfigures the leaves, and canker, which blights the young stems.

Ulmus glabra 'Camperdowni' – Camperdown Elm

There are two attractive weeping forms of our native Wych Elm.

The choicest form for gardens is Camperdown Elm, which forms a small dome of pendulous branchlets that are clothed to the ground in typical, but possibly slightly larger than usual Wych Elm leaves. It is normally grafted on to a 2 to 2·5 m (6 to 8 ft) stock of *U. glabra*. In winter outline, the straight trunk supports a dense head of contorted branches. In early spring, the weeping branchlets are covered in small flowers, quickly followed by winged fruits just as the new leaves appear. It makes an admirable lawn tree, growing 4·5 to 6 m (15 to 20 ft) in height, occasionally higher. It can be used to make a secluded arbour.

The weeping Wych Elm *U. glabra 'Pendula'* is a taller tree, with branches angled outwards at about 45° and their surface exposed when the trees are in leaf. Both grow well in most soils or situations, and especially in towns. Unfortunately, neither is immune to the ravages of Dutch Elm disease.

12

Garden Conifers

A selection of conifers for garden decoration, screening and shelter, including some dwarf variants.

There are three conifers native to Britain: Scot's Pine (*Pinus sylvestris*), Common Yew (*Taxus baccata*) and Common Juniper (*Juniper communis*). If all the introduced conifers and their cultivars are included there are now several hundreds to choose from.

Conifer literally means cone-bearing, but some conifers, such as Yew and Juniper, have fleshy fruits. Most conifers are evergreens and have needle or scale-like leaves, a feature which readily distinguishes them from broad-leaves. The tallest and most massive trees in the world, and the tallest trees in Britain, are conifers, but remarkably many have miniature counterparts that will not outgrow the proportions of a trough garden. Most are extremely hardy, originating from exposed mountain localities, and hence are adaptable to poor soils and harsh climatic conditions. In addition, conifers have tremendous appeal to gardeners because of their elegant forms and diverse colours. I have chosen the following as representative of the varied visual forms, and included a few others that are of practical use in providing screens and shelter in gardens.

Abies koreana – Korean silver fir

A broad conical tree, fairly slow-growing and rarely exceeding 9 m (30 ft). I doubt if this would be a distinguished garden tree, were it not for its interesting purple-blue cones, which sit upright on the branches like clusters of small barrels. Remarkably, these appear on plants only four or five years old, unlike other silver firs that rarely cone before the trees are fully developed.

Abies procera – Noble fir

This handsome conifer is essentially a forest tree, and is capable of growing over 30 m (100 ft) in height. It has beautiful blue-green foliage and graceful, downswept branches when open grown. Though not a tree for urban areas, it does, however, make a magnificent background or specimen tree in larger country gardens. Mature trees bear massive pale green cones.

Araucaria araucana – Monkey puzzle

Victorian gardeners were most enthusiastic about this unusual tree, and often planted it as a centrepiece for their front lawn flower bed. Unfortunately, it is a difficult tree to place, as its stiff, architectural outline and regular branching are not in harmony with the informality of many modern gardens. If, however, you have a formal garden, this tree can be used as a centrepiece, or perhaps as the focal point to punctuate a vista. Initially, monkey puzzles are slow-growing, and what appears to be one year's whorl of growth may actually have taken two, or possibly three years to grow. Eventually, however, they can grow to over 21 m (70 ft). They are best planted as young seedlings in well-prepared sites.

Calocedrus decurrens (*Syn. Libocedrus decurrens*) – Incense Cedar

Most specimens of this plant seen in English gardens are splendid narrow, columnar trees; but surprisingly, this is not the true habit of those found wild in Oregon and California, which have more open crowns. The beauty of this tree is the almost perfect column of rich, dark green foliage, with its fine texture. Its strong vertical lines look most effective when it is planted in groups. Incense Cedar has a good growth-rate and trees will put on 0·3 to 0·6 m (1 to 2 ft) in height each year; a few old specimens are now over 30 m (100 ft), but these are exceptional.

Cedrus atlantica – Atlas Cedar
Once established, this is a fairly quick-growing tree, whose stately proportions make it suitable only for spacious gardens. Cedars generally grow well on most soils, provided they have good drainage. Unlike several conifers, they also grow well in towns. The type has bright green needles, but the most commonly planted form is *Cedrus atlantica 'Glauca'*, often called Blue Cedar on account of its intense blue-green needles. These really are beautiful trees, but unfortunately they can grow to over 30 m (100 ft) tall, with a spread of over 18 m (60 ft) and are therefore not suitable for small gardens. Nevertheless, nothing can compare with the magnificence of a mature specimen with its low branches sweeping across a spacious lawn.

Cedrus deodara – Deodar
Undoubtedly, this is the most popular and elegant Cedar for gardens. Young trees have a conical outline with horizontal branches that have graceful drooping leaders. Young trees are fairly quick to establish, and you can expect 7·5 to 10·5 m (25 to 35 ft) of growth after 20 years. Eventually, however, they become large trees capable of dimensions up to 30 m (100 ft) by 18 m (60 ft) across.

Cedrus libani – Cedar of Lebanon
A tree often seen in the grounds of stately homes, where its distinctive flat-topped crown and horizontal branching make an impressive silhouette. In my experience it is a slow starter, but like those Cedars mentioned above, it eventually becomes a very large tree. Two interesting variants which can be accommodated in the smaller garden are *C. l. 'Sargentii'*, which has spreading, slightly pendulous branches. This plant rarely exceeds 3 m (10 ft), and has a spread of 3·5 to 4 m (12 to 15 ft). *C. l. 'Comte de Dijon'* is a perfect miniature form, suitable for the rock garden. This is a very rare plant, and grows exceedingly slowly.

Chamaecyparis lawsoniana – Lawson's Cypress
This is a most remarkable conifer: since its introduction in 1854, it has produced over 200 variants. Each one differs from the type

in either form, colour or texture, and there must surely be one to suit every garden-designer's need. It is also one of the most adaptable and accommodating conifers, being easy to cultivate and adaptable in its soil and situation requirements. It shows a preference for the wetter regions of the country and generally should be kept moist at the roots.

Unlike true Cypress of the genus *Cupressus*, Lawson's Cypress transplants well. It is a first-rate choice for a tall screen and if the situation demands, it can be clipped into a formal hedge. In such cases, keep the base open; otherwise, its lower branches become suppressed and the plant never refurbishes itself. Open-grown specimens develop into narrow conical trees, varying from 18 to 30 m (60 to 100 ft) in height. Multi-stemmed trees occur frequently and these usually develop a broader, conical shape. For gardens, the many cultivars have superior visual qualities, and I have selected the following to illustrate the diversity of this remarkable conifer.

C. l. '*Allumii*' – A form with blue-green foliage and a distinct spire-like habit.

C. l. '*Columnaris*' – One of the best blue-leaved forms, with a fairly narrow, conical shape.

C. l. '*Ellwoodii*' – On close examination, it will be seen that the foliage consists of small, soft, juvenile needles and not the scale-like leaves of a normal Lawson's. This is a compact, slow-growing plant, only reaching 1·5 to 2 m (5 to 6 ft) after ten years' growth, and thus ideal for small gardens. Its foliage is blue-grey in colour, although there is a more recent golden-leaved variant called *C. l.* '*Ellwood's Gold*'.

C. l. '*Erecta Viridis*' – A bright green, conical tree in which the foliage is in flattened sprays which are arranged vertically. This is a fairly quick-growing form which often unfortunately, has bare branches at the base which mar its beauty.

C. l. '*Fletcheri*' – This semi-juvenile form with blue-grey foliage is similar to *C. l.* '*Ellwoodii*', but generally its crown is broader and less dense.

C. l. 'Green Hedger' – Very aptly named, as its bright green leaves and dense habit make it the best Lawson's for hedging.

C. l. 'Intertexta' – An excellent Cypress with stiffer, more open sprays of foliage, giving a distinct elegance to mature trees.

C. l. 'Kilmacurragh' – This is a good substitute for Italian Cypress (*Cupressus sempervirens*) in British gardens. It has a stiff narrow, columnar habit and rich green foliage arranged in erect, flattened sprays.

C. l. 'Lutea' – Foliage of this tree is a distinctive pale yellow. It frequently bears an abundance of cones, and has the typical Lawson's habit.

C. l. 'Minima' – A dwarf globular bush, about 0·6 m (2 ft) across after ten years' growth, and ideal for rock gardens or tubs. There is also a golden-leaved variant called *C. l. 'Minima Aurea'*.

C. l. 'Pembury Blue' – This is regarded by many authorities as the best blue-leaved Lawson's on account of its intense, pale blue leaves. It has a slightly broader crown than *C. l. 'Columnaris'*.

C. l. 'Pottenii' – A cultivar notable for its bright green and slightly lax sprays of foliage, which give a delicate, feathery appearance to young plants.

C. l. 'Stewartii' – My favourite golden Lawson's, forming a broad column of rich golden-yellow foliage and making a superb tree up to 18 m (60 ft) in height.

C. l. 'Wisselii' – An unusual form with a fairly open habit and curious, spire-like sprays of foliage. It can grow to over 18 m (60 ft) in height.

Chamaecyparis nootkatensis – Nootka Cypress

I personally regard Nootka Cypress as visually superior to Lawson's Cypress. It forms a broad spire-shaped crown with graceful pendant branchlets that frequently bear small spiked cones. It seems happiest in the wetter western areas of Britain, and will grow reasonably well in most soils, with the exception of chalk. Mature specimens can attain a height of 27 m (90 ft), and because it is quick-growing, it should only be planted in large gardens. Less vigorous is the very elegant cultivar *C. n. 'Pendula'*, in which the branchlets drape from slightly drooping main branches.

Chamaecyparis obtusa – Hinoki Cypress

A Japanese tree of which there are two popular cultivars for use in gardens. *C. o. 'Crippsii'* is clothed in small sprays of bright yellow foliage that are almost dazzling in sunshine. It has a broad, conical crown that is fairly slow-growing but which eventually reaches 9 m (30 ft). *C. o. 'Nana Gracilis'* has small fan-shaped fronds of bright green foliage. This also forms a broad, conical bush, but is very slow-growing and rarely exceeds 3·5 m (12 ft). For this reason it is very popular in gardens, and is often seen planted on rockeries.

Chamaecyparis pisifera – Sawara Cypress

Another Japanese species very similar to Lawson's Cypress, which, like that tree, has produced many variants that are commonly seen in gardens. Sometimes it is still found in catalogues incorrectly named *Retinospora*.

C. p. 'Boulevard' – A broadly conical bush with distinctive blue-grey leaves. It seems to grow steadily but its ultimate height has not yet been reached. If it grows too large, it will respond to light pruning or even clipping.

C. p. 'Filifera Aurea' – A graceful dome-shaped plant with string-like drooping branchlets which in this cultivar are rich golden-yellow. Occasionally, odd shoots revert to the green form, and these should be pruned out as soon as possible. It grows slowly enough to be planted in rock gardens, but I have seen specimens cascading like golden fountains at a height of over 4·5 m (15 ft).

C. p. 'Nana' – This is a compact miniature form that looks like a mossy-green curling stone. Its dense, very compact habit and slow growth limit its use to rock or trough gardens.

C. p. 'Plumosa Aurea' – Soft, plumed foliage distinguish this species; in this cultivar, it is a pale yellow colour that looks best in spring. It makes a broad, conical bush developing into a tree with age.

Cupressus glabra 'Pyramidalis' – Smooth Arizona Cypress
An excellent, quick-growing Cypress with intense, blue-grey foliage that frequently bears heavy crops of large, globular cones. It has a formal conical shape and is capable of growing over 18 m (60 ft) in height. Tolerant to drought and dry soils.

Cupressus macrocarpa – Monterey Cypress
A very popular coastal tree in the south and west of Britain, and often seen as a seaside hedge. Young plants grow with exceptional vigour, sometimes too fast for their own good, as the top growth seems to outstrip root growth; resulting in wind-blown plants. It forms a columnar tree which broadens considerably as it matures, by which time it is frequently over 24 m (80 ft) in height.

Monterey Cypress is vulnerable to frost, and in severe winters even established specimens have been killed. Less extreme coastal temperatures account partly for its success in those areas. Unlike false Cypresses, true Cypress of the genus *Cupressus* transplant badly, and small, pot-grown plants are frequently used to ensure success. In recent years, golden-leaved cultivars such as *C. m. 'Goldcrest'*, *'Gold Spire'* and *'Donard Gold'* have become very popular for garden planting.

x Cupressocyparis leylandii – Leyland Cypress
This conifer has topped the sales charts of many nurseries for several years, and its popularity shows no signs of decline. The simple explanation for this is its rapid growth, which enables it

to furnish or enclose new gardens within a few years. Its vigour derives from its two parents, Nootka Cypress and Monterey Cypress; both are vigorous trees, but astonishingly, their offspring grow almost twice as fast and regularly add 1 to 1·2 m (3 to 4 ft) to top growth each year. The oldest known trees are now over 30 m (100 ft) high and still growing.

Young plants quickly fill out to make fine columnar trees of dark green, closely-textured foliage. I like to see them planted as specimens, or in informal groups where their strong vertical lines can contrast with other shapes. They respond exceedingly well to clipping and quickly make good formal hedges; alternatively, they can be grown on into taller screens and topped at the appropriate height. Both parents are reasonably suited to coastal sites, but Leyland Cypress develops a scorched appearance following exposure to salt-laden winds.

When planting, it is sensible and preferable to begin with young plants 0·4 to 0·6 m (1½ to 2 ft) in height. Apart from the additional expense, larger plants take longer to recover and are frequently unstable at the roots. Young plants in fact grow so rapidly that they soon overtake larger plants still struggling to recover from planting.

There is now a golden-leaved cultivar *x C. l. 'Castewellan Gold'*, but this is not quite so vigorous as the type.

Juniperus communis – Common Juniper

A native conifer forming a scrub plant of no special garden merit. However, several cultivars are highly ornamental:

J. c. 'Compressa' – A gem for rock gardens or miniature sink gardens, as it makes a very dense but perfectly formed column of bright green foliage. It rarely exceeds 1 m (3 ft) in height.

J. c. 'Hibernica' – Commonly known as Irish Juniper, this is almost a taller counterpart of the previous cultivar, and makes a dense columnar bush, rarely over 4·5 m (15 ft). It is always beautifully clothed to the ground in blue-green foliage.

J. c. 'Hornibrookii' – For complete contrast, this cultivar grows horizontally and rarely exceeds 0·4 m (1½ ft) in height. It can be regarded as a good ground-covering Juniper, carpeting an area about 3 m (10 ft) across in dense, finely-textured foliage. This form grows best in full sun. Junipers in this group are generally tough, reliable plants that grow well in most freely-drained soils and especially so on chalk and limestone.

Juniperus chinensis 'Pfitzeriana' (*Syn. J. x media*)
A popular, vigorous Juniper with a distinctive branching habit that contrasts well with vertical forms. On young plants, branches are inclined at slightly less than 45° with drooping tips. Eventually, they grow 2·5 to 3 m (8 to 10 ft) in height, with branches in a series of almost horizontal layers. There are two excellent golden variants, *J. c. 'Pfitzeriana Aurea'* and the more richly coloured *J. c. 'Old Gold'*. The cultivar *J. c. 'Hetzii'* is of similar habit, but with silvery-grey leaves.

Juniperus virginiana
Two good garden conifers are cultivars of this species: *J. v. 'Grey Owl'* is a spreading bush, eventually 1 to 1·2 m (3 to 4 ft) high and 2·5 m (8 ft) across, with decorative, silvery-grey foliage. In complete contrast is the very distinctive slender spire of *J. v. 'Skyrocket'*. This has blue-grey foliage and grows fairly quickly.

Larix – Larch
Basically, this is a forest tree grown for its timber, but it can be planted as a shelter to 'nurse' slower-growing trees. It is a very beautiful tree in its own right, providing you have adequate space for it to develop. Open-grown trees have graceful downswept branches that burst out in fresh, bright green needles each spring. These are superb again in autumn, when they turn butter-yellow before falling. Surprisingly, the Japanese Larch *L. kaempferi* fares better in gardens than European larch, *L. decidua*, as it has greater resistance to disease and tolerates town conditions better.

Metasequoia glyptostroboides – Dawn Redwood
Incredibly, this tree has survived from prehistoric times, and until 1941 was only known as a fossil. The discovery of living plants in the remote Shui-sha valley of Hupeh province in China was not immediately realised to be of botanical importance, but by

1944 specimens were collected and described, and by 1948, seed was being distributed around the world.

Now it is a popular garden conifer – and rightly so, for it is a highly ornamental and versatile tree. In many ways, it is not unlike the swamp Cypress. It is deciduous and has similar divided leaves, although here the leaves are slightly larger and the leaflets are in opposite pairs. There is a distinct elegance about its conical crown, and of the earliest trees introduced, most are around the 15 m (50 ft) mark after thirty years' growth. They are especially attractive in autumn, turning a glowing russet to orange. They seem to grow well on most soils, but growth is much improved where soil is kept moist.

Picea abies – Norway Spruce

Not my favourite garden conifer, as it is very rare to see good specimens. This is the type popularly used for Christmas trees, and no doubt many of the moribund specimens in gardens originate from this source. Generally, they grow poorly in towns, and are either thin in the crown or carry many dead branches.

Some of the slow-growing, dwarf forms, however, are excellent for rock gardens, notably *P. a 'Gregoryana'*, which forms a dense, bright green cushion and rarely exceeds 0·6 m (2 ft) in height and width. *P. a. 'Nidiformis'* has a more open habit, and develops into a small flat-topped plant with layers of short horizontal branches. It can grow up to 1 m (3 ft) high, but more usually tends to spread outwards. *P. a. 'Tabuliformis'* has very definite horizontal, plate-like branches with a flat top. It grows slowly: plants up to thirty years old attain only 1·5 m (5 ft) in height with a spread of 3 m (10 ft).

Picea breweriana – Brewer's Spruce

A supremely elegant tree with a conical habit and wide-angled branches, draped with long pendant branchlets that hang like green curtains. If possible, plant this in a position where its silhouette can be admired. Mature trees have been known to grow to 18 m (60 ft) and will give many years of pleasure in a medium-sized garden. Unfortunately, it rarely does well in town gardens.

Also, it has a strong dislike of chalk and prefers high rainfall areas.

Picea glauca var. albertiana 'Conica'
The natural form of this cultivar is a perfect, symmetrical cone, giving the tree a trimmed look. It is at its best in spring, just as the bright green needles flush into growth. It is quite slow-growing and is therefore suited to rock gardens. It is usually seen as a 0·6 to 1 m (2 to 3 ft) plant, but very old bushes have reached 3 m (10 ft).

Picea omorika – Serbian Spruce
I often think that this is the most underrated garden conifer. Few Spruces tolerate polluted atmospheres better than this species. Furthermore, it grows well in drier areas and tolerates a wide range of soils, including both acid and alkali. Visually, it has a distinctive narrow, spire-like crown, frequently over 18 m (60 ft), with short downswept branches that ascend slightly at the tips. Open-grown trees are always beautifully clothed down to the ground. It can be effectively used in groups or as a single lawn specimen.

Picea pungens 'Glauca' – Colorado or Blue Spruce
A popular Spruce for gardens, because of its intense blue-silver foliage, and one of the outstanding coloured-leaved trees. It has a broad, conical outline and a similar branching habit to Norway Spruce, and eventually can top 21 m (70 ft), although the majority of specimens range from 12 to 15 m (40 to 50 ft). This is another Spruce that does well in urban areas, and it will also thrive in the drier eastern counties. The best-coloured forms are 'named selections', and these are usually grafted; of these *P. p. 'Koster'* and *P. p. 'Moerheim'* are superb. For rock gardens, the spreading blue carpet of *P. p. 'Glauca Prostrata'* is unsurpassed.

Pinus – Pine
This is one of the largest genera of conifers, containing many useful and decorative garden plants. The following are a selection:

Pinus cembra – Arolla or Swiss Stone Pine
A very attractive Pine with dense, bushy foliage and a tidy, broad

columnar to conical shape. Growth is relatively slow – the tree usually increases about 22 cm (9 in) in height each year; but eventually it will grow to 15 m (50 ft), and is therefore suitable for medium-sized gardens. It looks best as an open-grown lawn tree, where it will remain clothed to the ground with foliage. The climate of north-western areas of Britain seem to suit it best.

Pinus mugo – Dwarf Mountain Pine
A spreading, open, bushy pine that only grows 2 to 2·5 m (6 to 8 ft) in height and width. It is not the most decorative Pine, but it will tolerate thin, poor soils and limestone areas. Perhaps more suitable in gardens is the slow-growing cultivar *P. m. 'Gnom'*, which is a compact dwarf form suited to rock gardens.

Pinus muricata – 'Bishop Pine'
This attractive bushy pine has proven to form a useful shelter against the salt-laden winds along the south and western seaboards. It grows between 15 and 24 m (50 and 80 ft), developing a broad crown as it matures.

Pinus nigra var. Nigra – Austrian Pine
A tough pine for exposed places, including coastal situations. This is a very hardy tree that will grow almost anywhere, even in poor or chalky soils. Its shoots are covered in dense tufts of stiff, dark green needles. Normally, it has a dense multi-branched crown that forms a pleasing, broad outline. This is quite unlike the closely related Corsican Pine *P. n. var. Maritima*, which is a quick-growing forest tree with a 'telegraph pole' trunk.

Pinus parviflora – Japanese White Pine
This is the outstanding species for small gardens, with a slow growth-rate and an ultimate size rarely exceeding 9 m (30 ft). This is the Pine found in Japanese gardens, and has characteristic flat branches, covered in short curly needles, a delightul blue-green in colour. For rock gardens, *P. p. 'Glauca'* is a splendid dwarf form with slightly more intense blue-green needles. This form often cones heavily as a young plant and is especially attractive when bearing its pinkish strobili (male flowers) in spring.

Pinus sylvestris – Scots Pine

A native conifer, but also an attractive garden tree. As a young plant it has a typical conical outline, with regular whorls of branches clothed in short, blue-green needles. Older trees become flat-topped, or develop irregular crowns. These have a distinct orange bark that glows when caught in the evening sunlight. They also look magnificent in silhouette, especially if planted in irregular groves. There are notable specimens over 30 m (100 ft) in height, but most trees are 18 to 24 m (60 to 80 ft). Scots Pine is the dominant native tree of the Scottish Highlands, where a few remnants of the great Caledonia forest persist; it is also found on sandy heathland in the south of England. Growth is poor in wet soils and on chalk, but it does not seem to mind the drier climate of eastern counties. In gardens, in addition to being planted as specimens, they can also serve for shelter screens or for copses. Mature trees, with their fairly lofty, open crowns, cast a dappled shade that is ideal for underplanted Rhododendrons.

P. s. 'Aurea' is an uncommon, slow-growing cultivar that turns golden-yellow as temperatures fall in winter, but tends to look a sickly green in summer. *P. s. 'Nana'* and *P. s. 'Beuvronensis'* are compact dwarf forms, both suitable for rock gardens.

Pinus wallichiana – 'Bhutan Pine'

A fast-growing species with long, soft green needles to clothe its spreading branches. It is only suitable for larger gardens, because it eventually grows to 24 to 30 m (80 to 100 ft) in height. The hybrid *P. x holfordiana* is similar, and when mature supports large pendant cones.

Sequoiadendron giganteum – Giant Redwood

This was a great favourite in the spacious grounds of Victorian houses, but is less suited to the modern suburban plot, as it frequently exceeds 30 m (100 ft) in height. 'Big Tree' is another appropriate common name for it – specimens in the famous Californian Redwood groves are the most massive trees on earth. It has a distinctive broad, spire shape, with downswept branches that clothe the tree to its base when open-grown; it also has a fascinating thick, fibrous bark. Growth is satisfactory in most soils and situations, but always bear in mind its eventual size.

Taxodium distichum – Swamp Cypress
An astonishing tree in the way that it has adapted to wet, swampy conditions; in the everglades of Florida it grows in several metres of water. Its survival in such conditions is dependent on its ability to produce pneumatophores, air-breathing roots that protrude above water and supply life-sustaining oxygen. Remarkably, it will also grow in quite dry soils. In many ways, this tree resembles the earlier-mentioned Dawn Redwood; it too is deciduous and has similar but smaller leaves, that turn russet and orange in autumn.

Taxus baccata – Common Yew
This is the third of the native conifers, and is an extremely useful and adaptable garden plant. It grows wild in woods on chalk, yet surprisingly, tolerates acid soils providing that they are freely-drained. Yew is perhaps used most often in gardens as a clipped formal hedge, for which purpose it is supreme. Remember, however, that its foliage is poisonous to stock and should not be planted adjacent to agricultural land that is likely to be grazed. I find Yew especially useful for underplanting in the dense shade of a young wood, to provide evergreen cover for shelter and screening.

Common Yew has dark, sombre green foliage, and whilst this is perfect as a background, there are more decorative Yews available for specimen planting. *T. b. 'Aurea'*, Golden Yew, is an excellent bright golden-yellow form, and less oppressive than the type when planted near buildings. *T. b. 'Dovastoniana'*, commonly known as 'West Felton Yew', has a very distinct spreading habit with long, horizontal branches arching out from the centre of the plant; these are draped with pendant branchlets. In complete contrast, *T. b. 'Fastigiata'*, the 'Irish Yew', has erect pinacle-like branches. Young plants develop as narrow columns, but mature trees have a rounded outline. 'Irish Yew' has a golden-leaved variant, *T. b. 'Fastigiata Aurea'*, which I think is preferable in gardens. *T. b. 'Repandens'* is one of several prostrate, or low-growing forms. This makes a spreading bush rarely more than 0·6 m (2 ft) in height, which can be used as a ground-cover plant in shady places.

Thuja occidentalis – American Arbor-vitae
A hardy, conical tree, similar in outline to Lawson's Cypress but with coarser, scaly foliage. This is another conifer with a proliferation of cultivars, of which the best for gardens is *T. o. 'Rheingold'*. This has a conical shape with rather loose, rich golden foliage which is quite superb during winter. It is a fairly slow-growing bush, and rarely exceeds 3 m (10 ft) in height. I have seen it used to good effect in rock gardens and heather beds, where its colour and shape provide an excellent contrast.

Thuja plicata – Western Red Cedar
A slightly misleading common name, in that it in no way resembles the true Cedars. Normally, this makes a conical tree that tapers broadly at its base when open-grown. Young stems are composed of thick, scaly leaves which give it a resemblance to a coarse-textured Cypress. This tree favours the wetter regions of the country, where plants over 24 m (80 ft) high are frequent. It is an adaptable tree, and tolerates both open and semi-shaded positions and most soils, including chalk. In gardens, its main use is as a quick-growing screen or hedge, and it will respond readily to clipping.

Tsuga mertensiana – Mountain Hemlock
A beautiful but sadly neglected garden conifer, with an irregular conical outline. It is a fairly slow-growing tree capable of growing over 18 m (60 ft) high in wetter areas, but more usually to 9 to 12 m (30 to 40 ft). Its beauty lies in the downswept branches, clothed in distinct blue-grey foliage which, on open-grown trees, is attractively furnished to the ground.

13

Climbers and Plants Suitable for Wall-training

Supporting, planting and training; a selection of plants for growing against walls.

In their struggle for survival, many plants have developed devices for climbing, twining or scrambling, and thrusting their canopies into sunlight. Gardeners and plant-breeders have selected and improved many of these, so that today we have a wide choice of suitable plants to furnish the walls of houses or outbuildings, and to embellish fences, trellises or pergolas. Climbing plants on buildings need regular maintenance to prevent them from becoming untidy and overgrowing windows or blocking gutters, but a wall well-furnished with plants is full of charm and character and is worth the effort.

Supports

Some plants support themselves by adventitious roots or adhesive sucker pads. These are quite capable of clinging to vertical surfaces without any additional help. Those plants with a lax, trailing or scrambling growth habit do, however, need a supporting framework on which to secure and train their shoots.

Horizontal wires

These are a most efficient method of providing support. The aim is to secure horizontal wires 22 to 30 cm (9 to 12 in) apart along the section of wall where you intend planting climbers. These wires are fastened to vine eyes (obtainable from ironmongers), which are screwed into previously drilled and plugged holes. Eyes are spaced along the wire at intervals of 2 to 2·5 m (6 to 8 ft). The wire is fastened to the end vine eye, threaded through intermediate eyes on the same plane and fastened off at the other end to a strainer eyebolt, which facilitates tensioning (see Figs 22 and 23). Use a strong gauge of galvanised wire. Green plastic-coated wire is the least obtrusive.

Vertical wires

This is an alternative method of support, suitable for plants with a twining habit. The wires are fixed in the same way, except spaced 22 to 30 cm (9 to 12 in) apart and running vertically.

Wall panels

Panels in wood, wire and plastic can be purchased from garden centres for fastening on to walls. Galvanised wire panels are more durable than timber. Remember that mature climbers are heavy and the pressure they exert on their supports will increase with the strength of the wind, so make sure to attach panels securely.

Wall nails

These are the cheapest form of support, but are unsuitable for many climbing plants. Ideally, nails are used to secure loops of durable fabric, such as plastic or rubber strips, as used for tree ties. These loops pass round the branches, leaving room for future stem expansion; the wall nail is then driven firmly through the tie to fasten the loop to the wall.

Planting

As with all planting, ground should be prepared throroughly. On new buildings, the base of the wall invariably contains a mixture

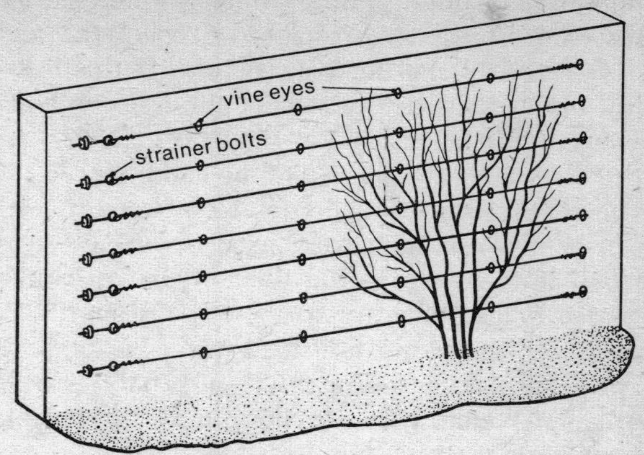

Figure 22 Detail of fixing wires to walls.

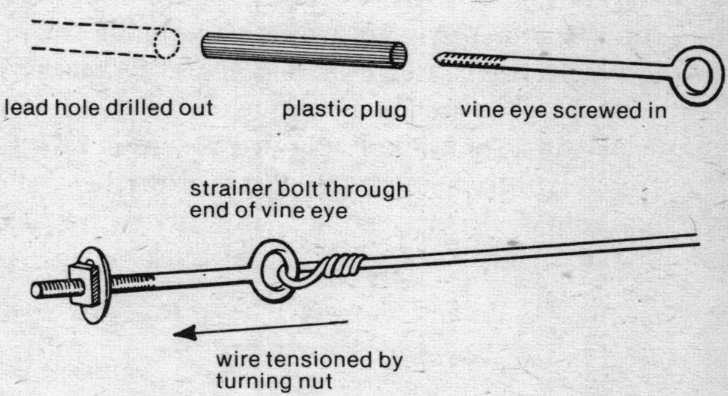

Figure 23 Horizontal wires.

of soil and building rubble and the rubble should be removed and replaced with good soil. Before planting, check the root systems of container-grown plants for constriction. If this has occurred, break up the root ball and spread out the roots as best you can. Set the stem no more than 10 cm (4 in) away from the wall and at its previous depth, before filling and firming in. Self-clinging plants are best pruned back fairly hard to within 10 or 12·5 cm (4 or 5 in) of their base, as it is the new growths that will attach themselves on to the wall. With non-clinging types, canes are used to lead the growths on to the supporting structure, where subsequent growth can be tied in.

After planting, water thoroughly – invariably, the base of a wall is fairly dry. Watering should continue until the plants have extended their root systems into moist soil.

Training

Self-clinging plants require little if any training, apart from being trimmed back to confine their growth. Other types do, however, need regular training, and their shoots should be carefully tied on to the supports whilst they are young and pliable. Plants which have strong, woody stems, *e.g. Pyracantha* and *Ceanothus*, should have their outward-growing shoots removed, to create a compact, flattened bush against the wall. Tying in is best done with durable twine, such as polypropylene string or tarred garden twine. Each tie should loop round the supporting framework with a loose, open loop round the stem, large enough to allow increase in girth without causing constriction.

The plants

Actinidia kolomikta

This is an unusual climber with large, heart-shaped leaves that have a unique variegation. The tips of its leaves are creamy white, which fades into shades of pink and purple on the newest foliage.

This remarkable colouration seems to be most impressive on plants grown in full sun. Normally, it grows 3 to 4·5 m (10 to 15 ft) in height.

Ampelopsis aconitifolia

A plant ideally suited to trellis or pergola, as it is vigorous, but weak-stemmed, and climbs by means of tendrils. It is hardy, with very decorative deeply-cut and lobed leaves; as its name indicates, these resemble those of Monkshood (*Aconitum*).

Ceanothus 'Gloire De Versailles'

This genus of sun-loving plants has been discussed in Chapter 9. Most Ceanothuses lend themselves to wall-training, and benefit from the warm, sheltered micro-climate of a south-facing position. This particular cultivar bears its profusion of pale blue flowers during the months of July and August. With established plants, it is beneficial to prune the flowered stems hard back each spring, as they bear their flowers on the new, current season's shoots. This popular plant is a vigorous grower that can be trained 4·5 to 6 m (15 to 20 ft) up a wall.

Clematis

This tremendous genus provides some of the most exquisite climbing plants, and regularly gives prolific displays of singularly beautiful flowers. Our native *Clematis vitalba* (Traveller's Joy, or Old Man's Beard) grows naturally on chalky soils, but it would be wrong to presuppose that this is an essential need of all Clematis. In fact, many grow well enough in neutral or slightly acid soils. Their favourite situation is a cool spot, preferably shaded, with moisture for the roots, where they can grow with their heads in full sun; spring mulches of leaf mould or farmyard manure are beneficial.

There are two problems that commonly arise: confusion about when to prune, and Clematis wilt. When to prune will depend on the species or hybrid group to which your plants belong. First come the spring-flowering species, such as *C. montana*, which flower on shoots of the previous growing season. Any pruning necessary to regulate their growth is done after flowering in May.

Next come those that flower in June with repeat performances during summer, for example, those favourite hybrids, *'Nelly Moser'* and *'The President'*. These are best thinned out by shortening back some of the flowered shoots after the first flush of growth. Old neglected plants that have become entangled with shoots can stand a drastic cutting back in February, but this will be at the expense of the first flush of flowers.

Lastly come the late summer-flowering kinds, for example *C. jackmanii 'Superba'* and *'Ville De Lyon'*. These flower on shoots of the current year and can withstand hard pruning each February, back to within 0·6 or 1 m (2 or 3 ft) of the ground. This treatment prevents them from becoming bare at the base and from developing a mop head of congested flowering shoots. As with all pruning, remember a spring dressing with a balanced fertiliser for a good response.

Clematis wilt is caused by a fungus which invades the stem and causes a sudden collapse of the plant, and is hard to treat. Stems may re-grow from the base, and if so, it is advisable to spray them with a copper-based fungicide. It is also helpful to prune out regularly any dead or dying shoots. From the many excellent climbers in this group, I have selected the following ten.

C. armandii 'Apple Blossom' – An evergreen species that must have a warm climate to succeed. On sheltered south-facing walls in the milder areas of Britain, it will provide a delightful display of white, blushed pink flowers in April and early May. It is not a vigorous grower, but once established is rather choice.

C. montana – This is a vigorous species and fortunately not susceptible to wilt. It can be wall-trained, or simply allowed to drape over poles and fences, and also looks effective when trained up an old rope into the canopy of a tree. During May, the plant is transformed into a cascading mass of white flowers. My own favourite is *C. m. rubens*, which is identical except for its rose-pink flowers. There is also a beautiful delicate pink cultivar called *C. m. 'Elizabeth'*.

C. tangutica – This species has beautiful butter-yellow, lanternlike flowers in July. It always flowers in great profusion and by late summer the plant becomes a mass of silky tassel-like seed heads.

Clematis hybrids:

C. '*Duchess of Edinburgh*' – A superb cultivar with double, white flowers that are slightly fragrant; at its best in May and June. Old flowered shoots should be pruned back soon after flowering.

C. '*Gypsy Queen*' – This cultivar bears an abundance of violet, purple flowers, which have the texture of velvet, from July to September. Prune hard back in February.

C. *jackmanii* '*Superba*' – This has a similar flower colour to '*Gypsy Queen*', but each bloom is larger. It flowers with gay abandon throughout late summer. Prune hard back in February.

C. '*Nelly Moser*' – This is probably the most popular Clematis hybrid, with large, very striking flowers. Each pale pink petal has a carmine pink band down the centre. Old flowered shoots should be pruned back immediately after flowering.

C. '*The President*' – One of the best, with rich, purple-blue flowers from June to September. Prune old flowered shoots after flowering.

C. '*Ville De Lyon*' – The best carmine-red Clematis. Each flower has a central boss of bright golden stamens. Flowering is from July to October. Prune hard back in February.

C. '*Vyvian Pennel*' – A lovely double-flowered Clematis coloured pale Lavender blue, suffused with a carmine blush, which flowers from May to July. Prune lightly after flowering.

Cytisus batandieri
Whilst this is not a true climber, it is so much at home when trained against a sunny wall that I have included it here. It is a deciduous shrub, growing over 3·5 m (12 ft), with handsome trifoliate leaves; these are covered in fine, silky down which gives

them a distinct silvery appearance. During July, it bears erect clusters of golden-yellow flowers; each cluster is about 12·5 cm (5 in) long, and has a delicious fresh pineapple fragrance. When wall-trained, old flowered stems should be pruned out to give you space to tie in some replacement stems.

Hedera – Ivy

A most valuable genus of self-clinging evergreens, that will find their own way up walls, posts or trees, by extending adventitious roots. These sprout along the stems, but are quite different from the roots in the soil, which sustain the plant with water and nutrients. It is a misconception to believe that these adventitious roots absorb water and nutrients; they should neither be parasitic when growing on trees, nor should they damage the fabric of sound brickwork, providing they are not allowed to get out of hand and are periodically clipped. Some authorities argue that Ivy benefits buildings by keeping them drier and warmer.

Most Ivies are extremely hardy and tolerate a wide variety of soils and situations. They grow remarkably well in dense shade, and thus often provide excellent ground cover in woodland gardens. Their versatility is shown by their popularity as indoor, pot-grown foliage plants:

H. canariensis 'Variegata' – This form is more often seen as an indoor foliage plant, but is suited to south-facing walls in milder districts. It has large handsome leaves, irregularly patterned with green, silvery-grey creamy yellow and white.

H. colchica – A vigorous Ivy with thick, glossy, oval-shaped leaves 12·5 to 17·5 cm (5 to 7 in) long. My preference is for the more decorative *H. colchica 'Dentata Variegata'*, which has a bold marginal variegation of creamy yellow and white. It is much hardier than *H. canariensis* and therefore a better choice for northern gardens.

H. helix – The native English Ivy that frequents woods, often seen scrambling up trees or over walls. A common belief is that Ivy is harmful to trees and slowly strangulates them. The truth is that they are often more prolific on old dying trees, where the sparse, open canopy provides more favourable growing conditions. The dieback of the tree is invariably due to other causes. Typical Ivy leaves are five-lobed, but they frequently display a great variety of leaf shapes. Some with permanent fixations have been selected and given cultivar names, as follows:

H. h. 'Buttercup' – A good golden-leaved variant.
H. h. 'Cristata' – This form has rounded, crinkled leaves.
H. h. 'Glacier' – A form with small three-lobed leaves that are silvery-grey with a white margin.
H. h. 'Gold Heart' – Often incorrectly called 'Jubilee', this has a distinct yellow splash in the centre of each leaf.

H. h. 'Sagittifolia' – This is a form with deeply cut lobes with a more prominent central lobe which gives the plant a distinct fine texture.

Hydrangea petiolaris – Climbing Hydrangea
This is a splendid self-clinging plant that will reach the top of a two-storey building in no time at all. During June, it is decorated with flattened clusters of pure white flowers that resemble the earlier-mentioned Lacecap Hydrangeas. It is perfectly hardy, and suitable for planting against walls with a northerly aspect. No more than routine pruning is required.

Jasminum nudiflorum – Winter Jasmine
An invaluable plant, on account of its habit of flowering freely from November to February; it thus brings winter cheer to the garden, and provides sprays of yellow, trumpet-shaped flowers for indoor decoration. It has a lax growth habit, and to clothe a wall effectively, new shoots should be tied in to supports.

Jasminum officinale – Common Jasmine
This is the hardiest of the sweetly scented Jasmine, but even this needs a warm, sheltered location in northern gardens. It can be trained up to 9 m (30 ft) on a wall, but it should be tied in until a framework of branches clothes the area. It is then allowed to cascade down and should only need occasional thinning out.

From June to September, its shoots bear terminal clusters of strongly scented, pure white tubular flowers.

J. polyanthum
This is the species with the most intense fragrance – but is not hardy. It can, however, be grown in a frost-proof conservatory.

Lonicera periclymenum – Honeysuckle
The perfect plant for training up a pillar or wall close to a patio or terrace, where its free flowering and sweet fragrance can be enjoyed and admired during the summer months. Its Honeysuckle flowers are borne in great profusion in flattened terminal clusters; these are followed by bunches of scarlet berries in autumn.

In woods and hedgerows it is naturally a twining plant, and it can be similarly trained over old tree stumps, or up a pole; alternatively, it can be fastened to a wall support. In the latter case, occasional thinning out is needed to prevent the plant from getting into a dense, heavy tangle.

Being a woodland plant it loves semi-shaded positions and its roots in particular should be cool and moist. The Dutch Honeysuckle *L. p. 'Belgica'*, with its bushy habit, is the form usually offered by nurseries. Another splendid Honeysuckle worth seeking is *L. x americana*. This is very free-flowering, and also delightfully fragrant.

Parthenocissus quinquefolia – True Virginia Creeper
A magnificent self-clinging plant that will quickly clamber up to 15 m (50 ft). It can, of course, be grown on smaller walls, but has to be contained by annual cutting back to prevent it from obscuring windows and blocking gutters. In autumn, its compound, five-lobed leaves become a flaming spectacle as the leaves turn into shades of orange, crimson and scarlet.

P. tricupidata – Japanese Creeper or Boston Ivy, (*Syn. Ampelopsis veitchii*). Often incorrectly called Virginia Creeper, this is also a vigorous self-clinging plant, with a marvellous blaze of leaf colour in autumn which accounts for its great popularity in gardens. Less common is an attractive cultivar, *P. t. 'Lowii'*, which has smaller, slightly crinkled leaves which give it a fine, close texture. Generally it is less rampant but its autumn colour is no less spectacular.

P. henryana – Leaves of this species are compound, with three to five distinct leaflets. These are an unusual greeny-bronze colour, with silvery-white and pink variegation down the centre. This is also self-clinging and has good autumn colour.

Passiflora caerulea – Passion Flower

The common name, said to have been given by Spanish Priests in South America, is derived from the construction of the flower and its symbolic representation of Christ's passion. Three stigmas represent the three nails, five anthers the five wounds; the corona signifies the crown of thorns and five sepals and five petals radiate, representing the ten apostles present at the crucifixion.

In favourable conditions, the flowers set seed which develop into large, egg-shaped, orange-coloured fruits; these, however, are not the edible 'passion fruits' produced by the tender species *P. edulis. P. caerulea* is generally regarded as the hardiest species, but even this will not survive severe frost, and a warm, sunny and sheltered site is essential. In the north, they can be grown in pots or tubs in conservatories or cool greenhouses, and put outdoors during summer. If you are unlucky enough to lose a plant, new ones are easily raised from seed, which can be extracted from the fruits. Climbing is by means of tendrils.

Polygonum baldschuanicum – Russian Vine

I am often asked to recommend something quick-growing to form a garden screen, and I doubt if anything can beat the speed of this plant in the British climate: it can extend its shoots up to 6 m (20 ft) in one growing season. It has a twining habit and will clamber and sprawl around any object in its path. This twining habit can strangulate trees, but the plant can be trained up dead stumps and is valuable for screening unsightly features such as old garden buildings or service areas. It is less well-suited to wall-training as its aggressive vigour is liable to get out of hand. During the summer months, plants become clouded beneath myriads of small, creamy white flowers.

Pyracantha coccinea – Firethorn

A stiff, erect evergreen shrub, suitable for hedging but seen to greatest advantage when trained against a wall. In such positions it will grow to 6 m (20 ft). In early June, its branches are densely packed with clusters of small white flowers similar to May Blossom. They come into their own during autumn, when the plant is transformed into a densely packed mass of orange-scarlet berries, which often persist until January. In areas where birds rapidly devour the fruits, displays can be protected by draping unobtrusive garden nets over the plants.

Training young plants requires a certain degree of skill. The lateral branches spreading from the leading shoot should be tied in horizontally, along wires, any misplaced laterals can be pruned back to within three or four buds of their base to form spurs. Once established, an occasional pruning to shorten back unwanted growth is all that is needed to keep plants tidy. In some localities, Pyracantha scab blackens the berries prematurely. This is a fungal disease that can be prevented by spraying with Captan at three-weekly intervals from March to June. Another problem in some areas is the plant's susceptibility to Fire Blight. Superior to the type is an excellent cultivar, *P. c. 'Lalandei'*, which has larger, more showy fruits.

Rosa – Roses

For sheer elegance, fragrance and beauty, nothing can surpass the delight of climbing Roses trained on walls, trellis and pergola. In their wild state, these forms scramble over other plants with their thorny stems to obtain their share of sunlight. The resulting tangled, thorny thickets would be unsuited to gardens. Fortunately, however, they are easily tamed by careful pruning and training into a supporting framework. There are many splendid species and cultivars available, of which the following ten are only a selection. Be guided by your personal preferences.

R. 'Alberic Barbier' – A rambler Rose with semi-double, creamy white flowers and good fragrance.

R. 'Albertine' – A rambler Rose with strongly scented, double, salmon-pink flowers.

R. '*American Pillar*' An attractive rambler Rose, very good for trellis work, which has bold trusses of single, rose-pink flowers with a distinct white centre.

These three cultivars above produce strong basal growths, which are tied into the places of older, flowered shoots when the latter are pruned out in September. If new basal shoots are sparse, the older ones can be retained with any lateral growths from these pruned hard back.

R. '*Danse Du Feu*' – This has splendid orange-red to scarlet flowers that are freely borne on established plants during the summer. Lateral stems from the main branches can be pruned back to five or six buds each autumn.

R. filipes '*Kiftsgate*' – A vigorous climbing Rose, growing up to 9 m (30 ft) and capable of spreading as much across – hence its need of a spacious wall. It carries enormous bunches of creamy white flowers that fill the surrounding air with their sweet fragrance. In autumn, its branches are decorated with small red hips.

R. '*Golden Showers*' – My favourite yellow-flowered climbing Rose with large-flowered (Hybrid Tea) flowers that open a rich golden-yellow, fading to pale yellow. It has a delicate fragrance and flowers perpetually through the summer months. Its flowers are borne on long stems that are perfect for cut blooms.

R. '*Madame Grégoire Staechelin*' – A cultivar with exquisite rich pink, fragrant flowers borne in great numbers. These appear in June, slightly earlier than most climbing Roses. It is a vigorous plant, quite capable of reaching the top of a 9 m (30 ft) wall.

R. '*Maigold*' – This has double, apricot-yellow flowers that are produced in great quantity. Trained along a trellis, it creates a very colourful screen, ideal for dividing the garden or as a background for other Roses.

R. '*Mermaid*' – A *R. bracteata* hybrid that is often regarded as the queen of climbing Roses. It is a vigorous, almost evergreen grower, but is slightly tender and needs the protection of a sunny, sheltered wall. Throughout the summer, it unfailingly bears large, single yellow flowers. Very little pruning is required, except to contain its growth, which is often over 9 m (30 ft) in height.

R. 'Zéphirine Drouhin' – A popular Bourbon climber, growing to 3·5 to 4·5 m (12 to 15 ft), with carmine pink, double flowers that are slightly fragrant. It produces vigorous, arching stems that are thornless. When tied in to a supporting fence these make a charming floral hedge, ideal for screens and partitions within the garden. I have found this Rose susceptible to Mildew.

Schizophragma hydrangioides
This plant has many similarities to the climbing Hydrangea (*H. petiolaris*), in that it clings by means of adventitious roots. It also bears similar clusters of white, Lacecap Hydrangea flowers during July. Flowering is best on a sunny wall, but it is quite happy clambering 12 m (40 ft) up a north-facing wall, providing it has good rich soil in its root zone.

Solanum crispum 'Glasnevin'
Strictly speaking, this is not a climber, but it is so ideally suited to wall-training that I have included it here. This particular cultivar is superior to the type in length of flowering season, flower-quality and hardiness. From July to October, it is clothed in bunches of mauve-purple flowers like those of the potato plant. Its preference is for a sunny position, and it also grows well on chalk.

Vitis coignetiae
A vigorous ornamental vine, capable of growing 15 to 18 m (50 to 60 ft), occasionally seen trained into the crown of trees. It has large, handsome vine-shaped leaves, that become spectacular in autumn, when they turn various shades of purple, crimson and scarlet.

Wisteria

A genus of vigorous, twining plants that give magnificent floral displays in May and June. They need a good-sized house wall to develop fully, and preferably one with a south- or west-facing aspect. They can also be effective trained along trellis or pergola, over arches and into the canopies of mature trees. Always begin with good ground preparation and during their formative years, train the young pliable stems to form a framework of branches to cover the wall or other means of support.

Mature plants on walls are best pruned in August, by cutting back the lateral stems to 30 cm (12 in). These shoots should be further pruned in winter to within 2·5 cm (1 in) of the old wood, to form spur shoots that will bear future flowers. Plants trained into trees need no pruning, but because of their twining habit it is best to lead them into the tree canopy on a suitably positioned pole or rope. The following selection includes the ones usually seen in gardens.

W. sinensis – Chinese Wisteria

This plant is capable of growing to 24 m (80 ft). It carries pale mauve to lilac-blue, pendant flower-clusters that are 20 to 30 cm (8 to 12 in) long. These are made up of numerous small pea-like flowers that hang like decorative lanterns. There is also a white-flowered cultivar, *W. s. 'Alba'*, but this is no match for the beauty of the type.

Wisteria floribunda – Japanese Wisteria

This species is not nearly so vigorous as *W. Sinensis*, and normally only grows 6 to 7 m (20 to 25 ft) tall. Its flower-clusters are also smaller, drooping 15 to 25 cm (6 to 10 in) except in the dramatic cultivar *W. f. 'Macrobotrys'*, which often has pendant spikes 0·6 to 1 m (2 to 3 ft) long. This plant needs an arch or pergola to display its flowers at their best.

In this section I have described a selection of plants with decorative foliage, flowers or fruits. It is also possible to make use of walls by training fruit trees up them. Most of these have showy flowers, for example, apples, pears, plums, cherries and apricots; others have ornamental foliage, such as hardy vines and figs. Fruits, however, require special selection and culture if they are to yield good crops. (See *Growing Fruit*, by R. Genders, in this series.)

14

Hedges and Screens

The horticultural value of hedges; planting, training and trimming hedges; plants suitable for use as clipped formal hedges, informal flowering hedges, hedges in exposed coastal gardens and taller screens.

Hedges should be a priority in any garden. A garden enclosed by hedges has a sheltered environment and consequently a microclimate that is more favourable for the cultivation of plants and for outdoor living. Hedges are preferable to walls and panelled fences, as they filter the wind and more effectively reduce its speed, unlike a solid barrier, which will create air turbulence on windy days.

Hedges may also be used to divide up space within the garden, separating a produce-growing area, say, from an ornamental garden. They are also useful for forming a screen to conceal unsightly objects or features – dustbins or compost heaps, for example. Occasionally, taller screens can also be strategically placed to obscure unsightly intrusions in the distant landscape. Visually, hedges provide the perfect foil for borders and plants, but equally, they may be an eye-catching feature in their own right.

It is important to recognise at the outset that hedges demand regular attention, and anyone contemplating a labour-saving garden should consider other alternatives.

Planting

Having decided where to plant your hedge, begin by marking out and preparing the site. Perimeter hedges should be planted within the confines of your own garden boundary, so that when they are mature they are not encroaching into your neighbour's garden. Mark out a strip of ground 1 m (3 ft) wide, centred on the intended line of the hedge. It is best to double-dig this strip, at the same time incorporating plenty of farmyard manure or similar bulky organic material. If possible, allow the soil to settle for a few weeks before planting, but if you are pressed for time, break the soil down to a reasonable tilth with a garden fork.

When choosing planting material, you may be tempted to buy plants that are already 1 to 1·2 m (3 to 4 ft) in height. It is a common misconception that these will produce a hedge more quickly. In fact, the quickest results are usually obtained from young plants 0·3 to 0·6 m (1 to 2 ft) in height. These suffer very little growth check after planting and will surpass the growth of the initially taller plants; apart from this, they will be considerably cheaper.

Planting should be done during the normal planting season of October to February, unless you plan to use container-grown plants. To achieve a straight planting-line, position a garden line down the centre of the prepared strip and peg this down at roughly 3 m (10 ft) intervals. Garden hedges should only require a single line of plants; double lines are sometimes used on boundaries adjoining farmland, where effective stock-proof barriers are needed. Planting distances vary from 0·3 to 1 m (1 to 3 ft) depending on the subject and the intended height of the hedge. After digging planting holes, set the plant against the line to check its depth and position, spread out the roots and finally fill in the hole with good friable soil, firming gently as you proceed.

After planting, some species such as Privet, Hawthorn and Myrobalan Plum, should be pruned halfway back, to encourage bushy, basal growth. Such treatment is not necessary for Cypress, Beech, Hornbeam, Yew and Holly – in these cases the leading shoots are left intact until the hedge has reached its intended height. Large plants may need the support of a cane or small stake until such time as the roots are firmly re-established. A dressing of high nitrogen fertiliser at the rate of 60 to 90 g per metre run (2 or 3 oz per yard run) of hedge can be applied and lightly forked into the soil. This dressing can be repeated each spring for five years after planting, to speed the rate of establishment. Beyond that stage only give nutrients if the plants look deficient, as lush growth will only need more frequent clipping.

Training and trimming

Leading shoots should be allowed to grow until they reach the required height. Initially, this means that the top of a hedge will be sparsely branched, but resist the temptation to clip or prune to encourage bushy growth – the plants will fill out satisfactorily, given time. Side growth can be trimmed in the normal way, and it is best to start trimming as the hedge is developing to stimulate dense, twiggy growth. During the formative years, this can be done with secateurs, so that the correct line and batter are established. 'Batter' is the angle to which the sides of a hedge are cut. In formal gardens, you will see hedges with vertical sides, but ideally a hedge should be trimmed so that the sides slope outwards towards the base 10° to 15° from the vertical. The broad, flat-topped hedges so frequently seen in suburban gardens should be avoided; these are not only difficult to maintain, but are liable to damage or permanent deformity when weighed down by a heavy snowfall. A good eye is needed when clipping to keep a straight line, especially along the top of the hedge, which can be spoilt by irregular undulations. Beginners will find it helpful to set up a guide line which can be supported on canes protruding above the hedge; it can also be used as a guide to batter. A taut line is essential and is achieved by guying the end canes firmly to the ground (see Fig. 24).

It is worth investing in a pair of good-quality garden shears, which should be kept well lubricated and sharp. Mechanical and electrical trimmers are becoming increasingly popular and these considerably reduce the manual effort. Informal hedges need not be clipped regularly, but occasional pruning to remove branches that protrude from the general line of the hedge will keep them in reasonable shape.

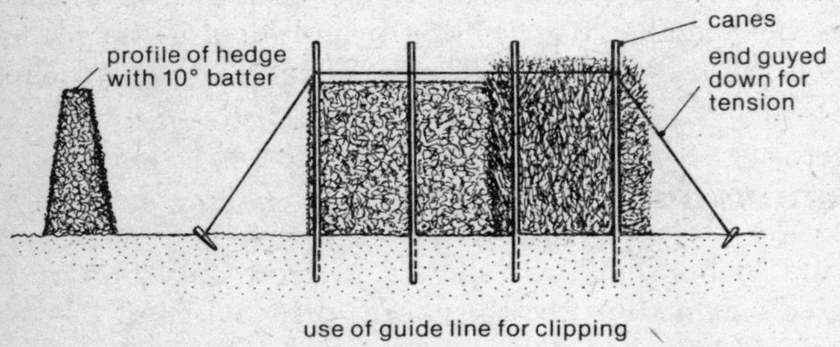

Figure 24 Hedge trimming.

The best time to clip hedges varies according to species. Some quick-growing plants such as Privet may require more than one trim in a season; conversely, a screen of Leyland Cypress may only need to be trimmed every four or five years. It is preferable to delay clipping until each season's new shoots are fully extended, and generally the period from July to October is best. Clipping after this date is permissible, but the task becomes more strenuous as the new shoots become woody. To reduce the frequency of clipping with quick-growing species like Privet and Lonicera, it is possible to spray the hedge after the first trim with a growth retardant such as 'Hedge Setter'. These products are based on growth-regulating chemicals which reduce shoot extension and thus remove the need for a second trim.

Plants suitable for hedges and screens

When deciding what to plant, priority should be given to the functional and visual requirements of your hedges. If, for example, you want a visual screen, then evergreens will be more effective than deciduous plants (unless you choose a deciduous plant like Beech, which, when clipped, retains its foliage during winter). Visually, your preference may be for a flowering hedge or one with a distinct foliage colour. The plant chosen must also be suited to the site in terms of soil conditions and hardiness. Other considerations are growth-rate, ultimate height and growth habit. For example, plants for formal hedges should have twiggy growth and be responsive to clipping. Finally, spare a thought for your neighbours. If, for example, your garden adjoins farmland, your hedge should be stock-proof; but equally, do not plant Yew or *Rhododendron ponticum*, which are toxic to browsing animals.

Plants for clipped formal hedges: Evergreen plants

Buxus sempervirens – Box
Few plants respond to clipping better than Box, and for this reason it is a popular choice for topiary work. The type can be used for formal hedges 1 to 2 m (3 to 6 ft) in height, but for traditional 'box edging', as used in Elizabethan knot gardens to weave intricate patterns through the flower beds, the cultivar *B. s. 'Suffruticosa'* is used. For a formal hedge, space plants 0·3 to 0·4 m (1 to 1½ ft) apart, but for edging, plants are usually divided up and spaced no more than 15 cm (6 in) apart.

Chamaecyparis lawsoniana 'Green Hedger'
This bright green cultivar selected by Jackman's Nursery is regarded as the best Lawson's Cypress for hedges. Seedling Lawson's makes a cheaper hedge, but these inevitably vary slightly in colour and texture, and produce a hedge of inferior quality. Plants are spaced 0·4 to 0·7 m (1½ to 2½ ft) apart, and allowed to grow on to their required height before topping. It is important to keep the base of a Lawson's hedge in full sunlight, otherwise lower branches will become suppressed and will never refurbish themselves.

x Cupressocyparis leylandii – Leyland Cypress
The perfect choice for the impatient gardener, as this remarkable conifer will form a good hedge 1·5 m (5 ft) in height within three years of planting. It responds admirably to clipping as a formal hedge, or it can be grown on into a tall screen and topped at any height. For formal hedging, plants are spaced 0·6 to 0·7 m (2 to 2½ ft) apart, and for informal, taller screens, distances of 1 to 1·2 m (3 to 4 ft) are used. Begin with young plants 0·3 to 0·4 m (1 to 1½ ft) in height; these grow very quickly and will soon overtake the more expensive 1·2 and 1·5 m (4 to 5 ft) plants, which inevitably take longer to recover from planting. Be wary of container-grown plants with 'pot bound' or constricted root systems, as these often become unstable and blow over several years after planting. Leyland Cypress has a general tendency to be weak-rooted, and in exposed gardens the erection of a simple post and rail fence down the centre line of your hedge will provide good support when the plants have grown up around it. In training Leyland, allow the leaders to run on to their required height, but keep their side growth clipped in, to form a bushy thicket.

The plant does not tolerate salt spray, and exposure to salt-laden gales will give hedges in coastal areas a brown, scorched appearance.

Ilex aquifolium – Common Holly
An excellent boundary hedge, which forms a dense thicket of prickly, evergreen foliage which will deter the intrusion of man and animals. It can be allowed to grow over 6 m (20 ft) high if needs be, but tall hedges such as these demand extra time and equipment when clipping. Holly can be successfully transplanted as 1·5 to 2 m (5 to 6 ft) specimens, if the plants have been prepared by root-pruning in the nursery. These are likely to be expensive, but they can be useful where an immediate screen is needed. Normally, 0·4 to 0·6 m (1½ to 2 ft) high plants are purchased, and these are spaced no more than 0·6 m (2 ft) apart, except where a taller screen is envisaged, in which case spacings up to 1 m (3 ft) are acceptable.

Clipped Holly makes a splendid background for your garden,

and to add interest variegated cultivars such as '*Golden King*' and '*Silver Queen*' can be used. However, when deciding where to use it, remember that the dried, old leaves are prickly. Holly is tolerant of shade and is therefore a suitable choice where hedge lines run beneath trees. It has a moderate growth-rate and only needs clipping once a year, usually in late summer.

Ligustrum ovalifolium – Privet
A quick-growing evergreen often found around the boundaries of suburban gardens. No doubt the reason for this is the ease with which it can be increased from cuttings. As a hedge, it has many virtues: apart from being a quick grower, it forms a dense, bushy thicket and responds to clipping better than most plants. Equally, it grows in almost any soil and situation, and has proved to be remarkably tolerant of smoky, town atmospheres. In recent years its popularity has declined, partly due to changing tastes, and partly because it is a plant that needs clipping two, and possibly three, times in a season to keep it tidy. This clipping frequency can, however, be reduced by using a growth-retarding chemical spray. Another disadvantage of Privet, especially in small gardens, is its over-vigorous root system, which greedily depletes the surrounding soil of water and nutrients. This makes the cultivation of plants in adjacent borders difficult.

More acceptable is *L. o.* '*Aureum*', Golden Privet, which has a broad golden-yellow margin to its leaves. It is less vigorous and has superb leaf colour all the year round. When planting Privet, use plants 0·3 to 0·6 m (1 to 2 ft) in height, and space them 30 to 37 cm (12 to 15 in) apart. Shorten all growths back to half their length to encourage strong basal shoots.

Lonicera nitida
The small evergreen leaves give this plant an extremely fine texture when kept tightly clipped. It is often seen as a garden hedge and, like Privet, is readily propagated from cuttings. It also has the same vigorous growth and needs trimming at least twice in a growing season. *Lonicera* is not a tall plant and will rarely exceed 2 m (6 ft) as a formal hedge. One disadvantage is that it can be killed back in severe winters; though it may regenerate from the

base, I would not choose this plant if you live in a cold district.

Prunus laurocerasus – Cherry Laurel
The large, glossy evergreen leaves of this plant give it a distinct coarse texture. It can be grown as a formal hedge or as a broad screen up to about 6 m (20 ft) in height. Formal hedges are established from young plants, and are easily raised from late summer cuttings. The plants are spaced 0·4 to 0·7 m (1½ to 2½ ft) apart. Normally, Laurel hedges are pruned with secateurs to contain growth as shears produce mutilated, unsightly foliage. One virtue of this plant is its ability to grow in dense shade – it is therefore suitable for boundaries overhung by trees.

Taxus baccata – Common Yew
This is undoubtedly one of the finest of all hedging plants on account of its rich, dark green colour and close, fine texture when neatly clipped. Initially, it may be a little more expensive to purchase than other plants, but the ultimate quality and long life are worth that bit extra. Start with young plants no more than 0·6 m (2 ft) in height, and space them 0·4 to 0·6 m (1½ to 2 ft) apart. Yew grows well in most soils, including chalk. One trim in late August is all that is required. It is often listed as a slow-growing hedge, and though it is true that it will not be as quick as some plants, a good hedge can still result within six or seven years, given good growing conditions and a spring application of high nitrogen fertiliser.

Deciduous plants for clipped formal hedges.

Carpinus betulus – Hornbeam
This plant has virtually the same qualities as Beech (see below), being similar in leaf and in its characteristic of holding its brown leaves through winter. It grows naturally in the same chalk soils as Beech, and has the additional virtue of being able to withstand late frosts better.

It can also be used for pleached hedges, which are hedges grown on an elevated stem to form a taller screen, or to create a shaded walk-way. Such hedges are a common feature of the classical formal gardens in the French style, and this technique can be useful in modern gardens where an elevated screen is needed. Initially, standard trees are planted and their crowns are then trained along a supporting framework of canes or wires to form an elevated hedge. These supports can be removed when the branch framework is well established.

Crataegus monogyna – Hawthorn or Quickthorn
There must be hundreds of miles of Hawthorn hedge in Britain, much of it planted by landowners to enclose their fields. It does not make a very interesting garden hedge, but it does respond to clipping, slashing and laying, and it is relatively cheap compared to most hedging plants. It is also a good choice for garden boundaries that adjoin open fields, to form a unified link with the distant countryside. Old, neglected Hawthorn hedges can be restored by 'laying', which involves partially cutting stems close to the ground and laying them down. They are then laced and secured between stakes. The resultant re-growth produces a well-furnished thicket.

Untrimmed hedges bear plentiful clusters of white flowers in late May and early June, and these are followed by dark red 'haws' in September. The haws provide food for birds, hence the fact that dense thickets are always well populated with nests. It is possible to manage hedges like this by cutting them hard back every four or five years, using a pair of loppers, thus providing visual and ecological interest in your garden.

At planting time, space young plants about 30 cm (12 in) apart and prune them halfway back to encourage a bushy base. A double line of plants can be used on field boundaries to provide a faster-growing stock-proof barrier. These hedges can comprise a mixture of other native hedgerow plants, such as Field Maple (*Acer campestre*), Hazel (*Corylus avellana*), Blackthorn (*Prunus spinosa*), and the occasional Dog Rose (*Rosa canina*).

Fagus sylvatica – Beech
A popular hedging plant that provides an effective screen throughout the year. The bright green spring foliage turns russet-brown in autumn. When beech is clipped, it exhibits the juvenile charac-

teristic of retaining its russet autumn leaves until the new leaves emerge. Beech can be trained to any height, and if necessary can be grown on to form a tall screen. Hedges are best established from plants 0·3 to 0·6 m (1 to 2 ft) in height, and spaced 0·3 to 0·6 m (1 to 2 ft) apart, or 1 m (3 ft) for a taller screen. Run the leaders on to their final height, but keep the sides closely trimmed. Clipping is best done in late summer, before the wood hardens. Unfortunately, this plant is frequently infested with beech aphis, which is a form of greenfly that causes sticky secretions on the leaves and the subsequent development of unsightly sooty moulds. A decorative effect can be achieved by inter-planting Copper Beech and normal Green Beech, but I must admit that I personally prefer hedges to be uniform in colour, as this 'tapestry' effect makes other plant arrangement difficult.

Prunus cerasifera – Myrobalan Plum
The type plant has green leaves, and it was once popular to interplant these with the dark purple-leaved cultivar, *P. c. 'Pissardii'*. The variation between the two plants is also evident in winter, as the stems are coloured green and purple respectively. Both are quick-growing plants and form dense thickets when clipped. They will make a hedge or screen up to 6 m (20 ft) if needed. Initially, plants are spaced 0·4 to 0·6 m ($1\frac{1}{2}$ to 2 ft) apart.

Plants suitable for informal flowering hedges

Various shrubs can be planted in lines to form broad, informal hedges, and periodically pruned to keep their natural outline. By limiting your pruning and not removing all the shoots, you will find you can make these hedges most impressive at the flowering season.

Berberis x stenophylla
This particular Barberry can almost stand clipping as a formal hedge, and is certainly one of the most reliable of flowering hedges. It is an evergreen with graceful, arching shoots hung with golden-yellow flowers during April. Any trimming is best done immediately after flowering. Being a very thorny plant, it is a good

choice for boundary hedges; plants should initially be spaced at 0·4 m (1½ ft) intervals. *B. darwinii* and *B. thunbergii* can be treated similarly, but these never seem to make the same quality of hedge as *B. x stenophylla*.

Escallonia macrantha
An excellent informal hedge for coastal gardens in the south and west of England, where it has proved to be remarkably tolerant of salt-laden Atlantic gales. Unfortunately, it is not fully hardy elsewhere. Young pot-grown plants, spaced 0·4 to 0·6 m (1½ to 2 ft) apart, are capable of growing to 2·5 m (8 ft) if planted in good, freely-drained soil. Two noteworthy cultivars are '*Crimson Spire*' and '*Red Hedger*'. Both bear masses of small red flowers in June.

Forsythia x intermedia 'Spectabilis'
This is the best Forsythia for an informal hedge, as others are either low-growing or have a lax growth habit. Space plants about 1 m (3 ft) apart, and then allow them to develop their natural shape. In April, they transform into a dense mass of bright yellow flowers. Any pruning needed to regulate the hedge outline can be done as soon as the flowers fade.

Fuchsia 'Ricartonii'
This hybrid Fuchsia, with scarlet and violet-purple flowers, can be grown as a 1 to 1·2 m (3 to 4 ft) high hedge in gardens on the south coast. Unfortunately, when grown inland, it is often cut back by frost and loses its hedge effect. Normally, it flowers in the summer months of July and August. The only trimming needed is a shortening back of the previous flower shoots in spring.

Rhododendron ponticum
A tough, shade-tolerant evergreen, making a broad, dome-shaped hedge that withstands hard pruning. Ideally, it needs an acid soil and given good conditions it produces an excellent shelter or visual barrier up to 4·5 m (15 ft) in height. During May and June, plants bear typical compact trusses of pale mauve flowers. Plants are easily raised from seed, which can be gathered from wild plants. To form a good screen, they are normally spaced about 1 m (3 ft) apart. Like Yew, its leaves are poisonous to stock.

Ribes sanguineum – Flowering Currant
This plant readily forms a hedge that can withstand clipping, which should be done immediately after flowering in April. It has pendant clusters of pink flowers in spring.

Rosa – Roses
The charm and fragrance of Roses give them an obvious appeal as a screen or hedge. Many climbing and rambling types can be trained on a suitable supporting fence or trellis, to provide the effect of a colourful hedge. A few Roses, notably the sweet briars derived from *R. rubiginosa* and the group called '*Penzance Briars*', will stand in their own right as informal hedges. These bear single flowers during June and July, followed by showy hips in autumn. They are also noted for their sweetly-scented foliage. Cultivars include '*Amy Robsart*' (pink), '*Anne of Geierstein*' (red), '*Lord Penzance*' (fawn-yellow) and '*Meg Merrilees*' (crimson).

Some of the *Rosa rugosa* hybrids can also be used for hedges 1 to 1·2 m (3 to 4 ft) in height. Suitable cultivars are *R.* '*Blanc Double De Coubert*' (double white), *R.* '*Roseraie de l'Hay*' (crimson-purple), and *R.* '*Sarah van Fleet*' (rose-pink).

Several hybrid Musk Roses have a habit that makes a good informal hedge, notably *R.* '*Cornelia*' (coppery pink), *R.* '*Felicia*' (pink), and the vigorous *R.* '*Moonlight*' (white). Among modern hybrids, *R.* '*Queen Elizabeth*' with its strong erect growth, healthy green foliage and abundant clear pink flowers, is a splendid choice. Most Roses used for hedges are planted about 1 m (3 ft) apart, extending to 1·2 m (4 ft) in the case of vigorous growers like *R.* '*Moonlight*'. Like all Roses, they respond to generous treatment; regular pruning is advisable to regenerate flowering shoots, and this must be coupled with the supply of nutrients, as prescribed for other Roses.

Plants suitable for hedges in exposed coastal gardens

Atriplex halimus – Tree Purslane
This grey, woolly-leaved plant is a semi-evergreen that forms a good first line of defence in seaside gardens. It grows into an

informal hedge 1·2 to 2 m (4 to 6 ft) in height; trimming is best done in late April after the spring gales.

Escallonia macrantha
See under informal flowering hedges.

Euonymus japonicus
An evergreen suitable for clipping into a formal hedge up to 2·5 m (8 ft) in height. Its smooth, waxy leaves resist salt injury, and the plant always has a clean, healthy appearance. It is also fairly tolerant of shade. The golden variegated cultivar *E. j. 'Duc D'Anjou'* is most colourful and makes an excellent hedge.

Hippophae rhamnoides – Sea Buckthorn
This is a pioneer shrub on coastal sand dunes, which shows how well this plant can adapt to harsh growing environments. Its grey, willow-like leaves remain unscathed even after severe storms. Hedge plants should be spaced 1 m (3 ft) apart and trimmed if necessary, but a broad screen gives more effective shelter. It is capable of growing to 3·5 to 4·5 m (12 to 15 ft) in height.

Oleria x haastii – Daisy Bush
A hardy evergreen shrub with a felty covering on the undersides of the leaf which protects it from wind and salt injury. This plant can readily be clipped into a formal hedge 1·2 to 1·5 m (4 to 5 ft) in height. In July and August, it bears white, small, daisy-like flowers. Spent flower-heads remain on the plant and detract from its otherwise tidy appearance. Plants should be spaced 30 cm (12 in) apart when planting.

Quercus ilex – Holm or Evergreen Oak
Mature hedges of this plant always impress me as being the best formal hedges for coastal gardens. They have a fine texture, good colour and, being evergreen, are effective all the year round. The only disadvantage is that they are slow starters and patience is needed to achieve the desired effect. It is a good idea to erect a temporary hurdle-type fence to provide immediate shelter until the hedge is satisfactorily established. Normally, pot-grown plants are used, and these are spaced 0·6 to 1 m (2 to 3 ft) apart.

Plants suitable for taller screens

Occasionally, a tall screen is needed to obscure some unsightly feature, or to give more privacy to an overlooked garden. The following plants are all fairly quick-growing and either have narrow crowns or respond to training into a dense screen.

Carpinus betulus – Hornbeam
See section on deciduous plants for clipped formal hedges.

Chamaecyparis lawsoniana – Lawson's Cypress
See section on evergreen plants for clipped formal hedges.

Cupressus macrocarpa – Monterey Cypress
An extremely fast-growing conifer, almost competing with Leyland Cypress in its young stages. It is best suited to coastal districts in the south and west of England; it is not completely hardy in the north and in inland gardens in cold districts. This plant cannot stand regular hard clipping but can be pruned back periodically to form a screen.

x Cupressocyparis leylandii – Leyland Cypress
See section on evergreen plants for clipped formal hedges.

Fagus sylvatica – Beech
See section on deciduous plants for clipped formal hedges.

Populus nigra 'Italica' – Lombardy Poplar
The male form is a narrow-crowned tree with erect branches often seen as a screen; but it can be a troublesome tree. Unfortunately, it has a vigorous root system that can invade drains and undermine foundations; it is not, therefore, the best of plants for a screen near buildings, especially in areas with clay soils which may shrink. Lombardy Poplar looks good when planted in groups, but does not really suit the straight lines of a screen.

Thuja plicata – Western Red Cedar
A fast-growing conifer with scale leaves that resemble a coarse-textured Lawson's Cypress. If clipped regularly developing plants make an excellent close-textured screen. The plant is hardy but

it tends to scorch in cold winds; young plants also suffer from frost injury, and are therefore a poor choice where there is a frost-pocket. It grows well on most soils, including chalk.

Tilia platyphyllos – Large Leafed Lime
If Limes are planted in a line 1·2 to 2 m (4 to 6 ft) apart, with their side branches trained along a supporting framework of wires and canes, a narrow 'pleached' screen can soon be formed. The only disadvantage of this method is the time needed for training and maintenance.

15

Ground-covering Shrubs

The uses of ground-covering shrubs; the desirable qualities of a ground-cover plant; a selection of ground-covering shrubs.

Observers of woodlands and natural vegetation will appreciate that there are three clearly definable layers of plants: the tree canopy, a shrub layer and, close to the ground, a carpet of ground-covering herbs and shrubs. I have always believed that this natural structure should follow in the ornamental garden. The preceding chapters have considered the tree canopy and shrub layers, and here I complete the picture with a look at the low growing, woody plants.

Visually, shrub borders are far more attractive when planted with a foil of low-growing plants. These ground-cover plants also reduce the maintenance required. By choosing the right plant, you can quickly form a dense carpet which prevents colonisation with weeds and thus obviates the need for regular cultivation or expensive herbicides. Ground-cover plants are also a useful solution to the problem of sloping sites and inaccessible corners. On steeply-sloping ground, their roots help to stabilise the soil: once vegetated, such areas need little attention.

Grass is often regarded as a good ground-cover plant, but this needs regular maintenance to keep it presentable. For those areas where such maintenance would be difficult, low-growing, carpeting shrubs are a good alternative.

For success with ground-cover plants, it is of paramount importance to clear the ground of perennial weeds before planting. With new borders, it makes sense to defer planting the ground-cover for one or two growing seasons, in order to allow the permanent plantings time to settle in and to establish their root systems before having to compete for water and nutrients. This time also provides the opportunity for clearing any remaining weeds, and allows for the multiplication of your ground-covering plants.

When planting, my policy has always been to put ground-cover at spacings of 0·3 to 0·6 m (1 to 2 ft), depending on the plant being used. This practice ensures the rapid development of a carpet of vegetation. One obvious disadvantage is that initially you need a lot more plants, and for this reason it is worthwhile choosing a few subjects that propagate easily, so that stock can be quickly bulked up from an initial purchase of stock plants. For example, I have propagated 300 hypericum plants in one growing season from an initial purchase of three stock plants. I did this by taking two batches of cuttings and by removing tops from the first batch to make more cuttings.

When choosing a ground-cover shrub, the following qualities should be considered. First, they should form a carpet of sufficient density to prevent weed growth. If they are to be used for soil stabilisation on sloping ground, those with suckering or creeping root systems are more effective. Over-vigorous and invasive plants should be used with discretion; in some places they are merely a nuisance. Shade tolerance is necessary where shrubs or trees are being under-planted. Finally, fairly permanent plants are desirable and visually, evergreens are preferable.

The following is a selection of suitable shrubs:

Arctostaphylos uva-ursi – Bearberry

A vigorous, dense, mat-forming evergreen with oval, dark green leaves about 2·5 cm (1 in) long. In April, it bears pinky-white, Erica-like flowers, with a few red berries in late summer. This plant grows well in both full sun and partial shade. I have young plants growing well in peat beds, but remarkably this is one of a few ericaceous plants that tolerate limestone areas. Its main need is for good drainage.

Calluna vulgaris – Heather or Ling

The carpeting effect of this plant is clearly evident on the mountains and moorlands of northern Britain and on the heathlands in the south. Apart from the common type, there are many named cultivars with differing flower and foliage characteristics, which are tremendously popular in gardens. Heathers have a strong preference for acid soils and open situations and as such are not suitable for ground-cover beneath trees and shrubs, apart from those with open canopies, such as Birch.

In open positions they can be effectively used for creating colourful ground patterns, and these can be further enhanced by association with the closely related Ericas and dwarf conifers. In rich garden soils, heathers can become straggly and untidy, and to prevent this it is advisable to trim them back after their main flowering display in August and September. Occasional replacement of a batch may also be needed, but replacement plants are readily propagated from cuttings inserted from July to early August. The following cultivars represent a selection for general planting.

C. v. 'Alba' – The popular white Heather that is traditionally a symbol of good luck. A clump is worth having for cutting.

C. v. 'Blazeaway' – A form with light mauve flowers, but grown mainly for its colourful orange-red winter foliage.

C. v. 'County Wicklow' – A compact plant up to 22 cm (9 in) high with double pink flowers.

C. v. 'Gold Haze' – A white-flowered Heather, but grown for its splendid golden foliage which makes an impressive carpet throughout the year.

C. v. 'H. E. Beale' – If you can only find room for one Heather, then this would be an excellent choice. It flowers with great profusion, bearing double pink blossoms often on spikes over 30 cm (12 in) long. Mature plants form a dense carpet 0·4 to 0·6 m ($1\frac{1}{2}$ to 2 ft) in height.

C. v. 'Hirsuta Typica' – This is a splendid grey-leaved cultivar with less significant pale mauve flowers.

C. v. 'Peter Sparkes' – A sport from '*H. E. Beale*', with similar double flowers, but a deeper pink.

Cotoneaster dammeri
An evergreen species that forms a dense mat of small green leaves 7·5 to 10 cm (3 to 4 in) above soil level. It bears small red berries, but these do not contribute significantly.

C. salicifolius 'Repens' – Another good evergreen species, but with larger leaves and a prostrate habit. It forms a thicker carpet of branches and is generally more vigorous than *C. dammeri.*

C. 'Scarlet Leader' – A rampant evergreen species ideal for cascading down banks. It is one of the best flowering and fruiting ground-covering Cotoneasters, with orange-red berries persisting into late winter.

C. 'Skogholm' – A vigorous hybrid of *C. dammeri*, making a dense mat of evergreen leaves.

Cytisus procumbens
A ground-hugging broom, forming dense mats several metres across. In May and June, it bears bright yellow, pea-like flowers. Full sun and freely drained soils are its main needs.

Erica cinerea – Scots or Bell Heather
An evergreen shrub 22 to 37 cm (9 to 15 in) in height, that is frequently seen growing amongst the Heather of our open moorlands. In gardens they also associate well with other Heaths and Heathers. To grow well, they need an acid soil, rich in peaty organic matter, and an open sunny site. For ground-cover purposes, the plants should be close together to form bold drifts. Like Heather, this has produced several cultivars, of which the following are noteworthy.

E. c. 'Alba' – A white-flowered cultivar in bloom from June to August.

E. c. 'C. D. Eason' – A popular favourite, with rose-pink flowers set against deep green foliage.

E. c. 'Eden Valley' – This cultivar has a spreading habit and only grows about 15 cm (6 in) tall. It has rose-lilac flowers, fading almost to white.

E. c. 'Pink Ice' – A newer cultivar, with soft pink flowers on compact, bushy plants.

E. c. 'P. S. Patrick' – An excellent purple-flowered cultivar.

E. c. 'Rosea' – A reliable and robust Erica with bright pink flowers.

Erica x darleyensis
This is an invaluable hybrid for ground-cover, as it is one of the few Heaths that tolerate a wide range of soils, including those with some chalk or lime content. It also adds a good deal of cheer to the winter garden, as it flowers right through from November to the end of April, quite undeterred by snow and frost. Plants eventually grow 40 to 60 cm (1½ to 2 ft) in height, in a dense carpet. You may find this plant listed in nursery catalogues as *'Darley Dale'*, with flowers a pale mauve-pink. Other good cultivars in this hybrid group are *E. x d. 'George Rendall'*, which has deep pink flowers borne from November to March, and *E. x d. 'Silberschmelze'*, which bears silvery-white flowers from December to April.

Erica herbacea – (*Syn. E. carnea*) – Winter or Spring Heath
This change of name is fairly recent, and most nurserymen are likely to list this as *E. carnea*. It is my favourite ground-covering Heath, and forms a dense, tidy carpet some 15 to 22 cm (6 to 9 in) high. After establishment it needs very little attention. Like the previous group, *E. herbacea* will also tolerate soil containing free lime, but prefers acid conditions. It is at its best from January to March, when it flowers with gay abandon through the severest frost and snow. There are several excellent cultivars that can be used to create interesting ground patterns.

E. h. 'King George' – This begins to open its rosy-crimson flowers in December and continues through to April.

E. h. 'Loughrigg' – Rich, purple flowers in February and March.

E. h. 'Springwood Pink' – A first-rate carpet-forming cultivar, with a vigorous spreading habit and pale pink flowers.

E. h. 'Springwood White' – In my view, this is the best ground-covering Heath. It has a vigorous spreading habit and is extremely floriferous, bearing its pure white flowers from January to March.

E. h. 'Vivellii' – In winter, the foliage of this cultivar turns an attractive bronze colour that intensifies as temperatures fall. From January to March it bears carmine-red flowers.

Erica vagans – Cornish Heath
A hardy Heath, making hummocks 0·3 to 0·6 m (1 to 2 ft) in height, but best seen planted to form carpeting drifts. Flowering takes place from July through to November; ideal for extending interest from a Heath and Heather bed. It prefers slightly acid soils, but will tolerate a small amount of lime in the growing medium. Full sun is needed for prolific flower displays. Like Callunas, these plants are best trimmed back after flowering to keep them compact and tidy. The following cultivars are recommended.

E. v. 'Cornish Cream' – This bears a profusion of cream-coloured flower spikes from August to October.

E. v. 'Lyonesse' – An excellent Heath, carrying masses of white flower spikes.

E. v. 'Mrs D. F. Maxwell' – A popular cultivar, with good deep, rose-pink, flower spikes.

E. v. 'St Keverne' – A form with bright pink flowers.

Euonymus fortunei var. radicans
A creeping shrub that is also capable of clambering 6 m (20 ft) up a wall by means of adventitious roots. It has decorative glossy, evergreen leaves, but no significant flowers or fruits. As a ground-covering shrub it is useful for both shaded or open

positions, and tolerates most soils. The more cheerful variegated cultivar makes a superb ground-cover plant, and one that can quickly be multiplied from summer cuttings. This has greyish-green leaves with a creamy yellow margin, turning to white. Moreover, it retains these striking colours all the year round in both sun and shade. As ground-cover it forms dense shrubs 30 to 60 cm (1 to 2 ft) in height; to maintain a tidy, carpeting appearance, they can be trimmed over with secateurs every four or five years to remove the occasional straggly shoots.

Gaultheria procumbens – Partridge Berry
An attractive carpeting plant that is limited to acid soils and moist, shaded positions. Given these conditions, it spreads rapidly by underground stems. In May, small white bell-shaped flowers protrude from the foil of glossy foliage; these turn into bright red berries in autumn.

Gaultheria shallon
This *Gaultheria* can grow 1 to 1·2 m (3 to 4 ft) in height but it is a very good shade-bearing plant, so I have included it for underplanting where dense shade is a problem. If needed for carpeting, it can be pruned or clipped back at appropriate intervals without detriment, although this practice departs from my principle that good ground-cover plants should need little attention.

Genista pilosa
A Broom with prostrate branches that eventually forms a dense mat about 30 cm (12 in) in height. The whole plant appears to turn bright yellow during May, as the myriads of small pea-like flowers open. This is an excellent plant for cascading down dry, sunny banks. Each one will spread to about 70 cm (2½ ft) across, but I would recommend closer planting, which achieves a dense carpet more quickly.

Hebe pinguifolia 'Pagei'
Few evergreen shrubs have such distinct blue-grey foliage. It forms low clumps 22 cm (9 in) high and 44 cm (18 in) across, but is best planted in bold groups to form a carpet. In May, small white flower spikes appear, but these always seem lost against the

intensely coloured leaves. It is quite hardy, but grows best in full sun on well-drained soil. Worn out plants can be rejuvenated by hard clipping back, but as they root so easily from summer cuttings I prefer to replant with young stock.

Hebe 'Carl Teschner'
This hybrid makes a delightful summer-flowering ground-cover plant. It has a prostrate habit that makes a flattened hummock 22 cm (9 in) in height, with a spread of 0·6 m (2 ft). When planted 30 cm (12 in) apart, plants soon merge into a dense and attractive dark green carpet. Each July, a great profusion of violet flowers spreads over them, creating a splendid effect; this, however, can only be achieved in full sun.

Hedera – Ivy
I have previously referred to the usefulness of Ivy as a climbing plant, but these plants are also first-rate for ground-cover purposes. Their main virtue is their tolerance to dense shade, and being creeping evergreens, they soon form dense mats of low-growing foliage. Both *Hedera colchica* and *H. helix* and their various cultivars can be used (see Chapter 13).

Hypericum calycinum – Rose of Sharon
An exuberant ground-cover plant, spreading rapidly by underground stems which can become invasive if left unchecked. This is a low-growing evergreen that flowers continuously during the summer months, with bright yellow, single blooms, each with a central boss of prominent stamens. You can treat this plant like a herbaceous perennial by cutting it hard back to the base each spring with a scythe or garden shears just before new growth breaks; this produces a close, flowering carpet 15 to 22 cm (6 to 9 in) high. Cuttings of summer shoots are easily rooted if you wish to increase your stock. This plant is first-rate for stabilising sloping sites with its vigorous network of underground roots and stems. It will tolerate semi-shade, but flowers more freely in full sun.

Juniperus communis cultivars – Common Juniper
Several cultivars of this plant are excellent for ground-cover.

Trees and Shrubs

These may be expensive to purchase compared to other plants, but once established, they form carpets of superb quality. Their use should be restricted to open, sunny positions. Junipers are excellent on chalk, but do well on most freely-drained soils.

The best forms for ground-cover are *J. c. var. depressa*, sometimes referred to as Canadian Juniper. This has slightly ascending branches with a spread of 1 m (3 ft). The bright golden form of this, *J. c. var. depressa 'Aurea'*, makes a dazzling contrast. I have already mentioned *J. c. 'Hornibrookii'*, which can be included here along with *J. c. 'Repanda'*, which forms a dense carpet of dark green needles.

Juniperus horizontalis – Creeping Juniper

Cultivars of this species are very popular with American gardeners, and the better forms are now finding their way into Britain. They are excellent carpeting plants with a trailing habit and upswept, fern-like branchlets. Young plants can be cut back to stimulate denser growth, and the clippings used for summer cuttings to multiply stock. *J. h. 'Bar Harbour'* is a vigorous spreading cultivar with blue-green foliage. *J. h. 'Douglasii'* has similar grey-green foliage, which takes on a purplish tinge during the colder winter months. Finally, *J. h. 'Wiltonii'* is a superb low-growing form with intense silver-blue foliage.

Mahonia aquifolium – Oregon Grape

Few ground-cover plants surpass this one. It is an evergreen shrub 0·6 to 1 m (2 to 3 ft) in height, with attractive pinnate leaves that have slightly prickly margins. This foliage is a useful foil for flower arrangements. From February until May, the young shoots bear clusters of bright yellow flowers, and blue-black berries, similarly bloomed to the small black grapes from which the common name is derived, follow later in summer. Underground suckers enable the plant to carpet the ground quickly and form a dense evergreen thicket. It grows exceptionally well in heavily-shaded positions beneath trees, and will tolerate most well-drained soils.

Pachysandra terminalis – Japanese Spurge

A semi-woody plant, with lustrous evergreen leaves forming a dense, even carpet 15 to 25 cm (6 to 10 in) high. This thrives in shaded positions and is excellent beneath shrubs or in woodland gardens. Avoid at all costs planting it in full sun, as it dislikes strong light and responds by turning a sickly yellow colour. It spreads by underground stems, and can be increased by division; if larger quantities are needed, summer cuttings can easily be rooted.

I always establish Pachysandra by planting at 15 cm (6 in) intervals; this produces a good effect within a year of planting. In March, it bears white flowers, but these are insignificant compared to the superb carpet of handsome leaves. The cultivar *P. t.* '*Variegata*' has decorative white-margined leaves, but I find this slow to establish.

Rosa 'Max Graf'

Generally, Roses are not suitable for ground-cover, but this one will meet my requirement of forming a dense carpet, provided its trailing stems are interlaced and pegged out along the ground. It is essential to begin with weed-free ground: pernicious perennials like Couch grass and Bishop weed can be a nightmare to eradicate. In mid-summer, the stems bear plentiful clusters of single pink flowers. A sunny position is needed for a good flowering display, and if you have a steep bank that needs covering, a cascade of '*Max Graf*' can create a delightful picture.

Sarcococca humilis – Sweet Box

This dense bushy evergreen is related to common Box, but only grows 30 to 40 cm (1 to 1½ ft) in height. It has spear-shaped, glossy leaves 2·5 to 5 cm (1 to 2 in) long, and small, fragrant white flowers during February and March. As a ground-cover, it forms a dense mat of splendid foliage but has the disadvantage of being rather slow-growing. The quickest effect is achieved by planting at 15 to 22 cm (6 to 9 in) intervals, and applying fertiliser to encourage rapid early growth. It is suited to most soils, including chalk, and will tolerate semi-shaded positions.

Vinca major – Greater Periwinkle

A rampant ground-cover plant, sending out long, wiry stems that take root where their tips contact the soil; this quickly creates a dense tangle of branches 40 to 60 cm (1½ to 2 ft) deep. Throughout the year it is clothed in glossy green leaves, and from April to June delicate blue flowers are scattered along its stems. Vinca grows with equal verve in both sunny and shaded positions, and is excellent for cascading down banks or carpeting woodland glades. Plants can initially be spaced 40 to 60 cm (1½ to 2 ft) apart, and as it multiplies so prolifically from natural layers or cuttings, supply from stock should be no problem. The cultivar *V. m. 'Variegata'* has prominent creamy white leaf markings and, remarkably, seems no less vigorous than the type.

Vinca minor – Lesser Periwinkle

By comparison this is a much tidier plant, forming a neat, dense carpet no more than 15 cm (6 in) deep. It has smaller, more pointed evergreen leaves and a greater profusion of delightful blue flowers from April to June. Good cultivars are *V. m. 'Alba'*, with white flowers, and the clump-forming *V. m. 'Gertrude Jekyll'* with glistening white flowers; *V. m. 'Azurea Flore Pleno'* has deeper blue, double flowers and *V. m. 'Multiplex'* has similar double flowers in wine red. All these cultivars are less invasive than *V. major* and are ideal for under-planting trees and shrubs.

16

Problem Sites

Selections of trees and shrubs where site factors may limit choice; soil limitations – acid soils, alkaline soils, wet soils, dry soils; other limitations – exposed gardens, seaside gardens, shaded places, polluted atmospheres and small gardens.

The main factors involved in successful cultivation of trees and shrubs are soil, climate, micro-climate and other localised elements affecting the growing environment. In the preceding chapters of Part II, I have endeavoured to indicate a plant's preference or dislike for certain conditions. This chapter summarises the main problems that arise, and gives short lists of previously mentioned plants that are reasonably tolerant of such conditions.

However, these lists should not preclude attempts to grow your own favourite plants. Many plants are remarkably tolerant of a wide range of soils and conditions, and seem to grow almost anywhere without fuss or bother.

Soil limitations

Acid soils

These are soils with a pH below 7. Most woody plants prefer slightly acid soils with a pH of 6·5 to 7, but when this falls to pH 5 and below, problems can arise with some plants. The main reason may be a lack of calcium, which is easily corrected by liming. On the other hand, problems may be caused by toxic metals like aluminium or manganese, or because the plant is unable to take up essential nutrients such as phosphate. Not all plants will respond in the same way to an acid soil; for example, although acid soils are unfavourable to Rose cultivation, they are excellent for Rhododendrons. This merely illustrates the importance of plant selection.

Shrubs suitable for acid soils

Arctostaphylos uva-ursi
Berberis
Calluna vulgaris, and cultivars
Camellia japonica, and cultivars
Colutea arborescens
Corylopsis pauciflora
Cotoneaster
Enkianthus campanulatus
Erica cinerea
Erica x darleyensis
Erica herbacea (*Syn. carnea*)
Erica vagans
Eucryphia glutinosa
Fothergilla major
Gaultheria procumbens
Gaultheria shallon
Hydrangea macrophylla
Kalmia latifolia
Magnolia sieboldii
Magnolia stellata
Magnolia soulangiana
Pernettya mucronata
Pieris formosa
Rhododendron, including *Azalea*

Trees suitable for acid soils

Abies procera
Acer cappadocicum
Acer davidii
Acer platanoides, and cultivars
Acer pseudoplantanus, and cultivars
Aesculus x carnea
Aesculus hippocastanum
Betula pendula
Cercidiphyllum japonicum
Chamaecyparis lawsoniana, and cultivars
Chamaecyparis nootkatensis
Cornus nuttallii
Crataegus
Embothrium coccineum
Liquidambar styraciflua
Malus
Picea breweriana
Picea omorika
Picea pungens
Pinus
Quercus coccinea
Quercus rubra
Sorbus

Alkaline soils

Alkaline soils are those with a pH above 7·0. Those containing free calcium carbonate (*i.e.* calcium carbonate which is chemically available to the plant) usually have a pH of 7·5 to 8·0, and are sometimes referred to as calcareous soils. These soils occur naturally overlying chalk or limestone, but similar conditions can be created by over-liming neutral soils. Many trees and shrubs can suffer from lime-induced chlorosis when the pH rises, usually above 7·5. This appears as a yellowing of the foliage and is caused by the plant's inability to absorb essential and minor nutrients. It is possible to correct chlorosis in some cases by watering with sequestrene, a soluble iron compound. Whilst slight acidity in soils can be corrected, it is impractical to acidify alkaline soils, and the sensible approach is to choose appropriate plants.

Shrubs suitable for alkaline soils

Aucuba japonica
Berberis darwinii
Buddleia davidii, and cultivars
Caryopteris x clandonensis
Chaenomeles
Cistus
Clematis
Corylus maxima
Cotoneaster
Daphne mezereum
Deutzia
Euonymus alatus
Forsythia
Hypericum 'Hidcote'
Juniperus communis, and cultivars
Kolkwitzia amabilis
Philadelphus
Photinia x fraseri 'Robusta'
Potentilla
Prunus laurocerasus
Ribes
Rosa
Solanum crispum
Syringa vulgaris, and cultivars
Viburnum x bodnantense
Viburnum carlesii
Viburnum opulus
Viburnum plicatum
Weigela florida
Weigela hybrids

Trees suitable for alkaline soils

Acer platanoides, and cultivars
Acer pseudoplatanus, and cultivars
Acer negundo, and cultivars
Aesculus x carnea
Aesculus hippocastanum
Carpinus betulus
Cedrus
Cercis siliquastrum
Chamaecyparis lawsoniana, and cultivars
Corylus colurna
Crataegus oxyacantha
x Cupressocyparis leylandii
Davidia involucrata
Fagus sylvatica, and cultivars
Fraxinus excelsior, and cultivars
Ilex x altaclarensis
Ilex aquifolium
Laburnum
Malus
Pinus nigra
Populus alba
Prunus avium
Prunus, and Japanese cultivars
Rhus typhina
Sorbus aria
Sorbus aucuparia
Sorbus intermedia
Taxus baccata
Tilia petiolaris
Tilia tomentosa

Wet soils

The majority of trees and shrubs need freely-drained soils if they are to grow well, and many will die if planted in waterlogged areas. Several, however, have adapted themselves to grow beside rivers and on flood plains, and their roots are more tolerant to permanently wet and at times waterlogged soil conditions. If you have water features or low-lying wetter areas that are difficult to drain within your garden, the following plants will succeed.

Shrubs suitable for wet soils

Bamboos
Cornus alba sibirica
Cornus stolonifera
Hippophae rhamnoides
Salix alba 'Chermesina' (coppiced)
Salix alba 'Vitellina' (coppiced)
Salix lanata
Sambucus
Viburnum opulus

Trees suitable for wet soils

Alnus glutinosa
Betula nigra
Metasequoia glyptostroboides
Populus
Quercus palustris
Salix
Sorbus aucuparia
Taxodium distichum

Dry soils

Sand or gravel soils and freely-drained sunny banks lose their moisture more rapidly than most soils. Irrigation can restore this loss and assist plant establishment, but in the long term a few plants tolerant to dry conditions are worthwhile.

Shrubs suitable for dry soils

Berberis thunbergii
Caryopteris x clandonensis
Cistus
Colutea arborescens
Cytisus
Escallonia
Genista
Hedera helix
Hippophae rhamnoides
Hypericum
Juniperus communis
Lavandula
Potentilla
Rosa rugosa
Santolina chamaecyparissus
Spartium junceum
Yucca

Trees suitable for dry soils

Ailanthus altissima
Betula papyrifera
Betula pendula
Cercis siliquastrum
Crataegus
Cupressus glabra
Gleditsia triacanthos
Ilex aquifolium, and cultivars
Pinus nigra
Pinus sylvestris
Pinus wallichiana
Prunus cerasifera
Pyrus calleryana 'Chanticleer'
Quercus ilex
Robinia pseudoacacia
Taxus baccata

Other limitations

Exposed gardens

Exposure is a common problem in many areas of Britain, and especially in new gardens devoid of vegetation. The constant battering of wind and gales damages stems, buds and leaves, as well as causing root disturbance through wind rock. In severe cases temporary protection will be needed to allow wind-hardy plants to grow; once these are established, more interesting plants can be grown in their shelter. The following plants are suitable for forming these first lines of defence against wind.

Wind-tolerant shrubs

Aucuba japonica
Berberis darwinii
Berberis x stenophylla
Colutea arborescens
Cornus alba
Cotinus coggygria
Cotoneaster conspicuus 'Decorus'
Cytisus x praecox
Elaeagnus pungens
Hippophae rhamnoides
Kerria japonica
Pinus mugo
Rhododendron ponticum
Ribes sanguineum
Salix lanata
Sambucus
Spartium junceum
Viburnum opulus

Wind-tolerant trees

Abies procera
Acer platanoides
Acer pseudoplatanus
Betula pendula
Chamaecyparis lawsoniana
Chamaecyparis nootkatensis
Ilex aquifolium
Larix kaempferi
Picea omorika
Pinus nigra
Pinus sylvestris
Salix alba
Sorbus aria
Sorbus aucuparia
Sorbus intermedia

Seaside gardens

In coastal gardens, plants not only have to tolerate the constant buffeting of wind, but at certain times these winds also contain salt spray which can be carried inland for several miles. The accumulation of salt on tender young leaves results in serious scorching, and subsequent poor growth. Gardens that are directly adjacent to the sea may also be subjected to the effects of sand blast. As with exposed gardens, the first task is to establish some form of protection, such as wattle hurdles, 'Netlon' windbreak or 'Paraweb'. Behind these screens, plants that tolerate wind, salt spray and sand blast can be planted. After these are established against the prevailing conditions, more exciting plants can be introduced.

Shrubs for coastal gardens

Atriplex halimus
Aucuba japonica
Berberis darwinii
Berberis x stenophylla
Colutea arborescens
Cornus alba
Elaeagnus pungens
Elaeagnus x ebbingei
Escallonia
Euonymus japonicus
Griselinia littoralis
Hippophae rhamnoides
Hydrangea macrophylla
Lavandula
Olearia x haastii
Rosa rubiginosa
Rosa rugosa
Sambucus
Senecio greyii
Spartium junceum
Tamarix pentandra
Viburnum tinus

Trees for coastal gardens

Acer pseudoplatanus
Crataegus
Cupressus macrocarpa
Ilex x altaclarensis
Ilex aquifolium
Pinus muricata
Pinus nigra
Populus alba
Quercus ilex
Salix alba
Sorbus aria
Sorbus aucuparia
Sorbus intermedia

Shaded places

Not all plants need full sunlight, and some in fact grow better in the shade. Where there are shaded places within the garden caused by overhanging trees or the proximity of tall buildings, shade-tolerant plants are needed. If you are fortunate enough to have a small woodland or copse, you can create delightful gardens using the following plants.

Shade-tolerant shrubs

Aucuba japonica
Buxus sempervirens
Camellia japonica, and cultivars
Choisya ternata
Corylopsis pauciflora
Eucryphia glutinosa
Euonymus fortunei
Fatsia japonica
Gaultheria procumbens
Gaultheria shallon
Hedera
Lonicera periclymenum
Mahonia aquifolium
Mahonia lomariifolia
Mahonia x media 'Charity'
Pachysandra terminalis
Pieris formosa
Prunus laurocerasus
Rhododendron, including *Azalea*
Viburnum opulus
Viburnum tinus
Vinca major
Vinca minor

Shade-tolerant trees

Fagus sylvatica
Ilex
Taxus baccata

Polluted atmospheres

Fortunately, since the introduction of the Clean Air Act, this is a less serious problem. In certain localised industrial areas, there are chemicals in the atmosphere that adversely affect plant growth, causing leaf scorch and occasionally defoliation. The main damaging chemicals are sulphur dioxide, fluorine, oxidised hydrocarbons and ozone. Sooty deposits also accumulate on leaves, blocking stomata and generally reducing their efficiency. If you have the misfortune to have a garden in such an area, do not despair: remarkably, there are plants that seem to thrive in such environments.

Shrubs tolerant of polluted atmospheres

Aralia elata
Aucuba japonica
Berberis
Cotoneaster
Hedera
Ligustrum
Lonicera
Mahonia
Prunus laurocerasus
Pyracantha
Rhododendron (hardy hybrids)
Rosa (modern hybrids)
Sambucus

Trees tolerant of polluted atmospheres

Acer platanoides, and cultivars
Acer pseudoplatanus, and cultivars
Aesculus x carnea
Aesculus hippocastanum
Ailanthus altissima
Alnus glutinosa
Carpinus betulus
Catalpa bignonioides
Cedrus
Chamaecyparis lawsoniana, and cultivars
Corylus colurna
Crataegus oxyacantha
Gleditsia triacanthos
Ilex
Laburnum
Malus floribunda
Malus 'Profusion'
Malus 'Golden Hornet'
Picea omorika
Platanus acerifolia
Prunus avium
Rhus typhina
Robinia pseudoacacia
Sorbus
Tilia
Ulmus glabra 'Camperdowni'

Trees for small gardens

Many gardens are too small to accommodate large-growing trees. All trees begin life as small plants, but if space is limited you must consider the potential height and spread of the chosen tree, in relation to the available space and surrounding features. The following selection are trees that are of the right proportions for the smaller garden.

Small trees with attractive flowers

Crataegus oxyacantha 'Paul's Scarlet'
Crataegus prunifolia
Laburnum x watereri 'Vossii'
Malus floribunda
Malus 'Profusion'

Trees and Shrubs

Malus 'Van Eseltine'
Prunus 'Amanogowa'
Prunus 'Cheal's Weeping'
Prunus 'Kanzan'
Prunus 'Pink Perfection'

Small trees with decorative foliage

Acer japonicum 'Vitifolium'
Acer negundo 'Auratum'
Acer negundo 'Elegans'
Acer pseudoplatanus 'Brilliantissimum'
Acer rubrum 'Scanlon'
Alnus glutinosa 'Imperialis'
Gleditsia triacanthos 'Sunburst'
Pyrus salicifolia
Rhus typhina
Sorbus aria 'Lutescens'
Sorbus 'Embley'
Sorbus 'Joseph Rock'

Small trees with ornamental fruits

Cotoneaster frigidus
Cotoneaster 'Hybridus Pendulus'
Ilex aquifolium 'J. C. van Thol'
Malus 'Golden Hornet'
Malus 'John Downie'
Sorbus aucuparia, and cultivars
Sorbus cashmeriana
Sorbus hupehensis

Small trees with attractive bark

Acer davidii
Arbutus x andrachnoides
Betula albo-sinensis var. septentrionalis
Betula jacquemontii
Eucalyptus niphophila
Prunus serrula

Small coniferous trees

Abies koreana
Cedrus libani 'Sargentii'
Chamaecyparis lawsoniana 'Ellwoodii'
Chamaecyparis lawsoniana 'Fletcheri'
Chamaecyparis obtusa 'Crippsii'
Chamaecyparis pisifera 'Filifera Aurea'
Chamaecyparis pisifera 'Plumosa'
Juniperus communis 'Hibernica'
Picea pungens 'Koster'
Pinus parviflora

Glossary of Terms

Aberrant form: a form which deviates from the type plant, *e.g.* *Fagus sylvatica* '*Pendula*' is a weeping form of *Fagus sylvatica* (Beech).

Acid soil: soil with a pH below 7·0 (*see* pH).

Adventitious roots: roots which do not originate from the primary root system. They usually arise from stems, as seen in *Hedera* (Ivy).

Air layering: a method of plant propagation in which a rooting medium is bound in polythene around a constricted stem until rooting occurs.

Alkaline soil: soil with a pH above 7·0 (*see* pH).

Anther: male part of the flower which bears the pollen and forms part of the stamen.

Anti-transpirant: a solution applied to the foliage of plants or cuttings. This forms a thin plastic film over the leaf surface, which for a time slows down the rate of water lost by transpiration.

Bare-root: a root system devoid of soil, *i.e.* one that is not bound with materials to form a root-ball nor grown in a container.

Bleeding: exudation of sap from a wound surface.

Botanical name: the classical name ascribed to a plant when it was first described or changed by a botanist.

Bract: a modified leaf often attached below a true flower and sometimes resembling a petal, *e.g.* as seen in *Davidiia* (Pocket Handkerchief tree).

Budding: a method of plant propagation in which a bud from the plant to be propagated is implanted into the stem of a closely related rootstock.

Calcicole: a lime-loving plant, *e.g. Clematis.*

Calcifuge: a lime-hating plant, *e.g. Rhododendron.*

Callus: new tissue produced from the cambium cells to heal wounds, *e.g.* at the base of cuttings, around graft unions and around pruning cuts.

Calyx: the outermost whorl of parts which make up a flower.

Cambium: the actively dividing cells found in the stem of a plant, which produce new phloem and xylem cells.

Carbohydrates: chemical compounds of carbon, hydrogen and oxygen found in plants.

Chlorophyll: the green pigment of plants.

Chloroplasts: the microscopic structures which contain the chlorophyll.

Clone: a group of plants which have all originated by vegetative propagation from a single plant.

Common name: the commonly used English name of a plant, *e.g.* Oak for *Quercus.*

Contact herbicide: a herbicide which kills those plant parts with which it comes into contact.

Container-grown plant: a plant with its roots grown in a container. This enables it to be transplanted at any time of year.

Coppice: the practice of cutting trees or shrubs hard back to ground level. In gardens, the purpose is to achieve an attractive display of colourful stems.

Corona: a crown-like appendage around the inside of a flower, *e.g.* as seen in *Passiflora* (Passion flower).

Cultivar: cultivated variants of plants which have not been found growing wild.

Cut-leaved: an aberrant form in which the foliage is divided into narrow segments.

Cutting: a detached part of a stem, root or leaf which forms a new plant.

Cyclic bearing: the bearing of good seed crops at intervals varying from two to five years, instead of annually.

Damping off: a fungal rot which causes the collapse of seedlings.

Dead-heading: the removal of spent flower-heads.

Deciduous: a plant which sheds all its leaves annually.

Dibber: a pointed wooden stick approximately 1 cm ($\frac{1}{2}$ in) in diameter and 10 cm (4 in) long, used to make a hole in the compost when pricking out seedlings or inserting cuttings.

Dieback: the death of a shoot tip which gradually progresses down the stem. This can also occur on pruned stems.

Dioecious: plants which bear unisexual flowers, *i.e.* male and female on different plants, *e.g. Salix* (Willow).

Dormancy: a period when growth-processes slow down to a state of virtual inactivity, *e.g.* in seeds and over-wintering deciduous plants.

Double-digging: turning over the soil to a depth of two spade blades.

Double-leader: the emergence of twin shoots on the main stem of a tree.

Dribble bar: an attachment for a watering can or sprayer, consisting of a perforated tube which enables herbicides to be applied without risk of them drifting.

Drip line: the furthest extent of a tree canopy.

Embryo: rudimentary plant within a seed.

Epidermis: outer layer of cells, which can be likened to the skin of a plant.

Evergreen: a plant which always bears foliage. Its leaves are shed intermittently throughout the year, but mainly in the spring, as new leaves arise.

Family: a sub-division of plant classification, comprising a group of related genera.

Fastigiate: a growth habit in which the stems and branches are strongly erect, as seen in *Populus nigra 'Italica'* (Lombardy Poplar).

Feathered tree: a young tree that has not had any of its side branches trimmed off.

Fertilisation: the fusion of the male cells (pollen) with the female cells contained in the ovule.

Field capacity: a state when a soil is holding the maximum amount of free-draining water against the force of gravity.

Frost pocket: an area where cold air accumulates. Because cold air is denser than warm air, it drains downhill and accumulates in low-lying hollows or places where its downward movement is blocked, *e.g.* when it meets a wall or a dense hedge.

Fruit: the seed-bearing product of a plant.

Fungicide: a chemical for controlling fungus diseases.

Genera: plural of genus.

Genus: a sub-division of plant classification, comprising a group of closely related species.

Girdle root: a root coiled around the base of the stem which may cause constriction.

Glaucous: blue-grey, or covered with a whitish, waxy bloom.

Grafting: a method of plant propagation in which a shoot of the desired variety is united to a closely related rootstock.

Grecian saw: a small handsaw used for pruning; it has a curved blade with its teeth set and sharpened to cut as the saw is pulled towards the operator.

Growth-regulator: organic or synthetic compounds which stimulate, inhibit or modify the growth of plants, *e.g.* auxin types which stimulate root formation in cuttings, or callus growth around pruning cuts.

Hardwood cutting: a cutting prepared from mature wood in autumn and winter.

Heartwood: the darker central part of a woody stem. This wood no longer transports water and food materials; its purpose is to provide strength.

Heel cutting: a shoot torn from an older shoot and trimmed to prepare a cutting which has a small portion of this older wood at its base.

Heeling in: a method of temporary planting to retain plants in good condition until they can be planted properly. It is achieved by laying plants on their sides, with their roots buried in a previously dug trench.

Herbicide: a chemical for killing weeds.

Hybrid: a plant resulting from a cross between two or more genetically different parents.

Hybridisation: the process of producing hybrids.

Hybrid vigour: the increased vigour often found in the first generation of a cross.

Insecticide: a chemical for killing insects.

Juvenility: the growth phase before the adult phase, when a plant does not bear flowers. In some conifers, this phase would appear to be permanent. Plants are generally easier to propagate whilst in the juvenile phase.

Kerf: the groove made by a saw cut.

Lateral bud: a bud which arises on the side of a shoot.

Layer: a stem of a plant which produces roots whilst still attached to its parent.

Layering: a method of propagation in which a stem is induced to root while still attached to its parent. (*See also* air layering.)

Leaching: the loss of dissolved nutrients from the topsoil into the lower reaches of the soil, and eventually into the drainage water.

Leader: the central branch of a tree, which thickens to form the trunk.

Leaf axil: the point where the leaf joins the stem of a plant; this usually contains a bud (the axillary bud).

Micro-climate: the climate specific to a small area, *e.g.* in a garden, the micro-climate of a shrub border will differ to that of an open space on a lawn.

Mist unit: a device which intermittently sprays a fine mist over a bed of cuttings to keep them covered with a film of water.

Monoecious: plants which bear both types of unisexual flowers, *i.e.* male and female, *e.g. Acer pseudoplatanus* (Sycamore).

Node: the part of the stem where the leaves arise.

NPK: the abbreviation of the chemical symbols for the three main plant nutrients: N – nitrogen, P_2O_5 – phosphate, K_2O – potash.

Ovule: female part of the flower which contains the ovum. After fertilisation this becomes the seed.

Perennial: a plant which grows on from year to year.

Pesticide: a chemical used to kill garden pests, *i.e.* insecticides, fungicides and herbicides.

pH: a logarithmic scale from 0 to 14 used for measuring the degree of soil acidity. Soil reactions can be classified as follows:

extremely acid	*below* pH 4·5
very strongly acid	pH 4·5 to 5·0
strongly acid	pH 5·1 to 5·5
medium acid	pH 5·6 to 6·0
slightly acid	pH 6·1 to 6·5
neutral	pH 6·6 to 7·3
mildly alkaline	pH 7·4 to 8·0
strongly alkaline	pH 8·1 to 9·0
very strongly alkaline	pH 9·1 *and above*

Phloem: a tissue forming part of the vascular system of plants, used for the distribution of food materials.

Photosynthesis: a physiological process within the green parts of plants, responsible for the manufacture of simple carbohydrates.

Pinnate: a compound leaf shape. This comprises a central leaf stalk with leaflets arranged along both sides and at the tip, as seen in *Sorbus aucuparia* (Mountain Ash or Rowan).

Pleaching: the training of trees, by interlacing branches to form screens or formal hedges for shaded walk-ways.

Pneumatophores: air-breathing roots, as in *Taxodium* (Swamp Cypress).

Pollen: spores borne by the anther, which are the male reproductive cells.

Pollination: the transfer of pollen from the anther to the stigma.

Pricking off: the transfer of seedlings from a seed bed, box or pan to single stations in another seed bed, box or pan.

Residual herbicide: a weedkiller applied to the soil which remains active for several months.

Respiration: a physiological process within plants, which absorbs oxygen and releases energy.

Root-balled: a type of root system in which the roots are contained in soil and bound with hessian or similar durable fabric.

Rooting medium: the compost into which cuttings are inserted to form roots.

Rootstock: the root portion of a grafted or budded plant.

Sapwood: the young wood which conducts the sap within a tree.

This surrounds the heartwood and is recognised by its lighter colour.

Scion: stem or bud used to provide the new shoot system when grafted on to a rootstock.

Seed: the product of a fertilised ovule containing an embryonic plant.

Semi-ripewood cutting: a stem cutting taken as the wood is beginning to harden.

Sepals: a division of the calyx found outside the petals.

Single digging: turning over the soil to a depth of one spade blade.

Softwood cutting: stem cutting taken before the wood begins to harden.

Species: a sub-division of plant classification, comprising a group of individuals which have the same constant and distinctive characters.

Sport: a sudden change in the vegetative cells of a bud, resulting in the development of a branch which has different characteristics (*e.g.* a variation in foliage colour or growth habit). Such branches, if propagated vegetatively, give rise to new cultivars.

Stamen: the complete male part of the flower, consisting of the filament (stalk) and the pollen-bearing anther.

Standard tree: a young tree which has had its lower branches trimmed off to leave a clear trunk (usually 2 m (6 ft) below its framework of branches).

Stigma: the receptive surface on top of the style which receives the pollen.

Stock: see rootstock.

Stomata: the small openings (pores) in leaves through which air and water vapour pass.

Stratification: the storage of seeds between layers of moist sand to enable completion of the after-ripening process.

Style: the structure which connects the stigma to the ovule.

Sucker: a shoot arising directly from the roots, below ground, *e.g.* as seen in bush Roses, when the rootstock sends up shoots of the wild rootstock.

Taxonomy: the science of classification.

Terminal bud: the bud at the shoot apex.

Topiary: the art of clipping trees and shrubs into fantastic shapes.

Translocated herbicide: a herbicide which when absorbed into the plant through the leaves or roots moves within it, finally killing it.

Transpiration: a physiological process, involving the movement of water through the plant and out through the stomata in the leaves.

Trifoliate: a compound leaf which has three leaflets, as seen in *Acer griseum* (Paper Bark Maple).

Turgid: fully charged with water.

Vapour pressure: pressure of moisture in the atmosphere.

Variety: a distinct geographical variant of a species.

Viable seed: a seed which is alive and capable of germination.

Virus: a microscopic agent causing disease in plants.

Whip: a seedling tree which has not yet developed side branches (feathers).

Witches' Brooms: abnormal clusters of short shoots which develop on the branches of trees.

Wounding: the slitting or removal of a sliver of bark from the base of a cutting.

Xylem: cells, fibres and vessels that form the wood of a plant.

Further Reading List

Bean, W. J., *Trees And Shrubs Hardy In The British Isles* (4 vols, 8th Edition, John Murray)

Bloom, A., *Conifers For Your Garden* (Floraprint, 1972)

Bridgeman, P. H., *Tree Surgery* (David and Charles, 1976)

Brown, G. E., *The Pruning Of Trees, Shrubs and Conifers* (Faber and Faber, 1977)

Chittenden, F. J., and Synge, P. M., (Eds), *Royal Horticultural Society Dictionary Of Gardening* (Clarendon Press, Oxford, 1969)

Den Ouden, P., and Boom, B. K., *Manual Of Cultivated Conifers* (Martinus Nijhoff, The Hague, 1965)

Hillier and Sons, *Hillier's Manual Of Trees And Shrubs* (David and Charles, 1977)

Johnson, A. T., *Plant Names Simplified* (Landsman's Bookshop, 1972)

Lancaster, R., *Trees For Your Garden* (Floraprint, 1974)

Lucas Phillips, C. E., *Climbing Plants For Walls And Gardens* (Heinemann, 1976)

Mitchell, A., *A Field Guide To The Trees Of Britain and Northern Europe* (Collins, London, 1974)

Seabrook, P., *Shrubs For Your Garden* (Floraprint, 1973)

Stearn, Dr W. T., and Smith, A. W., *A Gardener's Dictionary Of Plant Names* (Cassel, 1971)

Thomas, G. S., *Plants For Ground Cover* (J. M. Dent and Sons, 1977)

Wright, R. C. M., *Simple Plant Propagation* (Ward Lock, 1975)

Metric/Imperial Equivalents

Temperature

°F	°C
45	7
50	10
55	13
60	16
65	18
70	21

Length

in	*cm*
¼	0·5
½	1·0
1	2·5
12	30
24	60

Weight

oz/sq yd	*g/m²*	*oz*	*g*
1	35	1	28
2	70	4	113
3	100	16 (1 lb)	454
4	140	36 (2¼ lb)	1000 (1 kg)

Area

1 sq yd = 0·8 m²

1¼ sq yd = 1·0 m²

Volume

pints	*litres*
½	0·3
1	0·6
1¾	1·0

Note: These conversions are approximate.

Index

Trees and Shrubs